Praise for *Animalkind*

"Humanity's survival depends upon our learning to live in harmony with all other species. The second law of ecology is the law of interdependence. Without bees, phytoplankton, worms, and trees we cannot live; without dogs, cats, horses, elephants, and penguins we cannot be truly happy. We are a part of them as they are a part of us and together we are the planet Earth. Ingrid Newkirk and Gene Stone have done a wonderful service to us all with their stories of kindness and compassion. The book is truly inspiring."

—Captain Paul Watson, CEO and founder of
Sea Shepherd Conservation Society

"What *Animalkind* reveals only reinforces my belief that some of the most brilliant individuals you could ever hope to meet have fur, fins, or feathers."

—Alan Cumming, stage and screen actor

"We share this planet and the same kingdom with the animals and although we feel superior to them, they have senses that far surpass ours. This book shows how much we have to learn from them, beginning with compassion, simplicity, and unconditional love. It is a must-read."

—Dr. Marty Goldstein, author of *The Nature of Animal Healing*

"With wisdom and eloquence, Ingrid Newkirk and Gene Stone remind us of what we've always known, but too often forget: animals are deserving of our care."

—Jonathan Safran Foer, *New York Times*
bestselling author of *Eating Animals*

"This book makes the spot-on case that the future of laboratory research will not be based on four-legged or tail-wagging models, but rather on sophisticated, human-relevant, and high-tech animal-free testing methods. As Newkirk and Stone point out, these modern technologies are delivering better human health outcomes and are benefiting patients, physicians, and researchers."

—John Pawlowski, MD, PhD, Harvard Medical
Faculty Physician

"A resourceful guide and a treasure of greater compassion, integrity, and awareness, *Animalkind* is both a moving compendium of animals' remarkable intelligence and emotional complexity and a manual of all the ways we can stop accepting and contributing to their slaughter and exploitation."

—Joy Williams, author of *The Quick and the Dead*
and *The Changeling*

"This is the book to buy, read, and give to others so that everyone finally sees why they should respect and cherish all animals."

—Anjelica Huston, Oscar Award–winning actress

"*Animalkind* is a much-needed antidote to viewing other animals as second-class citizens and offers a fresh look into the cognitive and emotional lives of other animals. This thought-provoking and engaging book will change your view of who other animals are and how you should interact with them in respectful and compassionate ways."

—Marc Bekoff, PhD, author of *The Emotional Lives of Animals*

"Buy this book for anyone you know who harbors even the slightest doubt that animals aren't super-clever or that there aren't many ways to help them—because Newkirk and Stone show that animals are, and that you can."

—Edie Falco, Emmy Award–winning actress

"A fascinating look at animal behavior, as well as a treatise against cruelty toward animals . . . effectively nudges readers to think twice about their own use of products sourced, perhaps less than ethically, from the animal kingdom."

—*Publishers Weekly*

"This emotional and informative book should be required reading for everyone! I urge you to pick it up and embrace its beautiful message of compassion and understanding. The time is now for all of us to fall in love with *Animalkind*!"

—Mike White, filmmaker, actor, producer

"Wide-ranging and enlightening. . . . An impassioned plea for preserving animals' lives."

—*Kirkus Reviews*

"Explores research into animal intelligence, feelings, and communication . . . and suggests ways people can change their everyday lives to be more animal-friendly."

—*Phoenix News Times*

"Animals are our neighbors on this planet—this book shows how we can become better neighbors."

—Alec Baldwin, Emmy-winning actor

"Like me, Ingrid believes in protecting all the creatures we love."

—Sir Paul McCartney, musician

animalkind

Remarkable Discoveries About Animals and Revolutionary New Ways to Show Them Compassion

INGRID NEWKIRK & GENE STONE

Foreword by Mayim Bialik

SIMON & SCHUSTER PAPERBACKS

NEW YORK   LONDON   TORONTO   SYDNEY   NEW DELHI

Simon & Schuster Paperbacks
An Imprint of Simon & Schuster, Inc.
1230 Avenue of the Americas
New York, NY 10020

First Simon & Schuster trade paperback edition January 2021

SIMON & SCHUSTER PAPERBACKS and colophon are registered
trademarks of Simon & Schuster, Inc.

For information about special discounts for bulk purchases,
please contact Simon & Schuster Special Sales at 1-866-506-1949
or business@simonandschuster.com.

The Simon & Schuster Speakers Bureau can bring authors to your live event. For
more information or to book an event, contact the Simon & Schuster Speakers
Bureau at 1-866-248-3049 or visit our website at www.simonspeakers.com.

Interior design by Carly Loman

Manufactured in the United States of America

1   3   5   7   9   10   8   6   4   2

Library of Congress Cataloging-in-Publication Data has been applied for.

ISBN 978-1-5011-9854-0
ISBN 978-1-5011-9855-7 (pbk)
ISBN 978-1-5011-9856-4 (ebook)

To Nanci Alexander, who is responsible for the happiness of so many animals that it is impossible to count them, and to the memory of Gurudev Chitrabhanuji, the late Jain master, who asked everyone to regard all living beings as our brothers and sisters

Contents

Foreword   *ix*

Introduction   *1*

SECTION I: Remarkable Discoveries about Animals

The Mysteries of Navigation   15
The Channels of Communication   38
The Intricacies of Love   62
The Joy of Play   88

SECTION II: Revolutionary New Ways
to Show Them Compassion

Scientific Research   119
Clothing   155
Entertainment   181
Food   205

Afterword   *239*
Acknowledgments   *241*
Selected Sources   *243*
Notes   *267*
Index   *275*

Foreword

In the early 2000s, when I was working on my PhD in Neuroscience at UCLA, the world was a very different place. Our cell phones were just ... phones. Pluto was still considered a full-sized planet (tough break, Pluto!). Ringling Bros. and Barnum & Bailey Circus was still in business.

Twenty years isn't a long time in the grand scheme of the universe, but with technology and our 24-hour news cycle moving at warp speed, it feels as if we learn as much in a day as we once did in a year. And while it may sound trite, knowledge really *is* power—no matter how we receive it. *Animalkind* is a book that empowers readers with the knowledge to understand *who* animals are while dispelling the notion of "what" we assume animals are, and the power to change the way the world treats them.

As a neuroscientist and person who cares about animals, I seek to understand how we all think, feel, and communicate. Research in comparative neuroanatomy has fundamentally shifted the general scientific view of animals' abilities, as well as the public conversation about animals. We share far more in common with our fellow animals than most of us are aware of. We once thought that advanced cognitive abilities were uniquely human, but we now know that's actually not true. Animals have their own ways of communicating with each other, playing together, learning with each other, and—yes: loving each other.

The scientist in me appreciates *Animalkind* because it's full of scientific studies, captivating data, and surprising facts about animal behavior. The vegan in me loves this book because it shows readers how easy and rewarding it is to navigate the world without harming animals. Eating decadent, rich food, sporting fashionable purses and clothing that look and feel like "real" leather, and experiencing entertainment on screen or under the big top can still be a part of your life. All without harming another living being in the process.

As a vegan mother who is also a scientist, I raise my boys to question things and not accept the world as it is simply because it's convenient or easy or because everyone else is doing things a certain way. I teach them to be just and kind, and not complacent. I hope they grow up and continue to make life choices based on facts, but also on empathy. *Animalkind* is a book that can teach them—and all of us—how to live this way. Ingrid and Gene, thank you for teaching us how multifaceted animals are and showing us how simple it is to treat them with the kindness and respect they deserve.

—Mayim Bialik

Introduction

The dog who jumps for joy when you come home. The emperor penguin guarding his child through a subzero blizzard. The dolphin smiling at us from the water. The sleepy cat's purr of contentment. The manta ray's intricate underwater ballets. The lark's exquisite song. Animals delight, fascinate, and enrich human lives and thoughts every day of the year.

Through science, observation, and sometimes just luck, we are constantly discovering more about our earth's cohabitants. We learn that an albatross, not a sailor, was the first living being to circumnavigate the globe. We find that chimpanzees can defeat college students at computer games. We realize that a tiny desert mouse knows how to collect drinking water by placing a stone outside her burrow so as to drink the morning dew on a burning hot day.

We never seem to tire of our companion species and their antics. We watch documentaries that reveal the secret lives of urban street dogs, of river otters, and of ants who ford streams by making boats out of leaves or forming bridges with their own bodies. We visit wildlife parks, feed squirrels, go whale watching, and take camera safaris to Africa. Becoming a veterinarian is high on the list of young people's career choices, having an animal in the home is considered a treat and a joy, and spending our hard-earned money on dog treats, cat trees, and comfy beds for our beloved animal companions is de rigueur.

The news we read every day is filled with animal stories from the cute and ridiculous to the serious and sublime. We circulate videos of animals rescuing other animals, including human beings, from storms, fires, and other dangers—and videos of firefighters and everyday heroes reciprocating. New York's Museum of the Moving Image recently featured a wildly popular exhibit called "How Cats Took Over the Internet." Some cat videos have been watched one hundred million times. But it's not just cats—not long ago the Bat World Sanctuary posted a short video of an adorable orphaned bat being fed with a Q-tip—so many millions watched the video that the sanctuary's site crashed from all the viewers.

We marvel at animals' unique abilities, and as we've learned more in recent years, we've also come to marvel at all the things animals can do that we once thought were reserved for humans. For instance, animals can count: chickens and bears up to at least five; sheep can recognize at least sixty other sheep and can tell humans from other humans when shown photographs. The sheep's nemesis, a border collie named Chaser, has been taught the names of over one thousand toys. Renowned scientist Neil deGrasse Tyson put Chaser to the test on national television. Chaser performed spectacularly.

The more we know about the other animals, and the more we understand their abilities, the more we begin to question our relationship with them. Perhaps you remember that party question you might have been asked as a child: "If you were an animal, which animal would you like to be?" How would you answer that today? A bird? A wolf? An elephant?

If that question had been asked centuries ago, it would not have been easy to answer because for the most part animals were seen as good only for their usefulness to humans, from canaries sent down into the coal mines to horses used in war. Dogs had "masters" back then, not guardians. When did you last hear *that* word?

Of course, many people loved their dogs, even then, but there were limits. Stray dogs plucked from the streets in New York City were drowned in the Hudson; whale blubber lighted our lamps and whale bones were made into women's corsets; chicken was only *what* you ate, not a bird you sponsored in a farmed-animal sanctuary; a rabbit was "sacrificed" for every pregnancy test, and boys became men by being taken out with Dad to hunt. You can just imagine how else animals were used. The pickings were slim when it came to answering the question, "Which animal would you like to be?" Because for the most part, animals who had contact with humans suffered through difficult lives and came to a bad end.

Today, bad things still happen to good animals, but great changes have come about and more are in the offing. The biggest animal circus on earth has pulled up its tent pegs and the old beast wagon has been upgraded to showcase only terrific *human* talents and technical wizardry; the homing pigeon and the stagecoach horse have been replaced by electronic communications; beautiful animal sanctuaries for turkeys rescued from the holiday table and for bears liberated from roadside zoos are springing up all over the world; and that jacket collar is far more likely to be faux fur than real. Meanwhile, quite a few dogs and cats have their own luxury spas, day care centers, and even bakeries.

Thanks to animal behaviorists like Konrad Lorenz, primatologists like Jane Goodall, Biruté Galdikas, Frans de Waal, and Dian Fossey, undersea explorers like Jacques Cousteau and his family, and the thousands of animal rights activists who have been constantly and assiduously working to help animals, people's eyes are now opened to *who* animals are—and we like what we see. We have come to feel love, understanding, and respect for all animals and our delight in caring for them has entered a new era.

The first part of this book is a celebration of that relationship, an exploration of who animals are—their many talents, languages, and complex cultures. The second part of the book takes us to the next logical step—given our newfound understanding of all that is animal, how can we treat them in ways that respect their individuality and talents? Or, in other words, how can we conduct our lives happily and efficiently without having to exploit animals?

Be ready to be enchanted as you learn about animals who have performed tasks that baffle the imagination, who invent games, who undertake remarkable journeys, who stump scientists, who can achieve feats no human could ever do. Then be ready to be inspired as you read about computer-generated movie chimpanzees that are indistinguishable from real ones (but far more malleable on the set); cruelty-free medicines developed virtually overnight with the help of high-speed computers programmed with relevant human data; and chicken drumsticks that don't require any live chickens to produce them. Be ready to learn as you find out all the many ways that you can help all animals live the fulfilling and happy lives they deserve—or at least, to be left unmolested.

Perhaps, if all humans were to fully understand who and what animals really are, we may tread closer to the belief expressed by Jenny Leading Cloud of the White River Sioux, who once said:

"The buffalo and the coyote are our brothers; the birds, our cousins. Even the tiniest ant, even a louse, even the smallest flower you can find—they are all relatives. We end our prayers with the words *mitakuye oyasin*—'all my relations'—and that includes everything that grows, crawls, runs, creeps, hops, and flies on this continent."

SECTION I:

Remarkable Discoveries about Animals

Researchers at Germany's Max Planck Institute for Evolutionary Anthropology were dumbfounded. The excitement wasn't over a new fossil, or the discovery of a previously unknown human ancestor. It was over Rico, a border collie. In experiments conducted in 2004, the very normal-seeming, ten-year-old canine had learned to fetch more than two hundred objects on command—and moreover, remember them all a month later. Determined to discover the limits of Rico's abilities, the research team subjected him to a battery of cognitive tests that revealed astounding problem-solving abilities. Rico could easily retrieve from another room items he was familiar with, but when told to retrieve a new item—one he had never heard before—Rico correctly deduced that the unknown name must correspond with an unknown object and correctly retrieved it. The border collie's cognitive abilities were consequently compared to that of apes, dolphins, parrots, and, eventually, human children.

Researchers often end up comparing their animal subjects' intelligence to humans. But is intelligence truly easy to compare, animal to human, or even animal to animal? If Rico could use the process of elimination to correctly fetch a tennis ball, does that make him smarter than an arctic tern who journeys forty-four thousand miles each year between the north and south poles? Is a piano-playing cat more intelligent than a chimpanzee, who shares nearly 99 percent of her DNA with humans and can learn sign language?

Comparing the intelligence of animals is, in fact, no easier than comparing the intelligence of humans. Who's smarter: Aristotle or Plato? Newton or Einstein? Monet or Manet? The red-lipped batfish or Chinese giant salamanders? The Indian elephant or the African elephant? In the end, ranking the relative intelligence of animals is a futile exercise. What's more, a recent study found that less than 15 percent of the estimated nine million species on Earth have been discovered. Who knows what fantastical creatures reside at our oceans' crushing depths, soar high in the stratosphere, or creep deep in the densest jungles? What fantastic intelligence do they display? Or more so, what fantastic intelligence we can't even comprehend?

We often consider intelligence as the only factor in determining which animals deserve compassion and which don't. Yet we're still so limited in our understanding of human intelligence that it makes little sense to calibrate our animal brethren based on how similar their brains are to ours. Or, perhaps you could say, it's simply not an intelligent way to determine importance.

The goal in this book is not to merely question that superiority, or to show how animals think and act like us; it's also to show how they do not, and to honor those differences. How can anyone compare the mental faculties of a gibbon vaulting through the forest with a giant blue whale singing through the deepest oceans? Different animals excel at different actions. As we'll see in this book, animals think, navigate, communicate, love, and play in extraordinarily unique ways.

However, for many years scientists believed that intelligence was, indeed, all that mattered when it came to animals, and that intelligence consisted of a continuum, with humans at the most developed end. Every other species could fit neatly into that spectrum—a concept heralded by the great naturalist Charles Darwin, who wrote in his 1871 book, *The Descent of Man,* that "the difference in mind between man and the higher animals, great as it is, certainly is one of degree and not of kind." In essence, Darwin meant that because all animals share a common ancestor, they also share the same toolkit of mental abilities, but at different levels.

Not a new idea. Twenty-four hundred years ago, Aristotle presented his idea of a "Natural Ladder," or *Scala Naturae.* Like Darwin, Aristotle advanced that all life could be conveniently ranked, with "lesser" animals like worms on one end, "intermediate" animals like dogs and cats in the middle, and "higher" animals such as monkeys and humans at the far end. During the Middle Ages, Christian theologians expanded on Aristotle's teachings with the "great chain of being," a hierarchical scale that began with God at the very top followed by angels, humans, other animals, plants, and then minerals. Each layer of the chain also had its own hierarchy. Among humans, for instance, kings, aristocrats, and other noblemen sat at the top while peasants were relegated to the bottom. The highest-ranking animals were large carnivores like lions and tigers, who were untrainable and therefore seen as superior to docile animals like dogs and horses. Even insects were subdivided, with honey-producing bees ranked higher than mosquitos and plant-eating beetles. Finally, at the very bottom sat snakes—their lowly station a result of the serpent's deception in the Garden of Eden.

Even throughout the twentieth century, scientists clung to the notion that animals can be neatly ranked by their human intelligence. Scientists devised increasingly cruel experiments that could serve as universal tests for animal cognition, many of them led by University of Wisconsin–Madison psychologist Harry Harlow. Previously, Harlow was best known for a series of experiments from the 1950s, in which he removed infant rhesus monkeys from their mothers and provided them surrogate mothers made from wire. The traumatized monkeys' desperate attempts to be caressed by their inanimate mothers during times of stress became the basis for research into maternal separation, dependency needs, and social isolation. (Many historians cite Harlow as a factor in the rise of subsequent animal liberation movements.) Later, Harlow developed experiments called "learning sets," which effectively tested how well a subject could learn. For instance, an animal would be presented with two doors, one containing food. The test would be repeated until the animal learned the correct door. Much like Aristotle's *Scala Naturae*, by devising experiments like these scientists created their own interspecies "IQ test" to rank the world's animals.

At first the tests seemed to support traditional beliefs about brain size. In learning sets, humans outperformed chimpanzees, who outperformed gorillas, who outperformed ferrets, who outperformed skunks, who outperformed squirrels, and so on. But the more animals that were tested, the less neatly everything seemed to fit. Then scientists studied blue jays and other birds, who performed better than half the mammals tested. As one researcher said, "Pigeons can blow the doors off monkeys in some tasks."[1] Soon, scientists realized that the animal kingdom is far too complex to rank animals. Eventually, more of these experiments, many of which were physically and emotionally traumatizing for the animals, were halted. As one 1969 paper concluded, "The concept that all living animals can be arranged along a continuous 'phylogenetic scale' with man at the top is inconsistent with contemporary views of animal evolution. . . . The widespread failure of comparative psychologists to take into account the zoological model of animal evolution when selecting animals for study and when interpreting behavioral similarities and differences has greatly hampered the development of generalizations with any predictive value."[2]

Animal intelligence can only be understood, or at least studied, in the context of a particular species' evolutionary path. It's not just our upright posture and large brains that make us who we are; it's our sense of individuality, our art, our music. Our inventiveness allowed us to discover language, fire, and cooking. As we'll see in this book, however, many animals possess these skills too. And others rely on a far different set of traits that we cannot even comprehend.

Ants have evolved over more than 140 million years by honing their collective instincts. Have you ever watched time-lapse footage of an ant colony? Each ant has a specific role within a group, and each group has a distinct purpose. Anyone who has witnessed a session of Congress on CSPAN knows how easily communication between humans can devolve into a playground shouting match. Yet ant colonies can grow to hundreds of millions of ants, all working seamlessly together toward a collective good. Our six-legged insect friends may not be able to communicate with spoken words like humans do, but they coordinate reproduction, construction, resource gathering, and even war using a complex language of scent, touch, and sound. Who is to say the collective intelligence of an ant colony is any less profound than human individuality?

Even brain size is not a good indicator of intelligence. Humans' brains rank fourth in size, behind sperm whales, elephants, and dolphins. As for our brain-to-body mass ratio, we're a distant fifth behind ants, tree shrews, small birds, and mice. There is no obvious anatomical indicator to predict which animals are "smarter" than other ones—and if there is, there are far too many variables to study. It turns out that even with their relatively small brains, nerve cells, and neural connections, birds' mental abilities are mighty impressive.

Some of the greatest abilities come from the most surprising creatures. Slime molds, for instance, might not be the first creature that comes to mind when you think "smart." Not plants, not animals, and not fungi, slime molds are soil-dwelling amoebas containing a single cell. (For reference, the human body has an estimated thirty-seven trillion cells.) Slime molds can form exotic colors and shapes that resemble honeycomb lattices and rainbow popsicles, often growing into bulbous masses as long as ten feet. Then there's a charmingly named slime mold called "dog vomit," which, as you can guess, looks like its namesake. More than nine hundred species of slime mold exist on every continent, and scientists cannot stop studying them. (Says Frederick Spiegel, a biology professor at the University of Arkansas and a slime mold expert: "I thought they were the most beautiful, sublime things I'd ever seen."[3]) Scientists have identified specimens in New Zealand genetically identical to those in the United States, meaning they traveled, somehow, halfway across the world without wings, paws, or feet. Even if they are ripped in half, slime molds can continue to grow and reproduce unabated. And, as one fascinating study revealed, slime molds can even solve mazes.

Mazes are often used by researchers to determine the cognitive abilities of various animals, as they require significant memory and problem-solving skills to complete. In particular, mazes test the hippocampus, which is located in one of the most evolutionarily ancient regions of the vertebrate brain and plays an important role in the consolidation of information from short-term to long-term memory as well as spatial awareness, used for navigation. The development of a species' hippocampus is often considered a bellwether for its overall intelligence, and mazes are the easiest way to test this. Smidgens of slime mold at one end of a maze can actually reproduce and grow toward food placed at the other end. When the mold reaches a dead end, it retracts its branches, retraces its steps, and tries another way. Within hours, a slime mold can find the shortest possible path to its prize. In a later study, University of Sydney researchers found that slime molds even possess spatial memory, able to leave behind a trail of translucent slime so it can identify places it has already traveled. Who needs a brain when you have slime?

Slime molds may not be able to create art or fall in love (as far as we know), but their curious existence does makes us reconsider the definition of intelligence. By calling certain animals "smart," we are implying that there are "stupid" animals without bothering to understand their particular evolutionary path. For an animal to be alive today, her ancestors endured suffering far beyond our comprehension, surviving against all the odds to pass on their DNA to the next generation. Like slime molds, jellyfish may not seem to be highly intelligent beings, but they have traveled the seas for over five hundred million years, long before fins evolved into feet and before the continents separated, surviving everything from extreme ice ages to massive volcanic eruptions that obliterated 96 percent of marine life. The next time you see an ant crawling in your pantry, a pig in a factory farm, or even bacteria under a microscope, you might be looking at the smartest organisms who have ever roamed the Earth, just for the simple reason that they have endured and prospered.

At the turn of the twentieth century, the British psychologist C. Lloyd Morgan stated, "In no case is an animal activity to be interpreted in terms of higher psychological processes if it can be fairly interpreted in terms of processes which stand lower in the scale of psychological evolution and development." This declaration, known as Morgan's Canon, meant that anthropomorphizing animal behavior—that is, attributing human emotions and intentions to animals—was counterproductive when determining the relative intelligence of Earth's creatures. A human's mind is different than a dolphin's mind, which is different than a mouse's—trying to compare them is fruitless because their habitats and lives are so different.

Even comparing the cognition of animals within the same family can be difficult. For instance, take gibbons: Small, slender creatures with powerful tree-swinging arms, gibbons were for years considered mentally inferior to other primates. In studies, chimps could learn to distinguish between various tools and quickly learn simple tasks, while gibbons appeared clueless. It wasn't until the 1960s that the American primatologist Benjamin Beck, a researcher who helped tamarin monkeys prepare for release from zoos into nature, discovered why gibbons tested so poorly compared to their fellow apes. Unlike chimps, gibbons dwell exclusively in the trees. From their long, muscular arms to their hook-like hands meant to grasp branches, gibbons bear little physical resemblance to apes who live on the ground. The original set of experiments involved placing gibbons in cages and having them manipulate objects lying on a flat surface. Gibbons, with their hooked thumbs, were physically unable to pick anything up—behavior that scientists mistook for a lack of intelligence. When Beck repeated the experiment with the tools placed at shoulder height instead of the ground, the gibbons performed just as well as other apes.

As the physicist Werner Heisenberg wrote in his 1958 book, *Physics and Philosophy,* "We have to remember that what we observe is not nature herself, but nature exposed to our method of questioning." Heisenberg was referring to measuring atoms in the field of quantum mechanics, but the principle can be applied to the study of animals as well. We are doomed to compare the behaviors of mice to rats, of albatrosses to gulls, of cats to dogs—and, ultimately, of all animals to ourselves. In this book, we do something different. We believe that the navigational abilities of the blind mole rat—a furry species who lacks eyes and gets around by parsing the Earth's magnetic field—is every bit as amazing as the arctic tern who migrates more than forty thousand miles every year. The Adélie penguin dad who guards and keeps his unborn chick warm through the fiercest Antarctic weather is just as loving as a brown bear determined to protect her cubs at any cost.

In the following chapters we will explore the amazing, mysterious, and often incomprehensible ways that animals fly, crawl, slither, hop, swim, love, chat, and romp . . . in other words, how they live.

First we will take a look at the amazing ways animals navigate the world. Like humans, many animals use the sun and the stars to find their way, but they also rely on methods that humans are biologically incapable of using, from olfactory maps to internal compasses to echolocation.

Next we will explore the world of animal communication. Chirping birds, screeching owls, singing whales, burping frogs—this is the language of the animal kingdom. The latest science shows that what may appear to be a cacophony of random noise is actually an incredibly intricate system of communication.

We next dive into life's most powerful and mysterious emotion: love. While we can never hope to truly understand how animals love and care for each other, we can record the ways they cuddle, court, mate, and protect each other.

Finally, we'll examine perhaps the most universal activity on the planet: play. Like humans, animals love to play. From play-fighting to just a quick dip in the water, play transcends the species barrier in ways that scientists still cannot understand.

By learning about how animals move, chat, love, and romp, we learn more about who animals *are*—their many talents, languages, and fascinating cultures—and how we humans can benefit from our greater understanding of what makes animals tick.

The Mysteries of Navigation

How do animals find their way over apparently trackless country, through pathless forests, across empty deserts, over and under featureless seas? They do so, of course, without any visible compass, sextant, chronometer or chart.

—Ronald Lockley, naturalist and author of *Animal Navigation*

On a foggy night in Tobermory, Ontario, in May 2016, police responded to a distress call from a woman who had accidentally driven her Toyota into Lake Huron. After dutifully following directions from her GPS, she had taken a fateful turn onto a dock before plummeting into the murky waters below. (She escaped unharmed.)

A cursory Google search displays countless stories of navigationally challenged drivers blindly following their GPS onto train platforms, into oceans, down cliffs, into golf course sand traps, even through living rooms. The more sophisticated our technology becomes, the less we depend on our innate navigation abilities. Why read street signs when an app can tell you in which direction to walk? Better yet, why walk when you can Uber? Charles Lindbergh flew across the Atlantic using a compass. Today's airline pilots rely on sophisticated autopilot systems that can find their way to any airport on Earth. One 2015 study found that nearly half of junior doctors admitted to getting lost on their way to treat a critically injured patient.

As humans continue to set new lows in the brave new world of smartphone-dependent navigation, animals continue to confound us with their ability to travel from point A to point Z. Consider, for instance, the story of a common house cat. In November 2012, Jacob and Bonnie Richter took a trip in their RV from West Palm Beach, Florida, to Daytona Beach, a distance of two hundred miles. When they arrived, the Richters' cat, a four-year-old tortoiseshell named Holly, bounded out of the camper. She disappeared near the Daytona International Speedway. After a frantic search, the Richters abandoned hope and returned to West Palm Beach, assuming Holly was lost for good. Two months later they received a call: Holly had been found in a neighbor's yard, barely a mile away from their home. She had traveled two hundred miles up the Florida coast, dodging cars, alligators, and humans to return home.

Some chalked Holly's extraordinary journey up to coincidence: Perhaps she had hopped a ride in someone's car and jumped out at precisely the right time. The evidence suggested otherwise. Holly's paws were torn and bleeding, indicating a long journey by foot. Her claws were worn down to the nub. She had dropped from 13.5 pounds to just 7. According to the vet who treated her, Holly was barely standing when she reached West Palm Beach.

Holly was not the first cat to find her way home against all the odds. In 1989, a fellow tortoiseshell cat named Murka padded 325 miles from Voronezh, Russia, to her home in Moscow. In 1997, an eight-year-old Tabby named Ninja hoofed it 850 miles from a suburb of Seattle to his former home in rural Utah. And in 1978, Howie, a Persian who had always lived indoors, trekked more than 1,000 miles across the Australian Outback to return home.

How do animals navigate without the help of maps, GPS, and gas station directions? Achievements like Holly's are not just routine in the animal kingdom, but normal. In fact, the survival of many species depends on their ability to return to the exact same spot from thousands of miles away. From celestial navigation to magnetoreception, animals rely on prodigious skills that put even the most deft human explorers to shame.

WINGED NAVIGATION

Meet Klepetan and Malena, two long-legged, beautifully plumed storks who live on a tiny red rooftop in the remote Croatian village of Slavonski. Storks are migratory birds who typically fly south during the winter months. They are also extraordinarily precise, invariably returning to the same place on the same day, year after year. Each winter, Klepetan departs his red rooftop and flies five thousand miles to South Africa. Sadly, Malena does not join him. Shot by a hunter in 1993, she was rescued and nursed back to health by a local schoolteacher, who even helped her build a nest on his roof—but she can no longer fly. (She lives indoors with the teacher during the winter months.) Malena was spotted on that roof by Klepetan and the two have remained together ever since. Every summer the two storks bring up chicks and Klepetan teaches them to fly. Klepetan and Malena have become local celebrities, via a live webcam feed documenting their lives. Once Klepetan caused mild panic among the townsfolk when he did not show up at his expected time—he eventually arrived six days later to the collective relief of the locals, who knew what obstacles he had to overcome. In an age of Google Maps and turn-by-turn GPS, storks like Klepetan—and countless other birds—venture tens of thousands of miles every year and return to the same spot, often on the same day.

How Do Birds Fly?

For millennia, humans have marveled at birds soaring through the sky. From albatrosses who glide using their ten-foot wingspans to hummingbirds who propel themselves into the air by beating their tiny wings seventy times per second, birds vary dramatically in shape and size. But the same principles of flight keep them aloft.

The miracle of flight begins not in birds' wings or feathers, but in their bones. Unlike mammals, whose bones are filled with marrow, bird bones are hollow. This makes birds lighter and easier to lift, but hollow bones have a second party trick: they're pneumatic. They're full of tiny air sacs that can take in oxygen independently of the lungs, allowing birds to sustain the immense energy required to flap their wings and generate lift. The rest of a bird's body is aerodynamically shaped with no unnecessary parts, such as teeth. To grind their food, bird stomachs have a muscular, thick-walled component called a gizzard.

While the principles of flight remain the same, birds have many different ways of taking off. Loons—large aquatic birds with pointed bills and sleek, dark heads—charge furiously into the wind, sometimes for hundreds of feet. Peregrine falcons prefer to dive off cliffs and other high perches, allowing them to reach speeds as high as 200 mph—the fastest of any animal on the planet. On the other hand, hummingbirds, like helicopters, can take off vertically. But no matter how they reach the sky, all birds rely on a smooth, tapering layer of feathers that, like an airplane wing, serves as an airfoil.

Thanks to the feathers, air flows faster above the wing than below it, creating a pressure imbalance and "pushing" a bird higher into the sky. When a bird flaps her wings downward, she creates higher-pressure air below her wings and lower-pressure air above them, creating even more lift. Once airborne, birds rely on pockets of warm, lift-generating air, known as thermal air currents, as well as other natural phenomena like updrafts, which are generated when wind hits an obstruction and flows upward. The less a bird has to flap her wings, the more energy she conserves and the farther she can soar.

In the fall, migratory birds know the season is changing and depart for warmer climates where food is plentiful, and in the spring they return to more temperate regions. Of the world's 10,000 bird species, approximately 1,800 follow this pattern. (Other species are sedentary and remain in the same place year-round.) Some birds are determined to travel as fast as possible, while others prefer a more leisurely sight-seeing trip. The great snipe reaches speeds as high as sixty miles per hour and travels more than four thousand miles in two days. The bar-tailed godwit soars more than seven thousand miles on a single tank of gas, not stopping to rest or eat. The plump, long-billed American woodcock also prefers leisurely migrations, choosing to fly at night at low altitudes. While their small flocks may occasionally reach respectable speeds of up to thirty miles per hour, woodcocks often slow themselves to a mere five miles per hour. (No species of bird flies slower.)

The distance birds travel during their migration differs drastically. North American blue grouse occupy the mountainous pine forests of the Pacific Coast Ranges during winter months. When springtime arrives they summon the energy for their three-hundred-yard migration to lower altitudes to nest and feast on fresh leaves and seeds. At the other extreme, tiny arctic terns dart and zigzag more than forty-four thousand miles between Greenland and Antarctica each year. While the four-ounce birds' path might seem inefficient, they hopscotch from continent to continent following precise air currents so they never have to fly into the wind. Because they can live more than thirty years, arctic terns can end up flying the equivalent of three trips to the moon and back.

How are birds so precise? There are several possible answers. Science suspects hatching chicks imprint on the sun, stars, and local landmarks. Trace amounts of iron located in birds' ears may also interact with neurons in their eyes to help them determine magnetic north. The beak is another crucial navigational tool. Scientists believe that a kind of olfactory map helps birds smell their way from place to place. In addition, the trigeminal nerve in the beak may also sense magnetic strength, enabling migratory birds to sense how far they are from the Earth's poles.

The earth's magnetic field is quite weak, around forty millionths of one tesla. (For comparison, an MRI machine emits up to three teslas of magnetism.) Some theories suggest that birds have an inner compass made up of light-sensitive substances, known as photochemicals, imprinted directly on their retinas. When they come into contact with light, these photochemicals become susceptible to minute changes in magnetic fields—in theory, allowing birds to navigate based on how they perceive light. This might explain why birds often behave strangely or navigate erratically around high-voltage and communication equipment. German researchers recently suggested that birds "see" magnetic fields with photochemicals in their right eye. Interacting with the left brain, these molecules produce light or dark shadings based on the strength of the earth's magnetic field—essentially creating an easy-to-follow map to and from their destination.

Some birds likely use the sky as a navigational aid. While humans did not invent the sundial until about 3,500 years ago, and the sextant only 300 years ago, birds have long since mastered the art of celestial navigation. In the early 1950s, it was theorized that many species of birds navigate using a sun compass. After observing captive European starlings—beautiful birds with glossy black feathers and a shimmering metallic sheen—researchers noted the birds adjusted their migration patterns based on the position of the sun in the sky. Further research found that birds also rely on their internal circadian rhythms, allowing them to adjust for the sun's arc throughout the day. While humans nowadays need an iPhone to determine not just the time but their location, starlings and other migratory birds need only glimpse the sun to pinpoint where they are on Earth.

Pigeons have even more remarkable navigational abilities. Able to reach speeds approaching 90 mph and find their way home from as far as a thousand miles away, they've long been prized by humans for their talents. Little is known as to how they do it, but recent research suggests homing pigeons can remember the ultrasonic signature of their surroundings and effectively "hear" their way home. "They're using sound to image the terrain [surrounding] their loft," says Jon Hagstrum, a geophysicist who studies pigeons extensively. "It's like us visually recognizing our house using our eyes."[4]

In September 1918, a group of five hundred American soldiers were trapped at the base of a hill, surrounded by German gunfire. Within a day, barely two hundred remained. Even worse, American artillery stationed many miles away had mistaken the battalion's position for the Germans' and were raining down explosive shells. Unable to establish radio connection, the besieged Americans dispatched two homing pigeons pleading their artillery to end the assault, but they were quickly shot down by the Germans. Finally, Major Charles Whittlesey turned to his sole remaining pigeon, an eight-year-old named Cher Ami, and affixed a desperate message to his leg: "For heaven's sake, stop it." As soon as Cher Ami took the sky, he was met by a torrent of German bullets. Despite being shot in the breast and leg and blinded in one eye, Cher Ami maintained a blistering pace and made it twenty-five miles to Allied lines in just twenty-five minutes. Dangling from his mangled leg was a tiny metal capsule containing the life-saving message. The Americans stopped their assault, and the battalion managed to escape back to Allied territory. The grateful troops patched up Cher Ami's wounds and fashioned him a tiny prosthetic leg, and he was personally sent off home by General John J. Pershing, commander of the American Expeditionary Force.

While pigeons' abilities still mystify science, other birds rely primarily on their eyes to navigate, just like us. Most birds of prey have eyes on the sides of their heads, but owls have human-like eyes that face forward, allowing for greater depth perception during low-light hunting. Unlike humans' eyes, owls' eyes are fixed in their sockets, hence why owls must constantly spin their heads—by as much as 270 degrees, thanks to their fourteen neck vertebrae (compared to humans' seven). Their eyesight is also exceptionally sharp compared to ours.

Owls vary greatly in size, ranging from the five-inch, one-ounce elf owl to the twenty-eight-inch, nine-pound Eurasian eagle owl. Like humans, owls possess the ability to perceive a single three-dimensional image using two eyes, known as binocular vision. Until recently, however, scientists didn't believe owl brains were capable of processing large amounts of visual information—for example, of finding a moving target among a shifting background. This requires a high degree of visual processing, something previously only seen in primates. But a new study suggests that owls, and other birds of prey, actually make sense of the world very much as humans do. Israeli researchers attached cameras to the heads of barn owls as they watched moving black dots on a gray background, measuring how long it took the owls to process the direction changes of a target dot. Owls, it turns out, are able to distinguish distinct objects from their background and perceive individual objects, such as a mouse running in a windy field or a bird breaking away from its flock, indicative of a high level of brain development.

All told, the avian brain is far more complex than previously thought. Recent studies have shown that, ounce for ounce, birds have far more brain cells than most mammals, while possessing comparable problem-solving abilities to primates. After studying birds in depth, we can now safely say that having a bird brain is a compliment, not an insult.

Are Bats Truly Blind?

Contrary to popular myth, bats aren't actually blind. There are more than 1,300 species of bat, each with different habits and dietary needs. Some prefer flowers, others eat insects. Some have very poorly developed eyes while some species, such as Pallas's long-tongued bats, tiny creatures native to Central and South America who rely on their slithery tongues to extract nectar from plants, have special visual receptors enabling them to see daylight colors and even ultraviolet light. While many bat species can see as well as, or even better than, humans, they are predominantly nocturnal creatures who rely on echolocation to hunt.

Similar to the way naval ships emit sonar pulses to construct a map of the seafloor, bats send high-frequency calls and listen for echoes from nearby objects and animals. After calculating the time difference between their initial call and the subsequent echo, bats can pinpoint the exact distance to obstacles and prey. While humans generally cannot hear high-frequency sounds above 20 kHz, bats can hear sounds as high as 110 kHz. By emitting a full spectrum of calls, bats can detect and navigate around subtleties in their environment that humans easily miss even in daylight.

BRAVING THE SEAS

The oceans cover more than two-thirds of the Earth's surface and are home to 15 percent of its species—at least, as far as we know. Humankind may have reached the moon and sent probes into interstellar space, but more than 80 percent of the oceans remain unmapped, unexplored, and unseen. Water is eight hundred times denser than air, swallowing light even at shallow depths. At fifteen feet, you can no longer see the color red. At twenty-five feet you cannot see orange. You lose yellow at thirty-five feet and green at seventy. At just over seven hundred feet, the ocean becomes as dark as the farthest reaches of space.

The estimated one million species who live in the ocean must navigate with extraordinary precision. Some sea creatures cruise near the surface, relying on the sun for guidance. Green sea turtles, who glide across tropical and subtropical seas, are renowned for journeying immense distances between feeding grounds and hatching beaches. Every two to four years, female sea turtles swim as much as 2,500 miles to breeding beaches in Southeast Asia, India, and secluded islands in the western Pacific Ocean. While human sailors routinely were lost at sea until the invention of the chronometer allowed precise longitude measurements, female sea turtles return to the exact same beach on which they hatched, dozens of years later and from thousands of miles away. These majestic creatures—now endangered due to hunting (both legal and illegal), egg harvesting, and boat strikes—are likely guided by crystals in their brains that can detect the Earth's magnetic fields. But sea turtles might also rely on the sun to point them in the right direction. Researchers from Florida Atlantic University found that sea turtles likely monitor the sun's height in the sky, known as the azimuth, to calculate their position.

Most fish species are content to stay in their corner of the ocean or lake, but a few hundred species travel hundreds or even thousands of miles a year. Some even migrate between freshwater and saltwater in search of food. Perhaps the most curious of these rituals belongs to Pacific salmon, whose lives are the stuff of Hollywood blockbusters: a thrilling race against the clock that involves a laborious upstream dash, hungry grizzly bears, a furious but fleeting romance—and a heroic death.

For the five species of Pacific salmon—chinook, chum, coho, pink, and sockeye—migration is a one-way ride. After spending the first months of their lives in freshwater streams, Pacific salmon grow into adolescent fish called smolts, distinguished by their delicate, silvery scales. Over time their body chemistry begins to change, and the young smolts crave saltier waters. When they are large enough, smolts leave their childhood rivers and head for vast feeding grounds of the open ocean. For several years these young salmon eat as much as possible to grow bigger and more powerful. They need all the energy they can muster, for they have one final trip ahead of them.

Despite wandering thousands of miles in the ocean, Pacific salmon eventually return to the very same rivers in which they were born. Scientists are not sure how their navigation is so precise, but one theory suggests that salmon navigate via the Earth's magnetic field. Another idea is that every river has its own unique scent, and salmon can actually use their exceptional sense of smell to find their way home. Locating their river is the easy part. Rivers flow into the ocean, which means Pacific salmon must migrate against the current—a phenomenon known as a salmon run. By the beginning of their run, salmon have undergone dramatic physiological changes: their color has darkened, their tails have bulked up, and males have grown sharp teeth. Having developed strong muscles and high fat reserves during their time in the ocean, salmon use every ounce of energy to flop and dash upstream. They navigate rapids and waterfalls by leaping as high as twelve feet in the air while trying to avoid predators, including bears, eagles, and humans. Salmon swim nonstop and do not eat until their migration is complete, which can span hundreds of miles. Chinook and sockeye salmon from central Idaho must travel nearly nine hundred miles and climb seven thousand feet before they reach their home spawning grounds.

The Pacific salmon who manage to make it home are gaunt and depleted, with just enough energy for one last task. Female salmon build a spawning nest and lay up to five thousand eggs, known as roe, each about the size of a pea. Meanwhile, males bite and snap and chase each other, with the most dominant fish joining the females and depositing sperm alongside their roe. The adult salmon's bodies are no longer accustomed to the freshwater of their youth and their bodies rapidly deteriorate after spawning. With broken bodies and few sources of food, these exhausted salmon die in the same places they were born, their task complete. While the vast majority of salmon species die after spawning, a small percentage of female Atlantic salmon—a species found in rivers flowing into the North Atlantic—manage to escape back to the salty ocean, regain their strength, and live to reproduce again.

Longest Mammal Migration

Arctic terns hold the world record for the longest annual migration. They have the advantage of being able to fly. Among mammals, who are the current record holders? Researchers believe that title belongs to western gray whales (narrowly edging out their close relatives, humpback whales), who swim up to ten thousand miles annually between their breeding grounds near the equator and the food-rich waters of the Arctic and Antarctic oceans. These graceful, fifty-foot-long wonders travel nearly fourteen thousand miles from Russia to Mexico and back again.

The gray whale population was decimated by whaling until the International Whaling Commission granted them protection in 1949. Since then, their population has slowly rebounded, although certain subpopulations, particularly those in the northwest Pacific, are still considered critically endangered.

Most sea migrations have lower stakes than Pacific salmon. Great white sharks, found in all of the world's oceans, migrate thousands of miles each year, although it's less clear why. While films like *Jaws* have depicted great whites as ferocious man-eaters, great white attacks on humans are exceptionally rare. They don't display the same restraint toward other sea creatures. They feast on anything from sea turtles to dolphins to seabirds, but their favorite meals are fat-rich, slow-moving seals.

Until recently, great whites were thought to be territorial fish who stuck close to coastal waters, only traveling a few hundred miles here and there to follow the seal population. However, a 2009 study published in the journal *Proceedings of the Royal Society B* proved that great whites are actually transoceanic sharks, routinely traversing the most remote waters on the planet. A research team out of Stanford University discovered that instead of staying in one location, great whites can travel as far as 3,100 miles across the open ocean, where prey is scarce. Some great whites even dive to depths approaching 4,000 feet, possibly feeding on a dense vein of fish and squid known as the deep scattering layer.

While scientists have trouble finding migration patterns among great whites, certain locations are known for repeat visits. In the Pacific, for instance, great whites often make a curious midwinter migration between central California and a barren swath of ocean between Hawaii and Baja California. For no known (to humans) reason, they leave the rich feeding grounds of coastal California to congregate in these remote waters, often referred to as the White Shark Café. Once there, great whites begin mysterious, energy-intensive dives into the deepest reaches of the ocean. "The sharks are moving between 50 meters and 250 meters very fast up and down, up and down, all day and all night—sometimes over 100 times a day, swimming faster than their terminal velocity in water,"[5] said research scientist Sal Jorgensen, who has devoted enormous amounts of time tracking great whites. Scientists surmise they are looking for mates, or possibly a particularly delectable fish, but they don't really know, and as of now, have no way of finding an answer.

Are Fish Self-Aware?

One of the most specious myths about fish is that they cannot feel pain or feel emotions—and, therefore, that it's not cruel to catch them with hooks and let them suffocate on land.

Fish do feel pain, and they are aware of themselves as individuals. One way to test whether an animal possesses self-recognition is to place her in front of a mirror with a small section of her body painted. If she gazes into the mirror and then touches or investigates the mark, she likely recognizes herself in the mirror and is therefore self-aware. (It's worth noting that the mirror test is one of many tests for determining self-awareness; it's generally agreed that animals can be self-aware in ways not measured by human tests. And animals who are not traditionally self-aware still experience pain, trauma, and other emotions.)

Researchers from Osaka City University in Japan decided to try the mirror test on the cleaner wrasse, a small fish found along coral reefs from East Africa and the Red Sea to French Polynesia. These fish form mutualistic relationships with larger fish by "cleaning" them, usually by nibbling off parasites. Cleaner wrasses are quite entrepreneurial: They band together to create "cleaning stations" for larger fish, attracting new clients by wriggling their rears up and down in a dance-like motion.

In their study, the Japanese researchers placed a mirror in front of cleaner wrasses. At first they acted skittish and territorial—meaning they regarded their reflections as foreign fish. But over the course of several days the fish began to calm down, and by the end of the study they could clearly recognize their own movements. The fish even used their reflection in the mirror to help remove tags affixed by the researchers to their bodies.

TINY TRIPS

Despite possessing small brains—a half-millimeter wide with barely a million neurons—bees meander up to two miles from their hives before buzzing home. Even when they are unwittingly captured, such as by a car window or a nefarious scientist, and released in a nearby location, bees can reorient themselves and fly hiveward. How can such tiny creatures who measure their life span in days while lacking hippocampi, entorhinal cortexes, and other advanced brain structures find their way home? Scientists have no idea. Their hunch is that bees imprint a map of their territory on their diminutive brains and buzz home by navigating to familiar landmarks. Other research has suggested that bees monitor the position of the sun to orient themselves in conjunction with an internal clock—the bee equivalent of computing longitude and latitude.

A similar method is used by sandhoppers, tiny crustaceans who can often be seen bounding along sandy beaches near the high-tide mark after twilight. They are often called beach fleas, an unfortunate misnomer because sandhoppers are not fleas, nor do they bite. These creatures, who from a distance resemble dancing brown beans, commute from damp sands where they hide during the day to forage for food near the shoreline. Sandhoppers generally orient their movements along an east–west axis—the same route the sun takes across the sky. At night, they use the moon's rays as a guide.

Some insects navigate by the stars. The dung beetle, who prefers to go about his sordid business under the cover of darkness, uses the night sky to orient himself and return home with his bounty. Dung beetles spend their evenings rolling the excrement of other animals into balls and burying it in soft spots in the soil. They may not look particularly hardy, but according to researchers out of Queen Mary University of London, male dung beetles can haul more than 1,100 times their body weight—the equivalent of a human pulling six fully loaded double-decker buses.

Rolling a ball of poo is not quite as easy as it may seem to all of you who have never tried it. Dung beetles often have to shake off smaller organisms who try and hitch a ride on a dung ball. As a result, they can lose their way and must reorient themselves. Careful observations have found that dung beetles typically climb atop their freshly rolled scat and dance in circles before returning home—a complicated navigational process. "The dorsal (upper) parts of the dung beetles' eyes are specialized to be able to analyze the direction of light polarization— the direction that light vibrates in,"[6] researcher Marie Dacke told *Live*

Science in 2013. Dung beetles use the polarization patterns of the night sky to avoid moving in circles. In fact, researchers believe that certain subspecies of dung beetles navigate much more efficiently on clear, starry nights when the spiraling Milky Way galaxy is distinct.

From the lowly dung beetle to the monarch butterfly—a creature hailed as "one of the most spectacular natural phenomena in the world"—insects have honed remarkable navigational habits. The latter possesses one of the most amazing annual migration patterns of any animal—one requiring four generations of butterflies to complete. Beginning in March and April, the first generation of butterflies hatch after four days into caterpillars, also known as larvae. For about two weeks the baby caterpillars crawl around and consume milkweed plants until they are ready to begin the process of metamorphosis. After attaching themselves to a stem or leaf, the caterpillars spin themselves into a hard silk casing called a chrysalis. The chrysalis might appear sedentary from the outside, but within hides a spectacular process as the caterpillar's old body parts transform into wings. After about ten days, a monarch butterfly emerges, spreads her wings, and soars into the sky. Her life is as short as it is beautiful: She has just two to six weeks to lay as many eggs as possible before she dies.

The cycle repeats, and then again, with a second generation of butterflies born in May and June, and a third generation born in July and August. With each generation the butterflies follow the warm weather north, even as far as Canada. But the fourth generation, born in September and October, differs. Their journey is more arduous. As the weather turns colder, these butterflies must travel south to Mexico, and they must do it alone. Instead of two to six weeks, these butterflies live six to eight months, traveling up to 2,500 miles to over-winter sites— most notably the Monarch Butterfly Biosphere Reserve, about sixty miles northwest of Mexico City and home to nearly all of the wintering populations of eastern Monarch butterflies. (Monarch butterflies who live west of the Rocky Mountains generally spend colder months in southern California.) For the next few months they hibernate in oyamel fir trees until they are ready to commence the journey back north, to begin the four-generation cycle anew.

Scientists once believed that the monarch butterflies' migration pattern was the longest of any insect, but recent research suggests that this distinction belongs to a special kind of dragonfly appropriately called the wandering glider. With their multifaceted eyes, muscular wings, and elongated body, dragonflies are one of the most recognizable insects on the planet—and among the most misunderstood. Naturalists have long known that certain dragonflies are migratory, but due to their size and darting speed, tracking them for long distances is difficult. Powerful fliers, dragonflies can propel themselves in six directions and fly at bursts of thirty miles per hour. Many dragonflies aren't migratory, however, and don't travel more than a few miles over the course of their one or two months of life. Wandering gliders are different.

It was only in 2009, when biologist Charles Anderson presented his research in the *Journal of Tropical Ecology*, that the secrets of these mysterious insects were revealed. Anderson learned about wandering gliders the old-fashioned way: He watched them. After correlating observations from India, East Africa, and other locations with seasonal weather patterns, he found that many wandering gliders complete epically long journeys that, like monarch butterflies, require several generations of dragonflies to complete. Anderson was initially curious why these unassuming yellow insects would show up to his home in the Maldives—an island nation of tropical coral islands located southwest of India and Sri Lanka—and then mysteriously leave. After observing them for more than fifteen years, he discovered that wandering gliders hopscotch their way across the Indian Ocean by following the seasonal monsoon rains. Wandering gliders, it turns out, love to mate in torrential rain—so much so that they'll follow monsoons for nearly ten thousand miles.

Some animals don't need wings or feet to find their way home. In 2009, a senior citizen in England named Ruth Brooks was exasperated: Her garden was being overrun by marauding bands of snails. "They had eaten her lettuce, ravaged her petunias and devastated her beans,"[7] the BBC reported. Brooks was too compassionate to kill the tiny mollusks, so she relocated them to a nearby tract of land. It wasn't the very next day—garden snails top out at about 0.029 mph—but Brooks's hungry snails eventually returned to devour her petunias. No matter where she brought them, the snails found their way back. Brooks reached out to Dr. Dave Hodgson, a biologist at the University of Exeter, who devised an experiment involving sixty-five snails relocated to various corners of their home garden. The result: Nearly all the snails managed to navigate as much as eighty-five feet to return to their original location. Said Dr. Hodgson: "Now this needs some analysis, but as far as I am concerned this is quite spectacular evidence for homing instinct in the garden snail and it's so much better than I could ever have wished."[8]

LUMBERING ON LAND

It's easy to imagine birds and fish and flying insects—creatures who travel far above or below us—migrating long distances, but even the largest, slowest-moving land mammals are capable of navigating hundreds, or even thousands, of miles each year. In the days before the ivory trade decimated Africa's elephants—recent estimates suggest their population has declined by 97 percent since the early 1900s, from 12 million to just 350,000 today—these majestic animals would journey exceptionally long distances. Led by the oldest and wisest female of the herd, known as the matriarch, African elephants wandered hundreds of miles along tried-and-true migration paths, following the rains toward more fertile lands. Many of their routes were so trodden that they became the foundation of human roads. Today, elephant mobility is greatly hindered by human activity and poaching, and is generally restricted to protected reserves. But some elephant populations still retrace their ancestral routes.

Chief among these nomads are elephants who call home the Namib and Sahara Deserts in Africa. Known as desert elephants, these individuals spend their days migrating as many as thirty-five miles per day in search of water. As biologist Iain Douglas-Hamilton, founder of the nonprofit Save the Elephants, explains, desert elephants are "living on the edge, in the most extreme conditions."[9] Like all elephants, their primary threat is poachers. Although a massive conservation effort has helped the elephants rebound, Namibia's and Mali's desert elephant population stands around six hundred and four hundred respectively. Despite the risks, these elephants travel hundreds of miles per year, eating any sort of vegetation they can find including herbs, grass, shrubs, bark, leaves, seeds, and fruit. They can't afford to be picky, as desert elephants require up to 550 pounds of food and 42 gallons of water daily.

Unlike other animals, such as birds, who are born with their navigational abilities, elephants must learn from experience. A herd's survival is dependent on the matriarch, who has learned safe routes and reliable water sources in a landscape almost entirely devoid of either—knowledge that has been passed down for thousands of years. Over the years and decades, the matriarch remembers which routes are safe, which have become dangerous, and she can distinguish between friendly and unknown elephant calls. The wisest matriarchs can even tell the difference between male and female lion roars—a crucial difference as males are larger and more likely to hunt elephant calves. Matriarchs must navigate places like the northern Cunene Region of Namibia, where rainfall averages just four inches per year. When food is scarce, matriarchs must get resourceful; many herds, for instance, head to the Hoanib River in western Namibia to feed on the seedpods of Ana trees.

In one noteworthy study from 2008 led by the Tarangire Elephant Project, researchers followed twenty-one elephant families during an extended period of drought. Groups with the oldest matriarchs—those who had survived the previous major drought thirty years earlier—were much more likely to find food and water in far-flung locations that elephants rarely visited. Despite not visiting these places for de-cades, the matriarchs were able to summon ancient memories and navigate their families to safety.

World Record Migration

Land animals do not have the luxury of soaring high in the air. They must make their seasonal treks by paw or hoof. The most arduous journey of all belongs to caribou. Na-tive to northern regions of North America, Europe, Asia, and Greenland, every year three million of these antlered beings journey across the Arctic tundra, quite literally in search of greener pastures. During summer months they feed on the lush grasses of the tundra, feasting on as much as twelve pounds of plants each day. When snow begins to fall, they turn east toward more sheltered areas, where they feast on algae-like plants called lichens. Some caribou, notably woodland caribou found in Canada's remote Northwest Ter-ritories, migrate up to three thousand miles a year—the far-thest of any land mammal.

Near the eastern coast of Africa, another great navigational feat takes place each year. Hailed as "The Great Migration" or the "World Cup of Wildlife," each year more than 1.5 million wildebeest, 200,000 zebras, and some 400,000 gazelle gallop from the Ngorongoro Conservation Area in Tanzania to Maasai Mara National Reserve in Kenya—the largest terrestrial mammal migration in the world. The bulk of the migration occurs in the Serengeti, a twelve-thousand-square-mile ecosystem spanning from northern Tanzania to southwestern Kenya. Wildebeest, who make up the bulk of the yearly migration, are even-toed and horned with broad muzzles and shaggy manes, weighing up to 550 pounds and able to sprint up to 50 mph. (In the movie *The Lion King*, Simba's father, Mufasa, was killed during a wildebeest stampede.) The Great Migration begins generally in January and February in Tanzania, when female wildebeest give birth to approximately 350,000 calves, all born within several weeks of each other. The synchronized births offer wildebeests an evolutionary advantage, as their predators, mostly hyenas and lions, invariably engorge themselves all at once and leave the vast majority of calves alone.

Newborn wildebeest are on their feet and walking within minutes of birth—faster than any other hoofed mammal. They must be ready to move: By March the land begins to dry out and the wildebeest begin traveling north, following the rains and the growth of new grass. They then head to the heart of the Serengeti, toward small, freshwater lakes where they feed on the abundant grasses. By June, the wildebeest have arrived at the Grumeti Game Reserve, a picturesque park created in 1994 by the Tanzanian government to protect the path of the wildebeest migration. Perils remain: Throughout their journey the wildebeest are stalked by lions, hyenas, leopards, cheetahs, and other predators, and they must ford fierce and unpredictable rivers that can drown dozens of animals at a time. Finally, by August, the exhausted creatures have reached Maasai Mara National Reserve in southern Kenya, where they spend the next several months regaining their strength for the journey home. By late October, when the seasonal rains return, they begin the trek back to the Serengeti, this time traveling through its eastern woodlands. By the time they reach home, the females are heavily pregnant with the next generation of wildebeest who will complete the ancient migration path the following year.

Magnetoreception

Middle East blind mole rats—tiny, furry rodents known for their extravagant subterranean tunnels—are able to monitor their location underground by parsing the Earth's magnetic field. Blind mole rats are completely blind thanks to a layer of skin over their tiny eyes. This doesn't stop them from making long journeys to scavenge for onions and tubers and methodically depositing them in a complex network of tunnels to be retrieved later. Over short distances, mole rats rely on their balance and sense of smell to stay oriented, but over longer routes they rely on a more sophisticated navigational system—they use the Earth's magnetic field as a reference to help guide them. How mole rats use their magnetic compass is unclear, but it may be that mole rats have magnetite crystals embedded in their olfactory regions, allowing them to divine their way home.

Mole rats are likely not the only mammals who can sense the Earth's magnetic waves. For example, red foxes have been found to overwhelmingly pounce on their prey facing northeast. And if you have a dog, start paying attention to his bathroom habits: A two-year study published in the journal *Frontiers in Zoology* comprising thirty-seven breeds and more than five thousand observations found that "Dogs preferred to excrete with the body being aligned along the North–South axis."[10]

The ways in which animals fly, walk, swim, slither, gallop, and roll fascinate humans, because the more we learn about these complex processes, the more we realize how little we really know about them. How is it that birds with brains just a fraction of the size of our own can fly to the exact same place, thousands of miles away, year after year? How is it sea turtles can cross entire oceans to find the tiny, remote island on which they were born decades earlier? In short, how are animals so much better than humans are at navigating their way around this earth? Science keeps coming up with new explanations, but there are many mysteries we may never solve.

Humans will invent newer and greater smartphones that can lead us to any Starbucks on Earth. Self-driving cars will one day render road signs obsolete. Yet animals will continue to navigate the same way they always have—and as successfully as ever, without the downtimes or stoppages or battery failures. As for the estimated seven million species that have not yet been discovered, we can only guess what impressive ways they move about the planet—and perhaps learn from them as well.

The Channels of Communication

An animal's eyes have the power to speak a great language.

—Martin Buber

Around the turn of the twentieth century, Germany was in the thrall of a horse—specifically, a horse named Hans, an Orlov trotter whose owner, Wilhelm von Osten, claimed could understand human sentences and even solve math problems. By tapping his hooves, "Clever Hans," as he was dubbed by the media, could reportedly add, subtract, multiply, divide, compute fractions, keep track of time, and spell and understand German among many other advanced tasks. Von Osten exhibited Hans throughout the country, where he became such a sensation that the German board of education established a panel of experts, appropriately called the Hans Commission, to investigate the horse's seemingly miraculous language skills. The panel eventually determined that Hans, while indeed clever, was actually reacting to involuntary cues in von Osten's body language. By studying his trainer's facial tension, Hans could tell when another hoof tap was expected or when he should remain still. This phenomenon became known by comparative psychologists as the "Clever Hans Effect"—the tendency for researchers to inadvertently telegraph cues to their animal subjects when testing cognitive abilities.

The Clever Hans Effect raises questions that have long gnawed at scientists: Can animals communicate as we do? Do they merely *appear* to communicate? Or do they communicate in ways that we simply don't understand?

Human–animal communication has long been a feature of our folklore. The *Panchatantra*, one of the oldest collections of Indian fables, is wholly composed of stories about animals who talk with each other, and with humans. Russian folktales also feature anthropomorphized animals, notably the story of Baba Yaga, a mystical woman who can transform into animals at whim. During the early 1700s, a French bishop spotted an orangutan in a French zoo. The ape walked upright and appeared so human-like that the bishop, caught off-guard, declared: "Speak and I shall baptize thee!"

From our backyards to city streets to the vast Serengeti, animals are speaking all around us, and we are only now beginning to understand a little of what they are saying.

CANINE COMMUNICATION

Can animals understand the spoken word? Anyone with a dog will likely answer: "Of course."

Studies have shown that the average canine companion can understand and react to nearly two hundred human words—and with specialized training, even more. For years it was not clear whether dogs were reacting to specific words or to our tone of voice, but a study shines light on their complex linguistic abilities. Hungarian researchers at Eötvös Loránd University recruited thirteen family dogs and trained them to sit still in a functional magnetic resonance imaging machine. (The researchers stressed that the dogs were never restrained and could move around at any time.) After playing recordings of a trainer's words and studying the dogs' brain waves, the scientists found that the dogs could actually process tones and words separately. When the dogs heard words of praise, such as "good boy" or "well done," their brain's left hemisphere lit up—the same location where human brains process language. Moreover, the dogs processed positive and negative tones in the right hemisphere—again, as humans do. The researchers found that dogs only responded to words of praise when they were spoken in an upbeat tone. "Dogs not only tell apart what we say and how we say it, but they can also combine the two for a correct interpretation of what those words really meant," noted the study's lead researcher, Attila Andics. "Again, this is very similar to what human brains do."[11]

Further studies have shown that dogs do more than listen. To a human, a pack of dogs interacting might sound like a cacophony of growls, snarls, and yaps, but dogs alter their tone to produce a striking variety of sounds—each with their own meaning. Dogs modify the pitch, timing, and amplitude of their barks, which is believed to be a method for communicating intentions to their canine cohorts. For example, it has been determined that dogs produce a "food growl" when tussling over food, and a distinctly different "stranger growl" upon spotting an unknown human. When researchers played recordings of the growls to a dog circling a bone, he was far more hesitant to approach it when he heard the food growl compared to the stranger growl. Conversely, another experiment found that dozing dogs were more likely to jump to their feet when they heard recordings of stranger growls compared to food growls.

Dogs' close relatives, wolves, also have an intricate way of communicating. The gray wolf, or *Canis lupus,* is found in remote regions of Europe, Asia, and North America. Science once believed that today's canines evolved from gray wolves approximately ten thousand years ago, but recent genetic research suggests they share a common prehistoric wolf ancestor who lived in Europe between nine and thirty-four thousand years ago. Compared to dogs, wolves have lanky legs, slender bodies, and meaty paws allowing them to travel long distances in harsh environments. When a domesticated dog runs, he dashes and bobs with ebullient, if ungraceful, movements. A wolf, however, stalks rather than bounds, keeping her movements silent and smooth. Wolves also have much larger jaws capable of crushing bones. Dogs have fur and eye color that runs the gamut, but wolves generally have camouflaged white, black, gray, or brown fur, depending on their environment, with yellow or amber eyes.

Contrary to their lone-wolf moniker, wolves are highly social; they depend on extremely complex relationships and hierarchies to survive. Typically, groups of five to eleven wolves live together in packs consisting of two monogamous adults, three to six juveniles, and one to three pups. When juveniles reach sexual maturity they leave the pack to find a mate and begin a family of their own. In order to survive in harsh environments with limited food, wolf packs must work together closely to stalk and chase their prey, sometimes for many miles.

This is accomplished through a very intricate communication system involving three separate senses. The first is visual: Wolves rely on body language to impart basic rules of the pack—the foremost being that a pack consists of leaders and followers. The leaders are the parents, older, stronger, and wiser than the rest. They remind their children of this by standing tall and holding their tails high in the air. Other wolves display their submissiveness by keeping their tails down and slouching. Less dominant wolves will also lie on their side, displaying their vulnerable abdomen as a sign of submission. When a wolf is angry, she lets others know by sticking her ears straight up and baring their teeth. When afraid, she will flatten her ears against her head. When she wants to play, she will dance and bow like a dog. Like dogs, wolves also have an exceptional sense of smell—nearly a hundred times better than humans—which the pack uses to its advantage. By strategically marking trees and soil with urine, often every few minutes, wolves can stake out their territory and avoid areas belonging to other packs. Finally, when she howls, she does so very purposefully. It could mean a cry to rally the pack to defend young pups against predators, or it could be a social howl to locate her family. Other vocalizations include whimpering, used by mothers to encourage their pups to nurse and older wolves to indicate submissiveness, and growling, used to project aggression.

Why Are Dogs So Friendly?

When it comes to the human-canine relationship, it's less survival of the fittest and more survival of the friendliest.

While wolves continue to stalk the remote wilderness of North America and Eurasia, dogs prefer to live inside and make as many new human friends as possible. The bonds between dogs and humans are ancient and unwavering, and new studies show they run deeper than we thought.

In 2014, University of Chicago researchers published findings in *PLOS Genetics* revealing that several groups of genes in dogs and humans, especially those related to digestion and disease, evolved side by side for thousands of years—a likely result of their shared environments. As dogs and humans developed a mutual dependency, they increasingly lived in crowded environments, leading nature—and, eventually, humans themselves—to select for more friendly dogs. Because they lived and evolved together for so long—often developing similar habits for unhealthy foods—dogs and humans both share similar diseases, such as obesity, epilepsy, cancer, and even obsessive-compulsive disorders.

Dogs were so important to human development that, as research scientists Brian Hare and Vanessa Woods suggest in their book *The Genius of Dogs*, "We didn't domesticate dogs. They domesticated us."[12]

ANIMALS WHO READ

Some animals even appear to have rudimentary reading comprehension skills. For millennia we've known that horses are intelligent, highly trainable creatures able to learn a wide number of commands and tasks. While the Clever Hans episode extinguished for many years the belief that horses possessed communicative abilities, a research team at Norwegian University of Life Sciences discovered that horses can read symbols and use them to communicate a desire—in this case, whether they wanted a blanket. Published in the journal *Applied Animal Behaviour Science* in 2016, the study involved showing three signs to horses: one that was entirely white, one with a black horizontal bar on a white background, and one with a black vertical bar on a white background. After eleven days the horses learned to indicate a preference—to have a blanket placed on their back, to have an existing one removed, or to keep things the way they were—by nudging a corresponding sign. Moreover, the researchers found the horses were visibly excited with their newfound communicative abilities, suggesting they could understand cause and effect.

The ability to see a symbol and comprehend its meaning turns out to be more common to many species than previously thought. In one recent study conducted at the Oakland Zoo in California, a thirty-four-year-old elephant named Donna could associate a picture of a banana with the real fruit. When Donna scanned through various photographs and touched a picture of her favorite food, she knew that doing so would lead to a banana windfall. The ability to anticipate and plan ahead is a crucial marker of intelligence, as Caitlin O'Connell-Rodwell, an elephant expert at Stanford University, noted: "If you can imagine an object in your mind, that means you can think about that object and plan around that object. Does Donna understand that that picture of the banana represents a real banana? 'Cause that means that she can imagine that in her mind."[13]

THE TALK OF THE FARM

Domesticated animals who spend their lives on farms are no less able communicators. In fact, when it comes to cows, sometimes all that is needed is eye contact.

Kite's Nest Farm is a 390-acre organic farm located near the Cotswolds in south central England, home to lush, rolling hills and stone-built villages. Over the years, the farm's owner, Rosamund Young, has documented the fascinating ways in which cows living there interact. In her bestselling book *The Secret Life of Cows*, Young mentions the story of a cow named Christmas Bonnet. One winter's day Young brought a number of the younger bulls and their mothers across the farm to be counted for a government audit. This meant, as Young wrote, that Christmas Bonnet was left alone "with no family and *ipso facto* no friends."[14] The next day, when Young and her mother went to feed Christmas Bonnet, the cow simply stared at them. As they walked back and forth from their car, Christmas Bonnet fixed her eyes on Young and her mother in turn. It was painfully clear that she was not pleased. They apologized to Christmas Bonnet and promised to reunite her with her family as soon as possible. Evidently that was not good enough, for as soon as they left, Christmas Bonnet escaped, negotiating hedges, gates, and fences to find her own way back to her family.

Another farmed species, pigs, have an intricate way of communicating with each other. More than twenty of their oinks, grunts, and squeals have been identified for different situations, from wooing their mates to expressing hunger. Newborn piglets learn to run to their mothers' voices, and mother pigs sing to their young while nursing. Confirmed by a study in the journal *Royal Society Open Science*, these barnyard noises aren't just gibberish. "The aim of this research was to investigate what factors affect vocalizations in pigs so that we can better understand what information they convey,"[15] explained the lead researcher. After studying seventy-two male and female pigs in various social situations, the study confirmed that pig sounds are unique and repeatable. Pigs use "acoustic signals in a variety of ways; maintaining contact with other group members while foraging, parent-offspring communication, or to signal if they are distressed," one researcher explained. "The sounds they make convey a wide range of information such as the emotional, motivational and physiological state of the animal. For example, squeals are produced when pigs feel fear, and may be either alerting others to their situation or offering assurance."[16]

Cows and pigs aren't the only farm animals with highly developed communication skills. Leading animal behaviorists from around the globe know that chickens are inquisitive and interesting animals whose cognitive abilities are in some cases more advanced than those of cats, dogs, and even some primates. Like all animals, chickens love their families and value their own lives. The social nature of chickens means that they are always looking out for their families and for other chickens in their group. People who have spent time with chickens know they have complex social structures, adept communication skills, and distinct personalities, just as we do.

When in their natural surroundings, chickens form complex social hierarchies, also known as pecking orders. Every chicken knows his or her place on the social ladder, remembering the faces and ranks of more than one hundred other birds. Chickens have more than thirty types of vocalizations to distinguish between threats approaching by land or air. A mother hen teaches some of them to her chicks before they even hatch; as she clucks softly while sitting on the eggs, her chicks chirp back to her and to each other from inside their shells.

DEEP-SEA COMMUNICATION

There is a difference between understanding commands and actually conversing. When scientists study animal intelligence, they make a general distinction between animal language and animal communication. While dogs can parse individual words of praise and even adjust their growls, this is not considered a language in the traditional sense. The hallmark traits of human language include the ability to assign arbitrary sounds to words (e.g., there is nothing beak-like about the word "beak"), and the ability to communicate about ideas or things in the past or future. But in recent years, scientists have begun to rethink their assumptions about animals' inability to speak like us.

One such scientist is marine mammologist Denise Herzing, who for many years has been studying the cognitive and language abilities of wild spotted dolphins living off the coast of the Bahamas. Scientists have known for a long time that dolphins are smart. Like humans, they possess certain common measures of intelligence: They have the largest brain-to-body ratio of all aquatic mammals; they can recognize themselves in mirrors; and in some parts of the world they use tools to hunt. Highly social animals, dolphins live in pods comprising up to a dozen individuals. They can also be wonderfully empathetic: When one dolphin becomes sick or injured, others care for her. But Herzing's team was most concerned with figuring out the complexities of dolphin communication, composed of clicks, whistle-like sounds, and nonverbal signs.

Herzing set up camp in the Bahamas, renowned for its crystal-blue waters that offer near-limitless views of underwater life. Spending every summer for more than two decades on a sixty-foot catamaran, Herzing and her team monitored the same pod of dolphins, year after year, to figure out how they communicate. In her 2013 TED Talk, she described these creatures as "natural acousticians. They make sounds ten times as high and hear sounds ten times as high as we do. But they have other communication signals they use. They have good vision, so they use body postures to communicate. They have taste, not smell. And they have touch."[17]

Dolphins' skin is so sensitive that they can actually feel sound waves in the water. In fact, "dolphins can buzz and tickle each other at a distance," said Herzing.

Just as humans give themselves names, dolphins have their own distinctive calls: When a dolphin whistles, the rest of her pod knows who is speaking. But the true beauty of dolphin communication lies beyond the realm of the human auditory range. Dolphins also emit ultrasonic whistles, clicks, and peeps only perceptible to humans using specialized equipment. Herzing focused on burst-pulsed sounds that, when analyzed with a spectrograph machine, highly resembled human speech patterns. To test this theory, the team assembled a sophisticated two-way keyboard interface that could receive and transmit dolphin frequencies. The goal was to see if dolphins could be taught to associate artificial whistles with objects.

After observing dolphins playing a game of keep-away—dolphins are extremely playful animals—Herzing attached the keyboard to her boat and, with scuba equipment, brought down some of the dolphins' favorite play objects, including rope and seaweed. Using the keyboard, the team associated the objects with various whistles. Before long, the dolphins learned to request play objects from humans by emitting distinctive whistles. Moreover, when the dolphins were in possession of a toy, Herzing could play a whistle on her keyboard and ask them to return it to her—which they dutifully did. Herzing is currently working with Georgia Institute of Technology to create a mobile, more sophisticated keyboard that will allow her to further unlock the mysteries of dolphin communication.

Dolphins Don't Forget

Although we knew dolphins' memories were good, until recently no one knew how good. It turns out, very good. A recent study in the journal *Proceedings of the Royal Society B* reported that dolphins can actually recognize the whistles of others they hadn't seen in twenty years. In fact, the University of Chicago researchers found that dolphins were able to recognize the whistle of a companion they had last seen two decades ago just as easily as they recognized a friend they last saw six months ago. "This shows us an animal operating cognitively at a level that's very consistent with human social memory,"[18] the lead researcher, Jason Bruck, explained.

In the air, sound waves travel at roughly 760 mph. In water, they can move as much as five times faster, depending on ocean temperature and pressure; they travel like ripples, slowing down as they go deeper and deeper until they reach the thermocline layer—the depth where the ocean's temperature stops decreasing. There the sound waves ricochet back toward the surface, speed up, and can travel for thousands of miles. This means particularly loud sea creatures can communicate across vast distances—even entire oceans.

At nearly one hundred feet in length and weighing 170 tons, blue whales are the largest animals to have ever existed on Earth. Their hearts alone weigh 400 pounds. Long and slender with no natural predators, blue whales drift gracefully through the deep and are found in every ocean. Despite their size, their diet consists of some of Earth's smallest creatures: Using a filter-feeder system called baleen, they inhale tiny crustaceans, predominantly krill. A single blue whale can eat up to forty million krill, amounting to 7,900 pounds, in a single day. These whales, once abundant in the Earth's oceans, were hunted to near extinction by whalers. Their numbers have rebounded after they received protection from the International Whaling Commission in 1966, although they are still considered endangered today.

During the height of the Cold War, the United States Navy used hydrophones to search for Soviet nuclear submarines in the northern Pacific Ocean. Among the greatest sources of interference were blue whales, who seemed to be calling out to each other across incredible swaths of water. Studies have shown that whales of all species use sound for a variety of reasons, including navigation and detecting food, but even hundred-foot whales can lose track of each other in the depths of the ocean. With their booming voices, blue whales emit sounds as low as 14 Hz—well below the lower limit of human hearing—and as loud as 180 decibels, making them the loudest, if undetectable, creatures on the planet. Under the right ocean conditions, a blue whale's haunting hums and clicks can travel for hundreds of miles, ensuring that a mother and her baby can never truly be separated, even if they are an ocean apart.

Close relatives of blue whales, humpback whales are smaller—typically around forty-five feet long and thirty-nine tons—with a stocky body and, as their name suggests, a distinctive hump. Humpbacks are popular with whale watchers, as they routinely rush to the ocean surface and leap out of the water, a phenomenon known as breaching. Both males and females vocalize, but males are famous for producing beautifully complex songs. Whales do not have vocal cords, but they can call out using a larynx-like structure in their throats. As they don't need to exhale, they can sing continuously for hours at a time. Scientists aren't sure why males sing, but these songs—"probably the most complex in the animal kingdom,"[19] according to marine biologist Phillip Clapham—typically occur during breeding season, so they are likely designed to attract a mate.

"I had never heard anything like it," says Katy Payne, a researcher in acoustic biology at the Cornell Lab of Ornithology, regarding the first time she heard a whale song. With her husband, Roger, she was among the first scientists to study them. "Oh, my God, tears flowed from our cheeks. We were just completely transfixed and amazed because the sounds are so beautiful, so powerful—so variable. They were, as we learned later, the sounds of just one animal. *Just one* animal."[20]

Humpback songs are so complex that it takes a trained musician to truly appreciate them. After creating visual representations of the songs, called spectrograms, Payne could easily pick out patterns—the hallmark signs of melodies and harmonies. The songs are regionally diverse, with North Atlantic humpbacks singing one song and North Pacific humpbacks crooning another. But over years, individual whales subtly change the songs—an inflection here, a different pitch there, a fresh coda—until they are thoroughly unique. One whale Payne studied evolved his song from six elements to fourteen in just two years. "We don't know," Payne responded when asked why humpback males sing. "Ask the whale."

Talking Frogs

As for creatures who live on the fringes of land and water, possibly the first image that the phrase "talking frogs" evokes is the famous 1995 Budweiser Super Bowl commercial featuring three beer-loving frog puppets named Bud, Weis, and Er. In reality, frogs and toads create a rich variety of calls and songs during their courtship rituals. The caller, typically the male, projects his readiness to mate with any combination of whistles, chirps, croaks, ribbits, clucks, peeps, barks, or grunts, depending on the species. American bullfrogs, for instance, emit a very loud, low-pitched drone or bellow. Northern Pacific tree frogs prefer the more classic "ribbbbit." These "advertisement calls" serve several purposes for males, including establishing their territory, deterring rival males, and, ultimately, attracting females.

The Brazilian torrent frog, a tiny amphibian found in the Rio de Janeiro and São Paulo states of Brazil, has an especially intricate form of communication that employs tactile, vocal, and visual signaling. From squealing to head bobbing to arm waving, torrent frogs do whatever is necessary to make themselves seen, heard, and felt. In one study, researchers found that male torrent frogs call out during all months of the year—except, oddly, October—and will even conduct a bizarre breakdance routine involving snake-like figure-eight patterns, head bobbing, and feet shaking. Their vocal playlist includes peeps and squeals, and they often share special tactile signals with their female mates—the frog version of a secret handshake. Torrent frogs don't just reserve their moves for females, however. Sometimes they direct their routine toward approaching predators, perhaps to scare them off or to warn nearby frogs of danger.

SIGNING PRIMATES

The phrase "ape communication" conjures up the 1968 film *Planet of the Apes*, in which a human astronaut crew, after crash-landing on a strange planet, is confronted with a highly evolved society of apes who speak perfect English. The apes that we know, however, lack the anatomical prerequisites for verbal language, such as strong larynx muscles and nimble vocal cords. But just because apes can't speak like humans do doesn't mean they can't communicate.

The first inkling that species of apes were more human-like than originally thought came in Tanzania in 1960, when famed primatologist Jane Goodall observed a chimp squatting beside a termite mound. Unsure what he was doing, Goodall crept closer until she saw that the chimp was poking at the mound with a blade of grass to fish out termites. Later, Goodall observed chimps stripping leaves from twigs and using them to spear ants. These were breakthrough moments. Previously scientists believed that only humans possessed the ability to make and use their own tools. This belief was encapsulated by the anthropologist Kenneth Oakley, who explained in 1949 that "the most satisfactory definition of man from the scientific point of view is probably Man the Tool-maker."[21] But when Goodall telegrammed her findings to the renowned Kenyan paleoanthropologist Louis Leakey, he famously replied: "Now we must redefine tool, redefine Man, or accept chimpanzees as humans." Or, as the American biologist and author Jared Diamond suggested, we might consider humans to be the "third chimpanzee."

It's not likely that science will be so respectful as to reclassify chimps as humans, but their minds work remarkably similarly to ours. In 2012, an international research team confirmed that bonobos, dark-haired chimpanzees native to the rainforests of the Democratic Republic of the Congo, are humans' closest living relatives, sharing about 99 percent of our DNA. Humans and chimpanzees descended from a single ancestor who lived between six and seven million years ago. As

Diamond explains in his classic book, *The Third Chimpanzee,* chimps are more closely related to humans than they are to other apes. In fact, chimps are more closely related to humans than many animals of the same species are to each other, such as red-eyed and white-eyed vireo songbirds.

Since Goodall's observations, chimps have been repeatedly observed demonstrating human-like behavior, such as communities in the Congo who travel with two tool-like sticks, one for digging into ant nests and another for grabbing them. Chimps in Gabon have been seen hunting with an extraordinarily elaborate five-piece toolkit for harvesting honey, which includes a pounder for breaking open a hive, a perforator for opening the honey chamber, a channel enlarger, a collector to extract honey, and swaths of bark to scoop it. All told, says primatologist Frans de Waal, chimps "use between fifteen and twenty-five different tools per community, and the precise tools vary with cultural and ecological circumstances."[22]

Chimpanzees: Smarter than Trappers

Chimpanzees have keen intelligence and advanced cognitive skills—so much so that scientists observing wild chimpanzees in Guinea watched them deliberately set off snare traps designed to catch and kill them (and any other passing animal)—while avoiding harming themselves. Snare injuries to chimps are common across eastern and western Africa. But chimpanzees are increasingly learning to avoid and even intentionally set them off. Researchers believe that this lifesaving skill has even been passed down from one generation to the next.

In the 1970s, a psychologist at Columbia University named Herbert Terrace wanted to know if chimps could learn to communicate like human toddlers. While chimps lack the ability to vocalize words, they have extremely dexterous hands and fingers. (A recent study published in the journal *Nature Communications* found that human hands are in fact more primitive than chimps' hands, which are nimbler and enable them to climb trees with ease.) What if, Terrace wondered, we could talk with chimps using sign language? In an experiment that raised significant ethical concerns, Terrace brought an infant chimpanzee named Nim Chimpsky (a play on the famed linguist Noam Chomsky) to live with a human family in a brownstone in New York City. If Nim grew up with a human family just like a human child, Terrace reasoned, perhaps he could learn to understand English and communicate with sign language. For rather obvious reasons, the experiment was something of a mess: Chimps are used to living in lush, humid jungles, not stuffy apartment buildings. Nim did manage to learn around 125 signs, but many experts argued that he was merely reacting to the body language of his human trainers, much like Clever Hans earlier that century. "There was no spontaneity, no real use of grammar,"[23] Dr. Terrace conceded.

Other studies followed, some massively unethical. One experiment that began in the late 1960s involved a chimp named Washoe, who had been captured as an infant from her home in West Africa by the US Air Force for astronaut training. Eventually she found her way to the University of Nevada, Reno, where she was enrolled in a study to learn sign language. Like Nim, Washoe was raised like a human child, with a place at the dinner table, her own room, a bed, clothing, and a toothbrush. Washoe learned 350 words of sign language and could even teach signs to her adopted son, Loulis. Then, during the 1970s and '80s, scientists taught a female western lowland gorilla named Koko over a thousand signs, and she could understand more than two thousand words of spoken English. Koko became famous, met many celebrities (from Robin Williams to Betty White), and eventually died at a gorilla preservation in California.

In recent years, primatologists have taught a middle-aged bonobo named Kanzi living in the Great Ape Trust in Des Moines, Iowa, how to communicate using a specialized keyboard containing about four hundred visual symbols, called lexigrams. Scientists had their answer: With training, apes could indeed be taught rudimentary communication skills.

But at what cost? Our primate cousins are not meant to be torn from their loving mothers and raised in apartment buildings or research labs or zoos. They are not meant to sleep in a bed with sheets and be taught to wash dishes. If we are interested in how our closest animal relatives communicate among themselves, why abduct them from their natural habitats? Today's researchers have increasingly opted to conduct passive studies involving observation of primates in their natural habitat, much like the kind Jane Goodall pioneered decades ago. In 2011, the journal *Animal Cognition* published the results of an extensive study by University of St Andrews researchers who spent 266 days observing and filming chimpanzees living in a wildlife preserve in Uganda. After cataloging hundreds of hours of footage, the research team found that chimpanzees use at least thirty separate gestures for communication. "We think people previously were only seeing fractions of this, because when you study the animals in captivity you don't see all their behavior,"[24] lead researcher Dr. Catherine Hobaiter told *BBC News*. The team found that, for instance, a mother will hold out her left arm when she wants her child to climb on her back. "She could just grab her daughter, but she doesn't," Dr. Hobaiter said. "She reaches and holds the gesture while waiting for a response." The researchers documented more than five thousand exchanges between chimps.

A SYMPHONY IN THE SKY

Certain forms of animal communication are audible every day. Whether hiking a nature trail, strolling along the beach, or walking down Fifth Avenue in New York City, you are likely surrounded by bird calls. From squeaks, squawks, and warbles to trills, pops, and croaks, birds communicate to each other in unexplained ways. Not all use their voices. Ruffed grouse, for instance, beat their wings at a high intensity to create a vacuum, and the sound of rushing air creates a distinctive low-frequency hum discernible from a quarter mile away. The male Wilson's Snipe has special tail feathers that create a winnowing noise as he dives toward the ground—a tactic used to court females. Some bird communication doesn't even require noise. The peacock relies on his extravagant plumage to attract females, ward off rival suitors, and avoid predators. Male peacocks can quite literally make females' heads vibrate. When a peacock shakes his rear at a potential mate, his magnificent feathers emit a high-frequency noise that causes the crest of the female's head to vibrate vigorously.

The bird songs we hear every day are more than beautiful. They serve a practical purpose. Birds employ their voices to call their mates, find their flock, claim territory, scare off intruders, warn others about predators, and for countless other functions. For instance, Japanese and Swiss researchers recently discovered that Japanese great tits, small birds with jet-black heads and necks with prominent white cheeks, use syntax in their songs, just as humans do in their speech. Syntax is crucial to language. For example, if you say, "I love that restaurant," the message is clear. But not even Star Wars' Master Yoda could understand, "Restaurant love that I." Until recently, scientists believed that only humans could string together such vocalizations. The Japanese great tit, it turns out, is the first animal apart from humans (that we know of so far) who can use phonological syntax—the ability to combine sounds that individually have no meaning into a collective sound—that does. To instruct other members of his flock to scan for predators, or to attract a mate, a great tit must sing several distinct notes in the correct order—if the notes are sung differently, the study found, other birds will not react.

Some birds have evolved to use their songs to communicate with humans. In Mozambique's Niassa National Reserve, the appropriately named greater honeyguide jumps to attention when a human calls out, "*Brrrrrrhmmm.*" The tiny brown bird, weighing in at about 1.7 ounces, speeds toward the human and then guides him to the nearest wild beehive. Once there they share the bounty. The humans take the honey. The honeyguides take the beeswax. This human–avian relationship has persisted for many thousands of years. The birds do not have to be trained. From birth, they instinctively know how to work with humans. In fact, honeyguides will even "actively recruit appropriate human partners,"[25] a 2016 study by University of Cambridge researchers noted, by using a distinctive call to attract attention.

Singing in the City

To no one's particular surprise, studies continually show that urban centers are becoming increasingly loud—San Francisco, for instance, has gained six decibels a year on average since the 1970s. Anthropogenic sound—that is, caused by humans—comes from traffic, car alarms, construction, sirens, and other sounds that we tend to tune out. But birds cannot. They depend on their songs to attract mates and defend territory. If they can't be heard, they can't live. Thus, they adapt. In urban areas, birds have begun to sing in higher registers, enabling them to be heard over the cacophony of trucks, jackhammers, and sirens.

This has a downside, however. "You can tell a lot about a bird by how it sings, whether it's trying to attract a mate or defend its territory," explains David Luther, a biologist at George Mason University. "Because many noises are physically difficult for birds to produce, you can glean information about the health of a bird from its calls."[26] In a recent paper, Luther found that birds indeed sing louder and shriller around cities, but they hurt their voices. Consequently, rival birds and predators can pick up on their faltering voice and take advantage.

In early September 2007, Harvard University psychologist Irene Pepperberg bid a beloved parrot, an African gray named Alex, good night.

"You be good," Alex responded, as he always did. "I love you. See you tomorrow." The words were nothing new—African grays are renowned for their abilities to mimic human speech—but sadly, they were Alex's last. Pepperberg found him dead the following morning. He was thirty-one. Pepperberg was devastated, not just because she had lost a beloved friend, but because Alex was fundamentally reshaping human understanding of animal cognition right up until the day he died.

In 1977, when Pepperberg was a doctoral student at Harvard University, she spotted Alex in a local pet store. After purchasing him on a whim, she began teaching the one-year-old basic human words, which he gamely parroted back. But soon she wondered whether it was possible Alex could *understand* the meaning of the words he was repeating. Pepperberg devised a series of studies to test Alex's abilities to communicate and problem-solve. The African gray's vocabulary soon ballooned to 150 words, many of which he could place into categories like color, quantity, and size. Before long, Alex could perform basic addition with crackers and jelly beans and correctly put in order the numbers one through eight using refrigerator magnets. While remembering words is not unusual, Alex could actually identify objects verbally, distinguish between colors and shapes, and understand the concept of "bigger," "smaller," "different," and many more comparative phrases. He could announce what color paper was, what shape it was, and even what it was made of. Gazing into a mirror, Alex could even ask "What color?" and he learned the word "gray" to describe himself. Alex's knack for basic language tantalized scientists, many of whom wondered if animals living in the wild—their homes—display similar capabilities.

Feathered Primates

Parrots are so creative that scientists often call them "feathered primates." For example, Goffin's cockatoos—parrots endemic to lush forests across Indonesia—are some of the most adept toolmakers in the world. When confronted with a hard-to-reach food source, for example, one study found that cockatoos will tear cardboard into long strips to use as a tool. Cockatoos and other parrots are also notorious for clipping apart leg bands, satellite holsters, and other tracking devices fastened to their legs.

Parrots are famous for mimicking the human voice, but their communicative abilities don't end there. Researchers studying the yellow-naped Amazon—playful green parrots found along the Pacific coast from southern Mexico to Costa Rica—discovered that they communicate with each other in distinct dialects that remain the same over decades. Like humans, young parrots who relocate are more willing to learn dialects of their new home, whereas older transplants prefer to associate with each other and avoid learning to speak a new vernacular.

PARSING THE LANGUAGE OF THE ANIMAL KINGDOM

From ultrasonic chirps to barks to haunting whale calls from more than a mile underwater, the animal kingdom is in constant contact with others. All of these communications—from yodeling basenjis to barking koalas to screeching barn owls to bugling elks—serve a purpose. Recent research shows that the seemingly random growls, chirps, clicks, squawks, and bellows often mean a lot more than "I'm a male! Mate with me!" or "I'm a predator! Prepare to be eaten!" Using complex mathematics, scientists at the National Institute for Mathematical and Biological Synthesis demonstrated that even the most arbitrary-seeming squawk has far more nuance and purpose than we originally thought.

As the study showed, no matter how simple their vocalizations may seem, many animals have the ability to communicate intricate thoughts. For instance, a mockingbird can mimic more than one hundred distinct sounds and combine them into a complex sequence. And while the rock hyrax, a squat, furry creature found across sub-Saharan Africa, boasts a mere five discreet vocal elements, he, too, can string together long sequences to communicate complicated ideas. After recording vocalizations from free-tailed bats, Carolina chickadees, Bengalese finches, killer whales, pilot whales, rock hyraxes, and orangutans, the research team broke each animal noise into distinct musical notes, like A-flat, B-flat, C-sharp, and so forth. Initially the scientists expected the animal calls to be simplistic and random. It turns out that they more closely resembled human speech patterns, with the chickadee, finch, and whale calls especially complex. What may seem like noise to us may be an infinitely intricate language that we simply haven't learned to decipher.

Many animal sounds we hear may be two-way conversations—a trait that was once mistakenly believed to be uniquely human. The American robin may emit a sharp "tic tic" call when he spots a prowling cat or a thin "seeee" note when he spies a hawk, but his calls serve to warn the flock of a potential threat, not to begin a conversation with another robin. Until recently, scientists believed this "talking at" rather than "talking with" model was the full extent of animal communication. But a 2018 study published in the journal *Philosophical Transactions of the Royal Society B: Biological Sciences* suggests that animals hold two-way conversations. Among humans, there is typically a two-hundred-millisecond gap between turns in a conversation—that's the time it takes for the brain to recognize the other person has stopped talking, prepare a thought, and respond. The researchers found that animals, too, take turns to speak. Songbirds routinely wait roughly fifty milliseconds to reply during a conversation, while the more measured sperm whale collects his thoughts for two full seconds before responding. And just as humans consider it rude to interrupt someone, animals, too, have ways of dealing with impolite behavior. The researchers found that certain species, namely black-capped chickadees and European starlings, practice "overlap avoidance" while conversing—a fancy way of saying they politely wait to speak until it is their turn. "If overlap occurs," the scientists wrote, "individuals became silent or flew away, suggesting that overlapping may be treated, in this species, as a violation of socially accepted rules of turn-taking."[27]

Chirping Cheetahs

One of the fiercest predators on the planet, humans aside, cheetahs can accelerate from 0 to 45 mph in just 2.5 seconds and reach a top speed of nearly 70 mph. Cheetahs propel themselves twenty-three feet in a single stride using their long, muscular legs and semi-retractable claws for traction. Everything about a cheetah is built for speed, from their slender, aerodynamic bodies to their large hearts to their oversize nostrils and lungs that maximize oxygen intake. Due to their ferocity, you might expect cheetahs to have roars every bit as terrifying as their blinding speed.

Actually, cheetahs cannot roar. Big cats like lions, tigers, leopards, and jaguars have special two-piece hyoid bones in their throats that allow them to open their mouths wide and emit a fierce roar. But cheetahs—along with cougars, snow leopards, and clouded leopards—have only a one-piece hyoid bone. Instead of roaring, they produce a nasally, high-pitched whine often described as a chirp. Typically used to express excitement, such as when gathering around a kill, chirping is also used by mothers when searching for her cubs. And while the chirp may not be as fear-inspiring as a roar, it is practical: One study found that it can be heard from up to 1.2 miles away.

Animals may not be able to converse in a way that's familiar, or understandable to humans, and they may not be able to use language to compose poems and novels, but if you take a few minutes and step outside—no matter if you are high in the Himalayas, beside a quiet pond, in a city park, or merely in your backyard—you can hear myriad languages that are beautiful, efficacious, and mysterious. From bird songs to dolphin whistles to the haunting chorus of the cicadas at dusk, the language of the animal kingdom is the soundtrack to life itself.

The Intricacies of Love

*To me, the evidence for animal emotions is impossible to
deny, and it is widely supported by our current knowledge in
animal behavior, neurobiology, and evolutionary biology.*

—Marc Bekoff, professor emeritus of ecology and
evolutionary biology at the University of Colorado

In the Congo, the word *wounda* means "close to dying." Wounda was
the name given to a severely emaciated chimpanzee brought to the
Jane Goodall Institute's (JGI) Tchimpounga Chimpanzee Rehabili-
tation Center in the Republic of the Congo. Wounda's parents had
been killed by poachers. Left to fend for herself, she had succumbed to
disease before rescuers spotted her. As Goodall later said, "When I saw
the photographs of Wounda . . . I didn't see how she could possibly
have lived."[28] After being given the first-ever chimp-to-chimp blood
transfusion in Africa, Wounda received a liter of milk every morning
as she slowly regained weight. It took two years of dedication from JGI
staff to rehabilitate her, all while caring for dozens of other chimpanzees rescued from similar circumstances.

Finally, on June 20, 2013, the moment had arrived: Wounda was
ready to be set free into a sprawling animal sanctuary on Tchindzoulou
Island in the nearby Kouilou River. After a twenty-minute journey
by riverboat, Wounda and her caregivers reached the pristine island,
home to a growing population of rescued chimps who live in peace and
free from danger. After reaching a lush green clearing, volunteers slid

open Wounda's travel crate and she bounded out to absorb the beauty of her new home. But then she returned to bid farewell to the humans who had nursed her back to health. She leapt gracefully onto her crate, gazed at Goodall, and embraced her. In a viral video that was seen by millions around the globe, for several minutes Wounda lovingly hugged the woman who had saved her life before finally scurrying off into the wilderness.

A simple question has weighed on researchers for years: Can animals love? Any casual watcher of YouTube might reply, "Totally." From videos of euphoric dogs reuniting with returning soldiers to bromances between dogs and ducks, it certainly *seems* that animals are capable of loving. This question dogged even Charles Darwin, who in 1872 published *The Expression of the Emotions in Man and Animals*. As noted previously, Darwin believed that animal intelligence could be placed on a spectrum, with "primitive" animals like worms at the beginning and "complex" animals like humans and apes at the end. Toward the end of his life, Darwin became fascinated with the emotional lives of animals, writing that they experience "anxiety, grief, dejection, despair, joy, love, 'tender feelings,' devotion, ill-temper, sulkiness, determination, hatred, anger, disdain, contempt, disgust, guilt, pride, helplessness, patience, surprise, astonishment, fear, horror, shame, shyness, and modesty."[29]

Later, Darwin whittled his list of "core" emotions unique among all animals to anger, happiness, sadness, disgust, fear, and surprise. He based this conclusion on casual observations. "I formerly possessed a large dog who, like every other dog, was much pleased to go out walking," he wrote in *The Expression of the Emotions in Man and Animals*. "He showed his pleasure by trotting gravely before me with high steps, head much raised, moderately erected ears, and tail carried aloft but not stiffly." Darwin was describing the joy that every dog owner has witnessed. When Darwin cut short a walk, he wrote that his dog's "look of dejection was known to every member of the family . . . This consisted of the head drooping much, the whole body sinking a little and remaining motionless." But Darwin had more trouble identifying love among animals—mainly because, like so many poets, musicians, and philosophers before and after him, he had difficulty defining it. "With the lower animals we see the same principle of pleasure derived from contact in association with love," Darwin offered. "Dogs and cats manifestly take pleasure in rubbing against their masters and mistresses, and in being rubbed or patted by them."

While no one doubts the pleasure a dog experiences when his belly is rubbed, or a cat when her head is properly scratched, animals, like humans, experience love in a very complex way. Some animals have one romantic partner throughout their lives; others have hundreds or even thousands. More than 90 percent of bird species are monogamous, including pigeons and geese, while chimpanzees (and many other mammals, for that matter) are notoriously promiscuous.

Animals are every bit as capable of forming deep and powerful bonds as we are. This love may be very similar to human love, and it can be very different. From William Shakespeare to Taylor Swift, humans have struggled to describe the mind's most powerful emotion. Some express love by singing it to the world or by burying their significant other in an avalanche of kisses; others prefer to keep their true feelings hidden deep inside a diary, shut away from the world. Animals, too, express their love in strange and beautiful ways. Yet we can never expect to emphatically prove why and how animals love, or even hope to compare their forms of it to those of humans. The best we can do is celebrate the real, the familiar, and the exotic ways animals say, "I love you."

Worst Date Ever

Everyone has a worst-date story. But no matter how bad your date's restaurant choice or cologne was, at least you probably weren't afraid about surviving with your head intact.

Female praying mantises lure males with pheromones, enticing him to engage in a courtship dance. If his moves impress her, the much larger female consents to mate. But if the male misses a step and his prospective mate isn't intrigued, she bites his head off and devours his corpse. Studies show that female mantises exhibit such sexual cannibalism in 13 to 28 percent of encounters during breeding season. Some devious females even wait until after breeding to consume their mates.

The next time a Tinder date doesn't go as planned, remember that while love can break your heart, if you're a praying mantis, it can literally bite off your head.

CHOOSING A MATE

As with humans, sex is only a small part of what constitutes choosing a mate when it comes to animals. Countless species engage in deep deliberation when choosing a partner. Take, for example, southern right whales. These enormous, majestic creatures feed on plankton in the nutrient-rich Antarctic waters during the summer months and breed in shallow coastal waters near southern Australia, Brazil, and South Africa during winter. Their courtship is tender and elegant, with very little hostility between competing males. When courting, male and female whales gently touch their flippers, then begin a slow caressing motion. They roll against each other, locking their flippers, and roll upward, lying side by side. Then they dive and surface together in unison. If the female is not impressed with the male's moves, however, she breaks off their aquatic dance in search of a more graceful partner.

Other sea creatures aren't so picky. Despite having more than one hundred million years to hone their tastes, sea turtles are curiously casual when it comes to mating. These turtles are a family of reptiles comprising seven extant species: greens, loggerheads, Kemp's ridleys, olive ridleys, hawksbills, flatbacks, and leatherbacks. Like box turtles you see near ponds or in your local park, sea turtles' bodies are protected by a shell made up of smaller plates called scutes. (The only exception is the leatherback, whose back, like his name suggests, is covered by skin and oily flesh instead of a hard shell.) Capable of living in or out of water, sea turtles roam thousands of miles each year through the ocean, usually alone, but often return during mating season to the very beach on which they were born.

Males typically arrive on the beach first, anxiously awaiting the first females to arrive. This is because breeding is on a first-come, first-serve basis, with females generally unconcerned with choosing the fittest male for procreation. But this doesn't mean sea turtles don't take time to get to know each other. Males and females begin their courtship in shallow waters with gentle, coordinated circling. Then they rise to the surface to take a deep breath before the male latches onto her back and "hangs on for dear life for up to 24 hours,"[30] according to Dave Owens, a marine biologist at the College of Charleston. That's because during the mating process, other males may try to knock him off, even going so far as to bite his tail and flippers. Alas, sea turtle romances are over as quickly as they begin: After mating, the turtles usually go their own way to find a new flame.

Gender Through Temperature

For most species, gender is determined during the egg fertilization process and occurs entirely by chance. With most turtles, however—as well as alligators, crocodiles, and other reptiles—the temperature of the egg determines a baby's gender.

After successful mating, female sea turtles haul themselves up on sandy beaches to dig a circular nest in the sand twenty inches deep. There they lay a clutch of between 50 and 350 eggs, then carefully refill the nest with sand. After camouflaging the nest with vegetation, they bid their unborn babies farewell and return to the ocean. Eggs laid in cooler sand will generally become male hatchlings, while warmer sand produces females.

After fifty to sixty days of incubation, baby turtles break free of their eggs and crawl into the sea. But it will be some time until they, too, reproduce; for most sea turtle species, it takes thirty years to reach sexual maturity.

In the mid-1990s, divers off the coast of Japan discovered ornate circular patterns on the seafloor—not underwater crop circles created by an alien race, but nests created by a recently discovered species of fish called Japanese puffer fish. To attract a mate, the male puffer furiously flaps his fins and swims in a circular motion, carving the sandy sea bottom into precise peaks and valleys. Despite being only five inches long, over the course of ten days he uses his body to create elaborate circles that measure up to seven feet in diameter. For the puffer fish equivalent of chocolate and flowers, he decorates the edges with shells and coral fragments. When a female happens by, the male puffer fish eagerly stirs up sand at the center of the circle, hoping to make his nest appear as cozy as possible. If impressed, the lady puffer hovers at the center of the nest and beckons the male closer. The romance is short-lived. After mating and depositing her eggs in the nest, the female speeds away, never to return, leaving the male to remain with the eggs until they hatch six days later. Fortunately, the male's handiwork isn't entirely for show—the elaborate ridges he created can apparently reduce current flow by 25 percent, protecting the eggs.

Female puffer fish aren't the only animals who expect males to step up their game for love. Standing up to twenty-eight inches tall and weighing around ten pounds, Adélie penguins have the classic tuxedoed look of penguins in cartoons. Sporting lush black-and-white coats and pink feet, these energetic birds spend their entire lives on Earth's most frigid continent. Many species of penguins sail for warmer islands during the winter months. The nearly four million breeding pairs of Adélie penguins live in approximately 250 colonies situated along the Antarctic coastline. Whereas humans consider the diamond the ultimate symbol of devotion, for Adélie penguins the humble pebble is the most important rock of all. In the barren Antarctic landscape, small rocks are very difficult to come by, and males spend days meticulously gathering them—in many cases pilfering from other males. When a male Adélie has gathered the appropriate amount of pebbles, he digs a shallow depression in the ice and uses them to line the outside edges. After spotting a female, he stands tall and cackles, showing off his creation. If impressed, she exchanges bows with the male, who then scatters the pebbles into a comfortable nest for breeding. In many cases, Adélie couples remain together for life.

The elaborate ways in which other animals attract mates might seem alien to us, but how different are our own rituals? Just as human couples commonly hold hands to express their mutual affection, African elephants enjoy intertwining trunks with their soul mates. Densely packed with sensitive nerve endings, trunks contain over forty thousand muscles and play a central role in elephant communication. An elephant will use her trunk to stroke a sick or grieving loved one, engage in a friendly game of trunk wrestling with a friend, and even gently entwine it with a mate's during courtship.

And even the gaudier animal displays have parallels in our own lives. Is a human male who seeks to impress his date by picking her up in a sports car dissimilar from a peacock who spreads his iridescent tail feathers and struts to and fro, hoping to win over a potential mate with the flashiest, most impressive display? In a study titled "The effect of conspicuous consumption on men's testosterone levels," a duo of evolutionary psychologists reported how expensive bling greatly affects men's testosterone levels. When young men drove a sleek Porsche in downtown Montreal, tests showed, their testosterone levels were significantly higher than when puttering about in a beat-up sedan. Of course, there's then the risk of overdoing it, even in the animal world. In a Johns Hopkins report (one that will not surprise human females), male canaries with the most testosterone circulating in their blood sang the loudest, but were seen as less attractive by females, who preferred a soft, elegant chirp over a loud, toneless one.

When luxury gifts aren't available, both humans and animals have been known to get resourceful—maybe too resourceful. In late 1888, the famed Dutch Postimpressionist painter Vincent van Gogh severed his left ear and delivered it to the object of his affection: a young girl working in a café he often frequented. The episode did not work out well for van Gogh. A similar and more successful ritual takes place among large tropical seabirds called masked boobies. Male boobies offer gifts to potential mates, such as small stones, but will also pluck out their own feathers and offer them as well. Love can hurt, throughout the animal kingdom.

FIDELITY

Many humans stay monogamous for life, while others seem incapable of staying with the same partner for more than a few years (or even days). Likewise, in the animal kingdom there are many species who stay with a single mate forever, and there are many who breed and go their separate ways.

The humble prairie vole is an unassuming creature. But these rodents, known as "potato chips of the prairie," live an arduous life. Just five inches long, they are near the bottom of the food chain, the favored delicacy of weasels, hawks, snakes, and countless other predators. Finding respite in dry fields under the cover of grass and weeds, prairie voles cope with the near-constant danger of being eaten by forming deep and lasting bonds with their mates.

After breeding, male and female parents remain together for life, guarding their offspring zealously and even providing comfort during stressful moments. "When their partner is stressed they give them the equivalent of prairie vole hugs and kisses," said Jennifer Verdolin, author of *Wild Connection: What Animal Courtship and Mating Tell Us*

About Human Relationships. "They will spend upwards of 50 to 60 percent of their time together if not more."[31]

This level of monogamy is unusual among rodents. (In fact, just 3 percent of mammals are monogamous.) Even the prairie vole's nearly identical relative, the meadow vole, does not form such deep attachments. Scientists believe one reason is the unusual amounts of oxytocin—the so-called love hormone—released when prairie voles mate, which promotes emotional bonding. In fact, prairie voles are so loyal to their mates that their behavior has helped researchers understand the biochemical basis of human love.

Among all animals, however, few are as devoted as birds. And the biggest love of all belongs to the biggest of them all: the albatross. With wingspans reaching twelve feet long, albatrosses soar from the North Pacific as far as Antarctica. Despite their knack for wandering—studies find that albatrosses spend 95 percent of their life up in the air—these majestic birds almost never stray from their mate. As birder Noah Strycker explains in his book *The Thing with Feathers,* "These globe trotters, who mate for life and are incredibly faithful to their partners, just might have the most intense love affairs of any animal on our planet."[32] Because albatrosses lay only one egg at a time, young chicks are alone for much of their early lives as their parents travel hundreds or even thousands of miles in search of food. When they reach sexual maturity sometime after their fifth birthday, young albatrosses migrate to their native island to begin a curious mating ritual: dancing. As Strycker writes,

> [The] two birds face each other, patter their feet to stay close as they move forward and backward, each testing the other's reflexes, and point their beaks at the sky . . . Then, as they simultaneously utter a chilling scream, the albatrosses each extend their wings to show off the full 12-foot span, facing off while continuing to jockey for position. They touch beaks, throw their heads back again and scream.[33]

Albatrosses will continue to dance with more partners, over and over, until they find a favorite. Sometimes it can take years. But the wait is worth it, for albatrosses almost always remain together—which, for these elegant seabirds, can mean more than fifty years. According to ecologist Jeffrey Black, who studied nearly one hundred species of birds for his book *Partnership in Birds,* albatrosses are the most loyal bird animal on the planet, with not a single pair in his observations breaking up or mating with other albatrosses. Other studies have shown that when albatrosses do take up with a new mate, it's usually following the death of their former partner.

How do other bird species stack up, according to Black? Many are far more faithful lovers than humans, among whom in the US the divorce rate hovers around 40 to 45 percent. Swans, the lifelong lovers of fairy-tale legend, have a 95 percent rate of staying together. Swan couples, whose necks famously intertwine into a perfect heart shape, perform a courtship dance accompanied by a decidedly less romantic symphony of hisses and grunts. (The notion that swans only sing when they are dying is a myth.) Different species of swan have their own twists: Australian black swans, for instance, use their unique dark feathers to attract mates. Bewick's swans and whistling swans prefer to gently call out to each other. North American trumpeter swans are not shy about their love and enjoy honking wildly for the world to overhear.

Other species Black studied include masked boobies, who break from their mates at around the same rate as humans. Piping plovers, the plucky, sand-colored shorebirds common to North American beaches, break up 67 percent of the time, while the affable mallard duck stays faithful to his mate nine out of ten times. According to a recent joint study by the University of Sheffield and the University of Bath, birds of nearly all species are more likely to cheat on each other when a colony is heavily skewed toward one gender. Said Professor András Liker of the University of Sheffield: "If there is more of one sex than another, members of the rarer sex have a higher chance of getting a new partner for breeding than members of the common sex . . . Basically, the rarer sex has more opportunity to 'play the field' and either cheat on the partner or leave in favour of a new mate."[34]

The most promiscuous bird of all? Flamingos, says Black. These long-legged, pink-feathered wading birds common to warm coastal regions typically live in very large colonies often numbering thousands of birds, believed to help deter predators. But living in such large numbers also provides many opportunities for flamingo eyes to wander. Although they initially form strong pair bonds after an elaborate courtship involving synchronized dancing rituals and neck stretching, Black estimates that flamingo romance is as fleeting as a college fling, with 99 percent ultimately finding a new love.

Like many humans, birds often find love in the big city. Also known as city doves, feral pigeons like those found in New York are the descendants of wild rock doves, pale gray birds who dwell along crags and rock ledges across the world. Finding skyscrapers a suitable substitute for cliffs, feral pigeons are so abundant that jaded city dwellers have attempted increasingly dubious (and cruel) methods for controlling their population, including poison.

Nevertheless, says Brooklyn-based artist Tina Piña Trachtenburg: "A city without pigeons would be a sterile shopping mall. They add so much beauty and sweetness to our environment."[35] Mother Pigeon, as Trachtenburg is known in the neighborhood, is on a one-woman crusade to rehabilitate pigeons' reputation among New Yorkers. After feeding and later befriending a flock of pigeons on her rooftop, Trachtenburg has since rescued countless pigeons, including a baby named Lovely Rita, who fell from a seventh-story window and broke her legs. ("She had the cutest little leg casts," says Trachtenburg.) Trachtenburg even convinced her husband to walk around town in a pigeon outfit with a sign reading: "Pigeons mate for life."

Pigeons do, in fact, mate for life. Science journalist Brandon Keim tells the story of two lovestruck pigeons named Harold and Maude. Harold was the prototypical alpha pigeon: big and broad with crisp feathers, he strutted confidently along Keim's Brooklyn rooftop. Harold's mate, Maude, was not cut from the same cloth: "Head and neck feathers in patchy disarray, eyes watery, exuding a sense of illness that transcends several hundred million years of divergent evolution,"[36] Keim explained. Once, Maude couldn't take flight. She flapped her wings feebly and took a few feeble steps, but couldn't muster the energy to take off. Harold paced anxiously, waiting for her to follow aloft. Yet he always stayed by her side, even though he could have left to find a healthier, more robust mate.

This behavior is common among pigeons. Circulating in their brains are the hormones mesotocin and vasotocin—the avian versions of oxytocin and vasopressin, the hormones linked to mammalian bonding and love. Pigeons also have the reward-system neurotransmitters serotonin and dopamine, which regulate attraction and pleasure. Just like human couples, pigeons also share child-rearing duties. Mother and father take turns incubating the eggs to allow the other a chance to rest and eat. The doting parents are extremely protective once their chicks hatch, typically permitting them to leave the nest only once they are fully grown.

Musth-Dos

Human males can be loud, aggressive, and smelly, but at least they're musth-less. For reasons that remain unclear to scientists, sexually mature male elephants enter a period of musth, a term derived from the Persian word for "drunk," for one to two months per year. During musth, testosterone levels soar to as much as sixty times higher than normal, bringing even the most serene males into a frenzied and highly violent state.

Signs of musth are hard to miss, as males begin secreting a highly noxious blend of chemicals from temporal ducts in their cheeks, which swell to the size of basketballs. They also pass as much as eighty gallons of urine each day. During musth, males become obsessed with sex, not to mention fighting anyone from other males to giraffes to humans. Effects of musth aren't dissimilar to a human male in "roid rage," including aggressive outbursts after being disturbed, savage reactions to noise or sudden movements, and violent, unprovoked attacks toward familiar friends or even loved ones. If you happen upon a male elephant exuding sweat, urine, and testosterone-fueled rage, run. Unless you're a female elephant.

MOTHERLY LOVE

The most fundamental way animals experience love is recognizable by any parent: the bond between mother and child. The instinct for a mother to care for her young resides in the deepest, most primal recesses of the brain that transcend species and millions of years of evolution. Motherly instincts even appear in the most unlikely of species. The slimy, blood-sucking Australian leech may not be anyone's idea of a doting parent, but according to evolutionary biologist Fred Govedich of Australia's Monash University, these segmented worms are the earliest known example of an invertebrate caring for its young into maturity. "Although the word leech is often considered synonymous with selfishness and exploitation, many leeches are devoted parents,"[37] Govedich reported after studying the creature in-depth. Australian leeches are known to care for their young for many weeks after they hatch, carefully shuttling them to safe locations with few predators.

For more proof that big love can be found in small sizes: the wolf spider. Stout, solitary hunters who possess uncanny eyesight, these arachnids are known to pounce upon their prey with devastating precision. Yet while these lethal hunters are chasing down their victims, they also protect a sac of unborn young near their abdomen. After the spiderlings hatch from their protective silken case, they scramble up their mother's legs and seek refuge on her back until they are big enough to live on their own.

The Earth's great oceans are also home to fiercely protective mothers. While many fish use camouflage and other techniques to keep their young safe from predators, mouthbrooders—a family of fish that includes cichlids, sea catfish, pikeheads, and jawfish among others— use their enormous mouths to protect their unborn babies. In fact, mothers do not eat once their eggs are fertilized, keeping their lips clamped tightly to prevent any eggs from falling out. For some species, such as the African cichlid, this maternal fasting can last up to thirty-six days. Even after their babies are born and free to swim on their own, mothers stay close by in case predators approach—in times of danger, newborns instinctively know to swim back to Mom and seek protection in her mouth. Dad assists as well: In some species, such as the arowana and certain catfish, males, too, use their mouths to protect their young.

Perhaps no sea creature is as nurturing as the orca. Colloquially known as killer whales, orcas are actually dolphins. Found in every ocean on earth, they are famous for their black-and-white coloring, their symphonic whistles and clicks used for communication, and their unmatched hunting skills. Able to swim at speeds exceeding 30 mph, orcas travel and hunt together in tightly knit groups called pods. Orcas forge lifelong bonds beginning in childhood, when elders play a key role in passing on skills to the younger generation. Immediately after birth, mothers guide their infants to the surface to take their first breaths, and rarely leave their side for many years after.

Orangutan Love

Found deep in the rainforests of Borneo and Sumatra, orangutans are orange-haired great apes who spend nearly all of their time high in the trees. Solitary, intelligent beings, orangutans demonstrate the deepest mother–infant bonding seen in the animal kingdom.

Orangutan mothers give birth to one child at a time, and for years after they remain inseparable. During the first several months, mothers maintain a constant physical connection with their children. They will sleep, hunt, and play together. Mothers may even nurse their children through their ninth birthday. This bond runs deep. After studying museum collections, researchers found that orangutan teeth showed varying concentrations of barium, a chemical element found in milk, suggesting the apes nursed more or less depending on food supply. The rainforests of Southeast Asia are lush with fruit, orangutans' favorite food, but the supply can be extremely unpredictable. When times are tough, orangutan mothers can resort to hard nuts and seeds, but children must subsist on milk.

This might be why it takes so long for orangutan adolescents to separate from their mothers—and why their bonds are so strong. Even after young orangutans start families of their own, they are known to visit their mothers for many years after.

Mothers and daughters often have a special relationship. Some mother cows are overly controlling; others let their calves wander off free. And, like any human family, the relationship between mothers and daughters can be very complicated.

In *The Secret Life of Cows*, organic farmer Young tells the story of Dolly and her namesake, Dolly II. Dolly was an older, clever cow who successfully raised many calves by the time Dolly II came along. Dolly knew how much milk her babies needed, and knew when to ween them off it in favor of hay and grass. She even knew when it was time for her calves to learn to take care of themselves. For Dolly II, that moment came at about fifteen months, when her mother had another calf. "Dolly II was not spurned but was increasingly ignored until she understood that as an adult she must make her own friends and leave her mother to the job she was so good at,"[38] Young writes.

Sometime later, Dolly II was preparing to have her own calf. She had had little contact with her mother. When Dolly II gave birth, she was not near Young or her family. After a frantic search, they finally found her at the base of a faraway hill. Tragically, her calf was stillborn, and Dolly II was suffering from a displaced womb. Young helped make her comfortable, and a veterinarian soon arrived to stitch Dolly II's womb back in place. She slowly healed over the coming weeks, but it was clear she was depressed and still very weak.

One day, Young came to check on Dolly II, but she had disappeared. After another frantic search, she found Dolly II three fields away, back with her mother. Dolly was licking her all over her body. The two Dollys had not been together in ages, but in a moment of crisis, a mother made herself available to comfort her daughter. After six days, Dolly II finally left her mother and made a full recovery.

Gay in the Wild

In Japan, male macaques—also known as "snow monkeys"—tend to have a rough go of it. Not only do they have to compete with other males to win the affection of females, they often have to compete with other females, too. Not only is homosexuality common among Japanese macaques, in many cases it's the norm. Researchers routinely document female macaques mounting other females and stimulating their genitalia, among other sexual behaviors. Females also tend to groom each other, sleep together, and defend each other from threats.

Homosexuality and bisexuality are documented even in the tiniest of species. Male fruit flies, for instance, are bisexual for the first thirty minutes of life, when they try and mate with any nearby fly regardless of gender. Male flour beetles are largely bisexual, happy to copulate with both females and other males alike. And in the sea, male and female dolphins often exhibit homosexual behavior as a means of developing tight-knit social bonds.

Albatrosses, famous for remaining with a single mate for life, are also no strangers to homosexuality. Often found in Hawaii during nesting season, female Laysan albatross couples routinely raise chicks together. A study published in the journal *Biology Letters* found that in the event a father dies, or in the rare instance that he abandons his mate, a mother often bonds with another female, and together they raise their chicks.

On land, chimpanzees, especially bonobos, are promiscuous with both sexes. In fact, bonobos have so much sex with so many different partners that scientists call their dalliances the bonobo handshake. Sometimes sex between males can be transactional, with younger bonobo males using fellatio and other sexual acts to bond with larger, more dominant members of their social group. Others play games, scientifically defined as "penis fencing" by researchers, as a way to relieve tension. And, sometimes homosexual sex is used to comfort a depressed or grieving friend.

GRIEF AND MOURNING

On May 25, 2016, police officer Jason Ellis was shot and killed while on duty in Bardstown, Kentucky. Ellis was part of the division's K-9 unit and worked extensively with a four-year-old German shepherd named Figo. During Ellis's funeral, Figo padded up to the procession and, in a moment that broke millions of hearts as the footage swept across the internet, bowed his head and placed a lone paw on the casket. Figo's solemn gesture may prove just a small sign of grief, but stories about grieving animals, particularly dogs, are extremely common.

In one case, an Austrian man died and left his dog, Sultan, to live with his family. After the man was buried, his family could not locate Sultan for days until they found him at the cemetery, three miles away, lying over his old friend's grave. In a famous story from Japan, an Akita named Hachikō remained steadfastly loyal to his owner even years after his death. Every afternoon at precisely the same time, Hachikō left home to greet his caregiver, a university professor named Hidesaburō Ueno, at the nearby train station. But one day Ueno did not return from work—he had died from a massive cerebral hemorrhage while delivering a lecture. Nevertheless, every day for the next nine years, nine months, and fifteen days, Hachikō left home and sat by the train station, hoping that his old friend would reappear. Hachikō eventually became a symbol of the Japanese ideals of loyalty and fidelity. His likeness was placed on statues, he was featured in books, and he was the subject of a 2009 film, *Hachi: A Dog's Tale.*

Recent research appears to conclude that, indeed, dogs are heavily affected by loss. A study conducted by the American Society for the Prevention of Cruelty to Animals (ASPCA) found that after the death of a fellow friend, two-thirds of dogs demonstrate decreased appetite, clinginess, and lethargy—clear signs of grief. Researchers at the New Zealand Companion Animal Counsel took it a step further and studied data from 159 dogs and 152 cats. They found that 60 percent of dogs and 63 percent of cats continually checked the spot their former friends used to nap. Nearly the same percentage began craving more affection. Almost a third of cats and dogs ate significantly less food, and both were more likely to sleep for extended periods of time. As the researchers noted, these are behaviors commonly linked to grief in humans.

In a 2012 study published in the journal *Animal Cognition,* University of London researchers found that dogs were more likely to submissively approach a crying human than one who was visibly humming or talking, indicating that dogs possess an innate understanding of suffering.

Tika and Kobuk

For Tika and Kobuk, two beautiful dogs living in Colorado, love was complicated. As Marc Bekoff recounts in his book *Minding Animals*, the two were companions for life, and had even raised a litter of eight puppies, but Kobuk was not always the perfect gentleman. He'd sometimes wrestle Tika and steal her food, or whine when she got more attention than he did. But one day the dogs' caregiver, Anne Bekoff, noticed a mass forming in Tika's leg. She had bone cancer.

As Tika grew sicker, Kobuk's behavior changed entirely. He never stole her food, he let her sleep on the bed, and he even groomed Tika's fur. When Tika's leg was amputated and she struggled to relearn to walk on three legs, Kobuk comforted her when she fell. He even saved her life by barking to alert Anne when she fell into shock shortly after she returned home from surgery.

Of course, once Tika made a full recovery, Kobuk slipped back into his old ways—taking food, stealing attention, knocking her down. As the saying goes, friends show their love in times of trouble, not happiness.

Dr. Thom van Dooren, an Australian anthropologist, argues in his book *Flight Ways: Life and Loss at the Edge of Extinction* that "human exceptionalism"—the belief that mankind is superior to all other creatures—is a concept that has harmed our understanding of other animals. This is especially true with grief and mourning. As an example, van Dooren told *National Geographic* magazine that there is "very good evidence to suggest that crows and a number of other mammals grieve for their dead."[39] Medium-size birds with a mythological knack for showing up during foreboding times, the corvid family is composed of species more commonly known as crows, ravens, rooks, and jackdaws. Highly intelligent, corvids have been known to hold "funerals" for their fallen comrades. Upon the death of a friend, a flock of American crows (*Corvus brachyrhynchos*)—a.k.a. a murder of crows—will gather around the body for several hours. A study in the journal *Animal Behavior* suggests that this behavior isn't just to mourn, but to learn about the circumstances of the death so they can protect themselves in the future. Who knows? The researchers found that "crows learn places associated with conspecific death, and further demonstrate that crows can learn and remember people who appear complicit in these events."[40]

In 2016, a viral photograph touched hearts across the world: A female goose in China had been wrapped up onto the back of a motorcycle to be transported to slaughter. Her mate, whom she had grown up with, waddled over to her and cried out in obvious distress. Their craned necks shared a loving "kiss," and then the female was swept away along a dusty road to her fate.

Geese are loyal. They often mate for life and are protective of their partners and offspring. They'll often refuse to leave the side of a sick or injured mate or chick, even if winter is approaching and the other geese in the group are flying south. When a goose's mate dies, that bird will mourn in seclusion—and some geese spend the rest of their lives as widows or widowers, refusing to mate again. Multiple families of geese come together to form a larger group called a gaggle, in which birds look out for each other. There are usually one or two "sentries" who keep watch for predators while the others feed. The gaggle members rotate sentry duty, like sailors standing watch on a ship. Observers have noted that healthy geese sometimes look after injured comrades, and that injured birds will stick together to protect each other from predators and to help each other find food.

Geese in Love

Geese have exceedingly complex—and dramatic—social structures. In his book *The Year of the Greylag Goose,* famed ornithologist and Nobel Laureate Konrad Lorenz described the intense love triangle between three geese: Ado, Selma, and Gurnemanz.

In 1976, Ado was not in good shape. The love of his life, Susanne-Elisabeth, had been killed by a fox. He was depressed, withdrawn, and his social rank in the flock began to drop. "Then, in the spring of 1977," Lorenz wrote, "he abruptly pulled himself together and began an intensive courtship of a goose called Selma."[41] The two geese shared a torrid affair, but there was one problem: Selma was in a relationship with another male named Gurnemanz, with whom she had raised three children.

Gurnemanz was not at all happy about the new state of affairs. He tried to drive Ado off into the air, but Selma would follow him. This resulted in spectacular aerial chases, with the three geese typically exhausted afterward. Fighting quickly ensued as the two males snapped at and bit each other repeatedly and thrashed each other with the horn-like spurs located on their wing shoulders. Selma was stricken, unable to decide whom to choose.

Eventually Ado made the decision for her. He bested Gurnemanz in a brawl, forcing his opponent to flee for good. As Lorenz chronicled: "The victorious Ado then stood inflated with pride in a veritably eagle-like pose, his wings held so that the horny projections on the wing shoulders stood out as if he were brandishing brass knuckles." Just like Ado two years previously, Gurnemanz sank into a deep depression, stopped grooming himself, shuffled instead of walked, and generally lost interest in life.

Animals who live together in closely knit groups are the most likely to demonstrate ritualistic behavior after a family member dies. Ground dwellers native to the forests of central sub-Saharan Africa, gorillas are the largest living primates and our closest relative after chimpanzees and bonobos. Anthropologist Barbara King, author of *How Animals Grieve*, notes that gorilla "relatives may sit quietly at the body of the dead one, or touch the body quietly, or hold the hand of the body."[42] In 2008, an eleven-year-old gorilla named Gana living in a German zoo was found holding her lifeless three-month-old baby. For hours Gana gently carried and shook her son, her movements growing more desperate. At last she seemed to understand that he was dead, but fiercely guarded him even as zookeepers attempted to retrieve his body.

On October 10, 2003, in Kenya's Samburu National Reserve, an elephant named Eleanor collapsed. The matriarch of her herd at forty years old, she had been sick for some time: Her trunk was swollen and limp, one tusk was broken from a prior fall. Grace, a young elephant, rushed to her fallen friend and, using her tusks, tried to haul Eleanor back to her feet. But she was too weak. Grace called out in distress. Then, she seemed to understand. Instead of leaving, she remained next to her friend, gently stroking her. The following morning, after Eleanor had died, a parade of elephants gathered by her body, sniffing and stroking her. Over the next five days members of Eleanor's family stayed by her, and even elephants from separate, unrelated families came to pay their respects. A research team who observed the elephants concluded that it was "an example of how elephants and humans may share emotions, such as compassion, and have an awareness and interest about death."[43]

Compassion among elephants is well documented. In Kenya, researchers noted how adult elephants will help baby elephants escape from muddy holes, navigate swamps, and avoid electrified fences. In other cases, elephants removed tranquilizer darts from downed friends and spread dust on their wounds to protect against flies. A study published in the journal *PeerJ* found that Asian elephants can recognize when a member of their herd is in distress and provide gentle caresses. After studying twenty-six elephants from afar, the research team led by primatologist Frans de Waal found that elephants form protective circles around anguished friends and provide reassurance with rumbles and chirps. "They get distressed when they see others in distress, reaching out to calm them down, not unlike the way chimpanzees or humans embrace someone who is upset,"[44] de Waal told *National Geographic*.

In his book, *Stalking Big Game with a Camera in Equatorial Africa*, Marius Maxwell describes witnessing a hunter fire into a herd of elephants. The bullet passed through the brain of one bull, killing him instantly. Instead of fleeing in disarray, the herd hastily assembled into proper traveling formation and left the area. Yet, as Maxwell wrote, "They had among them the fatally wounded bull, which a few of the slowly moving titans succeeded in carrying away by pressing, with their heavy bodies in concerted action, against the flanks of their stricken brother." Despite imminent danger, the herd brought their fallen friend with them, carefully laying him to rest hundreds of yards away in a clump of brush where the hunter could not retrieve his tusks.

ANIMAL EMPATHY

The scientific community has been slow to acknowledge what observational studies have long shown: Other animals display empathy. Obviously you can't simply ask an animal if he is capable of love. When a young elephant tries to lift up the dying matriarch of her family after she falls down, skeptics may claim that the elephant is merely feeling *anxious*, not loving. So how do you prove that animals can feel love, grief, and pain?

In 1959, animal experimenter Russell Church demonstrated that caged rats trained to press a lever for food would stop when they realized the lever also shocked a rat in an adjacent cage. The inhumane nature of the experiment aside, scientists debated whether the rat was displaying anxiety, genuine empathy, or some combination of both. A few years later, in 1962, researchers at Agnes Scott College demonstrated in another ethically troubling experiment that a rat would attempt to free another distressed rat dangling from a harness in an adjacent cell by seeking out a lever he knew would lower the harness. If the harness held a piece of Styrofoam, on the other hand, the rat wouldn't bother to push the lever. Although the researchers concluded that "this behavior might be homologous to altruism,"[45] skeptical scientists claimed that the altruistic rat was merely trying to shut his squealing friend up—not save him.

Over the ensuing years, many more experiments attempted to demonstrate animal empathy—using decidedly nonempathetic means. One study even tried to show that rhesus monkeys would prefer to starve themselves rather than eat and subject a friend to electrocution. (One monkey went without food for eleven days rather than shock a monkey he didn't know.) At the same time, scientists who subscribed to so-called behaviorism—the theory that animal and human behavior can be explained in terms of conditioning, not individual thoughts or feelings—maintained that whatever altruism animals seemingly displayed was instead a trained response to stimuli.

This view remained predominant for decades, even as some scientists devised ever more barbaric experiments to try and prove just how deeply animals cared. During the early 2000s, geneticists at McGill University believed they had shown that nonhumans—in this case mice—were capable of consolation. The team's lead researcher, Jeffrey Mogil, designed experiments in which pain was administered to mice. "My sympathy is mostly reserved for chronic pain patients,"[46] he said when explaining why he was willing to hurt mice, to show the obvious. In a series of cruel experiments, Mogil's team dipped the tails of mice living together in a cage into hot water to determine their pain tolerance. By the end of the study, the mice who were forced to wait their turn and watch their friends shriek in pain were in significant distress by the time they were plucked from the cage. This meant that mice are able to not just observe pain in their friends, but feel that pain themselves in the form of fear. This so-called pain contagion is considered to be one of the most basic forms of empathy.

It shouldn't have to take scores of tortured mice to explain the obvious: Animals love. They grieve. They feel emotional pain. They worry. And they can anticipate pain. In early 2015, the Australian farm sanctuary Edgar's Mission rescued a dairy cow named Clarabelle who was about to be slaughtered because her milk production was declining. When she arrived at the sanctuary, volunteers discovered that she was pregnant. A week before her due date, Clarabelle began sneaking off the perimeter of the farm, avoiding staff, acting strangely. After a search, volunteers discovered that Clarabelle had already given birth and hidden her baby in a tall patch of grass. At dairy farms, calves are typically dragged away from their mothers immediately after birth so the milk meant for that baby can be sold for human consumption. Studies show that this is a traumatic moment for cows, who are exceptionally maternal creatures. Clarabelle, who had lost an untold number of babies over the years, assumed that her child would be dragged away yet again and tried to hide her. Fortunately, she was at a farm sanctuary, where she was able to finally raise her baby in peace.

Most cows don't get that luxury. In a similar story, a veterinarian in Upstate New York named Holly Cheever received a call one day from a puzzled dairy farmer. A Brown Swiss cow had recently given birth to her fifth calf, the farmer said, but her udder remained mysteriously empty even days later. It should have been swollen with many gallons of milk. Finally, nearly two weeks later, the farmer solved the problem. After following the mother out to pasture in the morning, he spotted her secretly nursing another calf in the forest near the edge of the farm. She had delivered twins, and knowing that one of her babies would be taken away from her—to be made into veal like most calves—in a "Sophie's Choice" moment she brought one baby to the farmer and kept one hidden in secret. As Holly later recounted:

> First, she had memory—memory of her four previous losses, in which bringing her new calf to the barn resulted in her never seeing him/her again . . . Second, she could formulate and then execute a plan . . . All I know is this: there is a lot more going

on behind those beautiful eyes than we humans have ever given
them credit for, and as a mother who was able to nurse all four
of my babies and did not have to suffer the agonies of losing my
beloved offspring, I feel her pain.[47]

In truth, we will never be able to comprehend the depth and beauty of
animal compassion. It is not solely a human characteristic to experience the ecstasy of love and the anguish of loss. All mothers, no matter
if they have two, four, or eight legs, understand what it means to lose
a child—that piece of themselves that can never be restored. Modern
science might offer inklings of the love possessed by dogs, cows, or any
other of the world's 8.7 million species, but even the most powerful
MRI machines will never penetrate that most peculiar of emotions.

For proof, look no further than mice, who live their lives avoiding
the gaze of mankind. Remember the mice in movies like *Cinderella*
and *Babe* singing their sweet, high-pitched tunes? It turns out that
real mice actually sing to each other in frequencies too high for the
human ear to detect. Using sensitive microphones, Austrian scientists
discovered that mice sing to each other during courtship—ultrasonic
ballads only they can hear.

If we can lie in bed oblivious to the love songs of our tiny friends,
then what else are we missing? The greatest love stories of our time may
be happening high in the sky, deep under the sea, inside the densest
forests—or perhaps under our own floorboards, in the dead of night.

The Joy of Play

Play is older than culture, for culture, however inadequately
defined, always presupposes human society, and animals
have not waited for man to teach them their playing.

—Johan Huizinga, Dutch historian

Dr. Marina Davila-Ross was intrigued. An expert in primate behavior at the University of Portsmouth in England, she had noticed something odd—after one gorilla would gently hit another, and then run away, the second gorilla would catch up to, and hit, the first gorilla. And run.

In other words: the gorillas were playing tag.

Curious if this behavior was normal, Davila-Ross and her research team analyzed videos of twenty-one gorillas from six colonies in five zoos across Europe. "Our findings on gorilla play show important similarities with the children's game of tag," she reported in July 2010. "Not only did the gorillas in our study hit their playmates and then run away chased by their playmates, but they also switched their roles when hit so the chaser became the chased and vice versa."[48]

As any parent can attest, toddlers squeal with joy when playfully chased, just as a high school running back feels a jolt of elation as he sprints for the end zone, dodging and juking his way around defenders. During the 1980s, American teens were enthralled by the arcade game *Pac-Man*, in which they controlled a plucky dot-gobbler as it eluded a host of pursuing ghosts. The thrill of chase is embedded in the deepest regions of our brain that transcend species. "When an animal is running from a real predator, the motivating force is fear," explains Peter Gray, a research psychologist at Boston College. "When an animal is practicing, in play, how to get away from a play predator, the motivating force is joy."[49]

Play is ubiquitous in the animal kingdom. It's found in humans and dogs, monkeys and crocodiles. Why is play so universal? The most common theory is that animals play to develop survival skills. Another theory is that play helps young animals navigate social hierarchies later in life. And yet, some animals—humans included—simply play for the fun of it.

PLAY TO SURVIVE

Back in the late nineteenth century, famed psychologist Karl Groos suggested that the universality of play can be explained by natural selection. "Animals can not be said to play because they are young and frolicsome, but rather they have a period of youth in order to play," he wrote in his 1898 book, *The Play of Animals*. "For only by doing so can they supplement the insufficient hereditary endowment with individual experience, in view of the coming tasks of life."[50] In other words, by playing, animals are practicing skills they will need later in life, when the stakes are far higher. So, according to Groos, gorillas playing tag might seem like an innocent expression of youth, but a higher evolutionary purpose is involved.

Observation seems to support Groos's theory. For one, play behavior is mostly seen in young animals, as it is in young humans. Studies have shown that among mammals, playful behavior decreases after puberty, meaning that by adulthood animals are ready to use the skills they learned through play for more useful ends, such as hunting. Groos divided play into various categories, including movement play, hunting play, fighting play, and nursing play. Observed animal play could then be neatly placed in the categories they ultimately promoted.

For instance, lions. Cue up YouTube and you can find hundreds of videos of young lions play-fighting. Young lions spend their days chasing, pouncing, pawing, wrestling, and nipping as they learn the skills that will one day keep them alive. Living together in tightly knit groups, or prides, lions are the most social of the big cats. Females, or lionesses, form the bedrock of every pride. Extremely defensive of their cubs and wary of outsiders, they often handle hunting duties, coordinating the movement of other lions to efficiently attack their prey. Because lions have relatively small hearts, their stamina is limited to very short bursts—they must be able to take down their prey with quick, powerful attacks. Cubs learn these skills after they are introduced to the pride, playing with others to strengthen muscles. This is especially important for male cubs, as in most cases they are expelled from the pride upon reaching sexual maturity at age three and must fend for themselves until they have a family of their own.

A trip to the Serengeti isn't needed to witness the play-for-survival theory for yourself. Chances are you've gazed out your window to see two squirrels dashing along power lines or up trees. Young squirrels chase each other to develop strength and coordination—crucial skills for an animal that routinely leaps to tiny tree branches and power lines dozens of feet in the air. Chase games also prepare squirrels for complex politics later in life. The most agile squirrels will chase and nip other squirrels who have begun feeding or harvesting acorns in their territory, so as to establish a squirrel "pecking order."

Squirrel Sleight of Hand

A 2008 paper published in the *British Journal of Animal Behaviour* asked an intriguing question: "Do tree squirrels engage in behavioural deception?"[51] In other words, do squirrels lie?

The answer is, apparently, yes.

Eastern gray squirrels are famous hoarders, stashing nuts

to keep themselves alive during cold, harsh winters. As "scatter hoarders," squirrels typically store their acorns in many different locations in case their booty is raided by thieves. Apparently realizing that rivals may be surveilling, squirrels employ sleight of hand tricks to hide their caches. The researchers found that squirrels will surreptitiously transfer acorns from their claws to their mouths just before appearing to bury them. When a would-be thief shows up to steal the nuts, they are met with an empty hole and leave with an empty stomach.

Chase is also a crucial component of mating. It is believed that male squirrels can smell when a female is ready to reproduce. In late winter and early spring, male squirrels will pursue females in order to catch a whiff of their scent. The more pursuit skills acquired as juveniles, the more likely they are to reproduce. A study of Belding's ground squirrels—who are found high up in the mountains in the western United States—concluded that play behavior "may ultimately influence long-term reproductive success."[52]

In the early 2000s, a team of researchers from the University of Alaska Fairbanks attempted to prove that play during childhood could help animals survive later in life. Located in the heart of Alaska, the researchers were fortunate enough to study one of the most playful mammals on earth: brown bears. Found in the mountains and forests of northern Europe, Asia, and North America, brown bears are among the largest carnivorous land animals, rivaled in size only by their close relative the polar bear. There are many subspecies of brown bears, including grizzly bears, found in Alaska, western Canada, and as far south as Wyoming, identified by gray or blond "grizzled" tips on their fur; Kodiak bears, who are darker than grizzlies and found along the Alaskan coast; and Eurasian brown bears, richly brown-colored bears found across Europe and Russia. Females typically give birth to one to three cubs at a time who are dependent on their mother for about three years. Males not only take no part in raising cubs, they will often kill young bears in hopes of mating with their mothers. For this reason, bear cubs must learn to defend themselves very early in life through play.

The University of Alaska researchers observed wild brown bears living on Admiralty Island, off the coast of Southeast Alaska in the Alexander Archipelago. The researchers followed ten individual mothers who gave birth to twenty-four cubs over the course of ten years. These cubs routinely played together, including wrestling, chasing, and other forms of play-fighting. "In our study," the authors wrote, "young bears that played more tended to survive best to independence. Our data support play as a survival factor."[53] Young bears love to play long and hard, strengthening their muscles as they rise up on their hind legs and wrestle with their siblings. Despite their hulking size and aggressive reputation, bear play is silent and bites are gentle—as if young bears understand they must work together to get stronger, for their mothers will not always be around to defend them.

Predators play. So do their prey. In order to survive, they must also romp to become stronger and more agile. White-tailed deer, common from Canada to Peru, have more than human hunters and automobiles to avoid. Wolves, cougars, alligators, jaguars, bobcats, bears, and wolverines—deer live in a constant state of tension. Fortunately, they can outrun most of their predators with bursts up to 45 mph and vertical leaps approaching nine feet. These skills are learned early in life when fawns play together to strengthen muscles and hone their reflexes. Fawns will dash around their mother in circles, often bucking and reversing course; sometimes they will walk backward from Mom and shake their heads back and forth like a puppy, beseeching her to join in the fun. If Mom is sure the risk of danger is low, she will indulge her young and play a game of chase. Play also helps fawns develop the social skills necessary to interact with other deer, such as mock fighting and aggressive and submissive postures.

Half a world away, another frequently stalked animal—the gazelle—must learn survival skills very early in life. A species of antelope, gazelles are found mainly in the deserts and grasslands of Africa as well as India and southwest Asia. All subspecies of gazelles are characterized by their swiftness, with some able to run at bursts approaching 60 mph. Their blinding speed is an evolutionary necessity—gazelles' predators include lions, cheetahs, leopards, jackals, hyenas, and even crocodiles. (As evidenced by ancient cave paintings, humans have also long hunted gazelles, although in recent years poachers have replaced spears with jeeps and high-powered rifles.) In a 2012 study, Chinese researchers revealed how play helps young goitered gazelles, who are found in the Middle East, India, and China, build the muscle strength to avoid predators. Unsurprisingly, the most common form of play was chase, with short, intense bouts involving frequent, high-speed direction changing, bucking, jumping, and kicking. This extreme agility allows gazelles to deftly outmaneuver predators like cheetahs who can achieve higher speeds but quickly tire from the repeated jukes, fakes, and dodges that gazelles master shortly after birth through play.

SOCIAL PLAY

Play may serve a purpose other than building physical survival skills.

By studying other primates, scientists have stumbled across a second theory for why animals play. Instead of—or, perhaps, in addition to—preparing for adulthood, play may serve to stimulate and strengthen regions of the brain associated with learning and cognition, which are crucial skills for highly social animals. Although primates are believed to be born with all the nerve cells, known as neurons, they will ever possess, it is thought that through play animals can strengthen connections in the brain, helping them to adapt and learn new skills. Species that enjoy playing, therefore, have an evolutionary advantage.

Research suggests that certain kinds of play are associated with specific skills. For instance, so-called nonsocial play, in which primates play alone with objects like balls, strengthens regions of the brain linked to tool use and creativity in adulthood. On the other hand, play with other primates is associated with complex behaviors, such as deception, used to navigate social hierarchies. The more primates play together, the larger the size of their cortico-cerebellar systems—a highly complex learning region of the brain that uses sensory information to develop muscle memory. Having fun makes us smarter.

In one disquieting experiment at the Yale School of Medicine several caged Rhesus macaques—monkeys native to South, Central, and Southeast Asia—were kept under stressful laboratory conditions and were taught how to play a modified version of rock, paper, scissors. Any human who has played this game understands the instantaneous pang of regret upon losing—*Why didn't I play rock?*—and monkeys, too, display competitive regret. In the study, when a monkey won a round against a researcher, he was rewarded with a glass of juice. When he tied, he received less juice. A loss meant no juice at all. The researchers found that when monkeys lost a round, they were far more likely in the following round to deploy the gesture that would have won the previous one—behavior that doesn't just demonstrate highly intelligent planning and problem solving but regret for making a poor decision. Forcing imaging equipment and implanting electrodes into the monkeys' brains, the researchers showed that when the monkeys didn't win, their brains lit up in two regions associated with regret: the dorsolateral prefrontal cortex, which involves planning, memory, and abstract thought; and the orbitofrontal cortex, which involves decision-making and the emotional aspect of regret.

A small argument among primates, including humans, can quickly escalate into a full-blown brawl. When a fight does occur, wise individuals can quickly defuse the situation and reconcile. These tactics were first observed by the Dutch primatologist Frans de Waal in the mid-1970s. His paper, published in the journal *Behavioral Ecology and Sociobiology*, explained that "After agonistic interactions among chimpanzees, former opponents often come into non-violent body contact . . . They tend to contact each other shortly after the conflict and show special behavior patterns during these first contacts."[54] This reconciliation behavior includes kissing, embracing, submissive vocalization, and hand-holding. Other studies found that reconciliation among chimps led to better relationships later in life and a reduced likelihood of aggressive behavior. Just as you feel relieved after you make up with a loved one after a fight, chimps are less stressed out after hugging it out.

Primates likely learn how to reconcile when they are juveniles. In a later study, de Waal found that after a host of especially pugnacious macaques were housed together for a few months, their ability to reconcile after a squabble increased threefold. And what do these young, forest-dwelling monkeys enjoy doing together? Playing. By roughhousing together—and, invariably, fighting—the macaques learned that to live in peace, they must learn to make up. This theory was confirmed in a 2016 study involving chimpanzees, when British researchers found that "immature chimpanzees commonly reconciled using social play."[55] Just as young humans learn to resolve disputes by tussling on the playground beyond the watchful eye of a teacher, our primate cousins learn many crucial social skills through roughhousing.

PLAYING FOR KICKS

Some animals play to learn survival skills; some play to develop tight social bonds. Still others seem to play for no discernible purpose, as in the case of meerkats—small insect-eaters belonging to the mongoose family. Found in the Kalahari Desert in Botswana, the Namib Desert in Namibia and Angola, and parts of South Africa, meerkats live in groups of about twenty called mobs. Weighing about five pounds, meerkats have long, slender bodies with large tails that aid in balancing when they stand upright on their hind legs.

Meerkats live underground in interconnecting tunnels with multiple entrances. When not scavenging for food outside, they groom each other in their tight living quarters. Meerkats also have specific roles in a mob, such as standing sentry to warn of approaching predators or babysitting newborns. As pups, meerkats crawl around and on each other, gently gnawing on limbs, ears, and noses. By a week old they are standing on their hind legs and wrestling much like sumo wrestlers do: teetering on their stubby legs as they push and heave, trying to topple their opponent. When one meerkat pup finally wins, he leaps onto his foe's stomach and nibbles his ears and paws.

There doesn't seem to be much evolutionary sense to meerkats' play routines. They tend to romp outside, in the full view of their predators, including eagles and jackals. A particularly frolicsome meerkat could twist his leg or hurt his claw, making him less likely to survive and pass on his DNA. Over millions of years, natural selection tends to weed out behavior that reduces a species' chance of surviving, from the tiniest rodent to the most ferocious predator. Meerkats have shown us that sometimes animals just love to play. Survival be damned.

Lynda Sharpe, a biologist at Australian National University, has been studying meerkats in South Africa for years. In one experiment, she followed forty-five meerkat pups until they reached adulthood. Meerkats have so many natural predators, Sharpe reasoned, that they wouldn't risk playing outside unless it was very important. The most likely answer was that playing formed social bonds, thus strengthening a mob's chance of survival when pups reach adulthood, or perhaps play helped them develop battle skills. Sharpe spent weeks wading through thigh-high sour grass and evading bees to observe the meerkats play. "Everyone leapt and bit and rolled at such a furious pace I couldn't identify who was doing what," she later wrote. "Often the whole group joined in (up to 30 animals), creating a seething ball of fur and waving limbs."[56]

Finally, she had her data. Did lots of juvenile play make meerkats better fighters as adults? Did the most vigorous players later become skilled statesmen who looked out for the collective good of the mob? "No, no, no!" Sharpe grumbled. "Play had no affect [sic] on any of these things." It turns out that even the most rambunctious meerkat pups were not better fighters as adults, nor were they any more likely to be upstanding members of the mob. For meerkats, play is only about play.

If play does not always serve a discernible purpose, then why does such a potentially dangerous activity exist? Perhaps the answers lie closer to home, among some of the most studied creatures on the planet.

ROMPING PUPPIES

Anyone who shares a home with dogs knows about the dozens of soggy tennis balls hidden in various rooms around the house. Or that, when you come home from work, your companion may likely leap across the room to greet you and immediately beg to play—or perhaps, beg to go to the dog park where they can jump and sprint for as long as you let them. What are they up to? Is that chihuahua mix who loves a belly scratch really learning how to become a better predator? Is that pound puppy catching a frisbee meticulously practicing a new survival skill? While science explains why young lions and bear cubs play-fight, it's less clear why dogs enjoy romps at the beach, ball games, and other seemingly useless activities. And unlike other animals, who tend to stop playing after reaching adulthood, even the most wizened old dog is up for a game of fetch. If meerkats cannot unlock the mysteries of play, scientists reasoned, dogs could.

In a 2017 study published in the journal *Applied Animal Behaviour Science*, researchers found that canine "play is not one type of behaviour—there are several types that each serve a different purpose."[57] First, dogs play to develop their motor skills. If you look closely at playing puppies, they chase, roll around, nibble, pick up and move objects with their mouth, and play tugging games. Through play, dogs learn to use their bodies, understand their limitations, find food, and defend themselves in a fight. Second, dogs learn to train for the unexpected. Playing with humans and other dogs can be a volatile activity full of knocks, tumbles, and yelps. By learning to be okay with unexpected pain and unfamiliar faces, dogs prepare to deal with real-life stressors. That's why your dog might be excited to see a new ball or chew toy, but an unfamiliar vacuum cleaner will give him a fright. Finally, the researchers found evidence that play helps dogs develop cooperative, but not dominant, relationships later in life—crucial skills for pack animals that once lived and hunted together.

At the very least, play reveals how dogs are capable of complex emotional thought. After observing footage of dogs playing, scientist Marc Bekoff concluded they display a range of emotions including joy, indignation, guilt, and jealousy. For instance, if several dogs are playing in the park and one play-bites too hard, the others may ignore him for the rest of the day. This, Bekoff explains, is a basic form of morality. Even more tantalizing, dogs appear to display the skill known as theory of mind—which, as we saw in the previous chapter, is the ability to understand what another animal is thinking.

For instance, Bekoff says, when one dog wants to play, she will first try to get the attention of a second dog, such as by gently nipping him or bounding into his field of view. The first dog understands that her playmate is not attentive, and will not initiate play until she has gained their attention. This might seem like a rudimentary skill but theory of mind is the backbone of empathy and a hallmark of human intelligence.

POUNCING KITTENS

Compared to dogs, cats tend to be more in tune with their predator instincts. Their play more closely resembles that of lions, tigers, and other large cats who must learn to survive at an early age. By the time kittens are just one month old, they are learning basic techniques rooted deeply in their evolution, including play-fighting, bird swatting, fish scooping, and mouse pouncing. Kittens who grow up in a litter universally practice play-biting the backs of their siblings' necks, which mimics techniques used to take out rodents. This sort of wrestling, known as social play, typically peaks around twelve weeks. Kittens are working to improve their paw–eye coordination by learning how to shuffle and leap sideways, pounce, and ambush unsuspecting siblings. For humans who adopt a single kitten, ankles and unsuspecting canines can bear the brunt of this play-aggression.

Before long, kittens advance to object play. While we prefer our young feline friends to play with approved toys like stuffed mice and scratch posts, they invariably graduate to toilet paper and paper towel rolls. That's because cats' eyesight is adept at catching sudden movement, whether it's a scurrying mouse or tissue paper dancing under a ceiling fan. When objects, siblings, or ankles aren't available for ambush, cats often engage in "self-directed" play, such as tail chasing and pouncing on imaginary targets. Like most mammals, cats play less after they reach adulthood, but they don't entirely stop. Even as adults, cats continue to place their siblings in paw-holds, nibble their ears, and enjoy high-speed pursuits around, under, and atop living room furniture. Cats will often take turns taking the role of the aggressor—a key way to determine if cats are playing or actually fighting. This sort of play reinforces the social bonds between cats, releases pent-up energy, and reduces stress.

Cats' predisposition to hunt rodents and birds is rooted deep in their evolution. Over thousands of years cats have capitalized on their close relationship with humans to colonize every continent except Antarctica. Geneticists believe cats were first domesticated approximately ten thousand years ago by farmers who prized their varmint-hunting skills. Cats were venerated by ancient Egyptians by about 3000 BCE, and often afforded the same mummification privileges typically reserved for the wealthiest humans. Throughout the Middle Ages, cats were staples on sailing ships to control the rodent population—a crucial reason why cats are found nearly everywhere on the planet.

This has led to what some people have found a sadistic form of feline amusement: "playing" with their not-yet-dead prey. Cats are not feline Hannibal Lecters; they are practicing a skill they acquired very early in their evolution. Mice, rats, and other rodents have sharp teeth and fight back when they are injured, while birds can deliver painful pecks. Because cats have short muzzles, their eyes and face are susceptible to attack. For this reason, cats seem to play with their food to tire them out—say, by allowing a mouse to hobble away before clawing him back. When her prey is sufficiently dazed, a cat will deliver the death blow in the form of a devastating bite to the spinal cord. Instead of experiencing amusement in the human sense, cats are simply following their predator instincts, however gruesome they may seem.

FUN ON THE FARM

Goats are curious creatures. Descended from the wild goat of Southwest Asia and Eastern Europe, today's domesticated goats are raised for their milk, meat, fur, and skin all across the world. When not confined to a farm, goats are natural grazers whose curiosity leads them on travels far and wide. Extraordinarily intelligent and agile, goats test their pens and repeatedly exploit weaknesses, often by climbing high fences. Nearby goats watch their friends closely and learn the same tricks. This often leads to massive prison breaks. In August 2018, more than a hundred goats broke through a wooden fence and escaped their pen in Boise, Idaho. Eyeing greener pastures, the goats had gone for a stroll to munch on the well-manicured lawns of a nearby residential neighborhood.

When goats aren't busy escaping, they enjoy being around happy humans. Sometimes all it takes to win over a goat is a sweet smile. In one study, after testing twenty goats, researchers found that goats behave very similarly to dogs in their ability to read humans. The goats were presented with photographs of humans with various facial expressions, including grinning and scowling. The goats overwhelmingly made a beeline for smiling humans and spent about 50 percent more time with them. Said the lead researcher: "The study has important implications for how we interact with [farmed animals], because the abilities of animals to perceive human emotions might be widespread and not just limited to pets."[58]

Pigs likewise exhibit keen senses of intelligence and playfulness. In fact, they're so thought-provoking that former president Harry Truman once said, "No man should be allowed to be president who does not understand hogs." When in their natural surroundings—not on filthy, joyless factory farms—pigs are social, playful, protective animals who bond with each other, make nests, relax in the sun, and cool off in the mud. Pigs are known to dream, recognize their own names, learn "tricks" like sitting for a treat, and lead social lives of a complexity previously observed only in primates. Pigs have been documented showing empathy for other pigs who are happy or distressed. Many pigs even sleep in "pig piles," much like dogs. Some love to cuddle and others prefer space.

People who run animal sanctuaries that include pigs note that they are more similar to humans than you would guess. They enjoy listening to music, playing with soccer balls, and getting massages. Pigs can even play video games. Researchers found that pigs eagerly controlled a ball onscreen using their snouts and a joystick. They quickly grasped the basics of the game: Roll the ball into shaded areas at the edge of the screen, which grow smaller as the game progresses, and win a real-life treat. Of course, in nature, rather than in a laboratory, pigs can be seen playing happily all the time.

Rescue Pigs

Pigs have been known to save the lives of others, including their human friends. As reported by London's Daily *Mirror,* "A pet piglet called Pru was praised by her owner . . . after dragging her free from a muddy bog." The owner said, "I was panicking when I was stuck in the bog. I did not know what to do and I think Pru sensed that. . . . I had a rope with me that I use as a dog lead and I put it around her. I was shout-

ing 'Go home, go home' and she walked forward, slowly pulling me out of the mud."[59]

In addition to Pru, there is Priscilla, a pig who saved a
young boy from drowning; Spammy, who led firefighters to
a burning shed to save her calf friend Spot; and Lulu, who
found help for her human companion, who had collapsed
from a heart attack. A pig named Tunia chased away an
intruder, and another, named Mona, held a fleeing suspect's
leg until the police arrived.

ELEPHANT SHENANIGANS

In 1942, when the Japanese invaded Burma, a British man named
James Howard Williams joined the Fourteenth Army, a military unit
specializing in guerrilla warfare. Surrounded by the enemy, Williams's
company was forced to endure a treacherous journey across several
mountain ranges to escape to India. As they marched, Williams came
across elephants who were previously used to carry timber but had
been pressed into service to aid the evacuation of Burma. Williams had
become familiar with elephants by working as a forest manager prior
to the war, and during the retreat he documented the astonishing ways
elephants could adapt to any situation, even violent battles. During the
desperate retreat, elephants were forcibly removed from their families
and endured terrible beatings and other cruel training techniques to
quickly teach them to haul logs used to build bridges in places where
heavy equipment could not be brought.

During the retreat, Williams noticed a peculiar trait among the
elephants: humor. One elephant, Bandoola, enjoyed playing a game
with his handler. When rolling bridge logs up to the bank of a river,
Bandoola would sometimes pretend to run out of strength at the last
moment, huffing and puffing and straining to move the log one last
inch into the water. After waiting for his handler to complain, Bandoola would use his trunk to flick the log into the river like it was a

stick. Those who told the story swore they could see the elephant smiling, satisfied with his practical joke.

Elephants play, for all kinds of reasons and in all kinds of places. For example, mud baths. Under the harsh African sun, extreme heat and ultraviolet radiation can quickly weaken the animals if they do not stay cool. By covering themselves in mud, elephants form a protective layer on their skin to shield themselves from the sun, as well as providing relief from insect bites. Mothers encourage their babies to dash into pits, and while there, they romp, wrestle, and lather themselves in glorious mud.

Water, too. Although they're the world's largest land mammal at nearly thirteen thousand pounds, they have no problem diving into oceans and swimming long distances. Elephants develop strong swimming muscles from walking dozens of miles each day in search of food and water, and because of their heft, they remain buoyant even when they stop swimming. African elephants have been observed swimming up to thirty miles continuously, and many experts believe the ancestors of elephants living in Sri Lanka swam there from southern India. Elephants swim low in the water to avoid waves, using their trunks as a snorkel. From the age of about five or six months old, young elephants love to dive into the water and splash in the waves, repeating the process again and again until exhausted. However, captivity deprives them of all such pleasures and natural behaviors.

AVIAN AMUSEMENTS

Humans have observed play mostly in land mammals. But play exists elsewhere as well. As noted in the previous chapter, crows hold funerals, but they also enjoy hamming it up when in lighter spirits. As with human toddlers who learn skills like problem solving and spatial awareness by building with blocks, there also may be an evolutionary purpose to crow play. In particular, there might be a link between crows' tendency to play and tool use, as they have been observed plucking insects from tiny crevices in trees using hooked sticks and folded leaf edges.

But other tools don't seem quite as useful. YouTube features numerous videos of crows snowboarding down rooftops using a plastic lid. The crows aren't using the lid to sneak up on an unsuspecting cricket or to save energy from flying: After reaching the roof's edge, they clutch the lid in their beak, fly back to the top, and slide down again. (Crows have also been observed rolling and sliding down slippery roofs, playing pranks, and launching themselves into sharp gusts of wind and floating back down.)

Scientists call this snowboarding "unrewarded object exploration." That's a fancy way of saying that the crow is having fun. A dog who fetches and shakes is expecting a treat, but there is no reward for snowboarding down a rooftop. It has been speculated that perhaps crows played with seemingly useless objects to test if they could be used as a tool for more serious purposes. Six crows, in laboratory conditions, were able to play with toys, such as a stick, then trained to use those toys for certain tasks, such as poking food out of a tube. Those who studied them thought the crows might interact with the toys differently once they understood their purpose. They didn't. Even though the birds understood a stick could also be used to acquire food, they still played with it the same way. A 2018 study found that crows can even construct their own tools using disparate parts—for example, by combining shorter sticks together into an extralong one to reach a chunk of larvae in a box. "The finding is remarkable because the crows received no assistance or training in making these combinations, they figured it out by themselves,"[60] said Auguste von Bayern of the Max Planck Institute for Ornithology and the University of Oxford.

Herring gulls, commonly referred to as seagulls, are found in coastal regions across the world. Known for their characteristic "long calls"— a series of notes made by dipping and raising their heads, used for anything from courtship to threats—herring gulls are typically white with a gray back, gray wings, and black wing tips. They have extremely varied diets, feeding on anything and everything from mussels, crabs, sea urchins, and squid to fish, insects, and discarded human food.

If you've ever driven near the beach, you might have heard your tires crunch against shells. Seagulls often pluck clams and other mollusks from the water and shatter them on hard surfaces for a juicy snack. But younger seagulls often turn this activity into a game. Mischievous seagulls sometimes intercept their friends' clams or oysters mid-drop and play keep-away. This game is played more often over soft rather than hard ground, suggesting that the birds are consciously deciding to play a game rather than eat. Moreover, this behavior is more common with high winds, adding to the challenge and thus the enjoyment.

Caged Birds

Captive birds lead difficult lives. All caged birds have either been captured in the wild or bred in captivity; birds are smuggled into the US more frequently than any other animal. Many are force-fed and have their wings clipped and their beaks taped shut before being crammed into anything from a spare tire to carry-on luggage. It's not unusual for 80 percent of the birds in a smuggled shipment to die. Birds bred in captivity don't fare much better. Because birds older than eight to ten weeks don't sell well at pet shops, they are kept for breeding and condemned to small cages with virtually no human contact for the remainder of their lives.

There is no such thing as a "cage bird." In the wild, these enchanting beings are never alone. If they become separated from their flockmates for even a moment, they call wildly to them. They preen each other, fly together, play, and share egg-incubation duties. Many bird species mate for life and share parenting tasks. Unfortunately for birds, the very qualities that we find admirable and fascinating about them—their brilliant colors, speech capabilities, intel-

ligence, playfulness, and loyalty—have made them the third
most popular type of animal companion in the US, where
an estimated forty million birds are kept caged and often
improperly cared for—bored, lonely, and a long way from
home.

FROLICKING MOLLUSKS

Octopuses are mollusks with soft, malleable bodies, two eyes, a beak,
and eight limbs, which are traditionally called "arms." They live all
across the world's oceans, from coral reefs to intertidal zones to the
seafloor. They vary greatly in size, ranging from the star-sucker pygmy
octopus, less than an inch long and weighing in at 0.04 ounces, to the
appropriately named giant Pacific octopus, who grows as large as 150
pounds and can propel herself at 25 mph for short bursts.

Outside of these basic facts, octopuses are difficult for humans to
understand. Even one of the fathers of Western philosophy, Aristotle, maligned them. In his *History of Animals,* written in 350 BCE, he
wrote: "The octopus is a stupid creature, for it will approach a man's
hand if it be lowered in the water." Then, after mentioning a few oc-
topoid tidbits, Aristotle dismisses the three-hundred-million-year-old
cephalopod: "So much for the mollusca."[61]

Aristotle was mistaken. Octopuses are extremely intelligent. Studies have revealed how well they can solve mazes, use tools, distinguish
between shapes and patterns, and learn through observation. The
veined octopus, found in tropical waters in the western Pacific Ocean,
regularly refashions discarded coconut shells into makeshift shelters,
even using them as shields as he moves across the ocean floor. Some
species can recognize individual faces. Octopuses can communicate
with each other by activating special skin cells to rapidly change color
and pattern—a skill also used to camouflage themselves when hunting or avoiding predators. Reports routinely surface about octopuses
who escape their aquariums, and they have been known to board fish-

ing boats and break into their holds to eat crabs. In 2016, an octopus named Inky living at New Zealand's National Aquarium managed to slip out of his tank, slither across the floor, navigate through a fifty-foot drainpipe, and escape into the ocean.

And, octopuses like to play. While many animals, especially invertebrates, will cast away objects that can't be eaten, octopuses don't. For instance, a 2006 study observed an octopus playing with Legos by tossing them between his arms. "Do octopuses have the cognitive complexity to show play behavior?" the authors wrote. "Yes they do."[62] Octopuses can also use their funnel—a tubular opening located behind the head that can expel water at high speeds—to blow objects around and back again, much like a child bounces a ball against a wall.

As discussed earlier, comparing the relative intelligence of animals is almost impossible (and, arguably, pointless, since different animals are better at different things), but it's especially futile with octopuses. While vertebrates all have basically the same nervous-system architecture—a centralized brain, protected by a skull—octopus nervous systems are quite literally all over the place. Only part of the octopuses' nervous system is found in their brain. Two-thirds of their neurons are located in clusters of interconnected nerve cells called ganglia located on their body and arms. Yet some restaurants chop these arms off, bit by bit, while the animals are still alive, leaving the octopus with only one or two arms until the next customer orders."

All told, octopuses have the highest brain–to–body mass ratio of any invertebrate—and greater than some vertebrates. With so many neurons in their arms, octopuses have astounding control over their circular, adhesive suckers. Take a moment and grip your thumb and forefinger together. This is known as the pincer grip, a crucial component of humans' ability to interact with their environment. Without it, we would likely not have evolved into the world's dominant species. An octopus can manipulate both sides of each sucker to create a hundred separate pincer grasps, making them perhaps the most deft and graceful sea creature.

Ultimately the true extent of octopus intelligence is probably inexplicable to humans. As one research paper concluded: "A chief roadblock in investigations of octopus learning abilities has been their relative intractability as experimental subjects."[63] They break lab equipment, escape from their tanks, refuse to learn dumb tricks—and, quite simply, do not appreciate being plucked from their homes to be poked and prodded by humans.

Octopoid Facts

1. *Octopuses don't have tentacles.* There are many misconceptions about octopuses—chief among them that they have tentacles. Octopuses have eight arms, but *arms* are not synonymous with *tentacles*, although the difference is a bit technical: If there are suckers along the entire limb, it's an arm. If the suckers are only at the end, as with squid and cuttlefish, it's called a tentacle. Some octopuses have even been observed crawling out of the water and walking along the shoreline.

2. *Octopuses have three hearts.* One heart pumps blood throughout the body, while the other two circulate blood to the gills. The first heart is deactivated when octopuses are in motion, which is why they tire quickly. This is the main reason they prefer to walk along the seafloor rather than swim.

3. *Octopuses escape enemies like James Bond.* Under an octopus's digestive gland is an ink sac. Like 007's Aston Martin, octopuses can escape danger by expelling a camouflaging "smoke screen"—in this case a dark cloud of ink mixed with mucus. Thanks to a toxic compound called tyrosinase, the ink also physically harms enemies by causing a blinding irritation in their eyes.

4. *Octopuses are blue bloods.* Many species of octopus live

in extremely deep waters, where temperatures hover around 30 degrees Fahrenheit. Most animals have blood containing hemoglobin, a component of which—an iron-based compound called heme—gives blood its characteristic scarlet color. Octopuses, however, have copper-based blood, which allows their tissue to more efficiently absorb oxygen in frigid environments. It also turns their blood blue.

5. *Octopuses die after mating.* During reproduction, males insert packets of sperm into the female's mantle cavity using a special arm called a hectocotylus. Soon after, males undergo an intense aging process called senescence, in which their cells can no longer divide and grow. Within a few weeks they are dead. Females, meanwhile, secure tens of thousands of fertilized eggs in rocks and crevices in the ocean floor, where she guards them for about five months. So devoted is the octopus to protecting her unborn children that she does not even eat. She lingers until her babies are born, and then she dies. (Sometimes this process takes longer. In 2014, a research team reported that a female deep-sea octopus guarded her eggs continuously for four and a half years before they hatched, and she could finally die.)

CROCODILE SMILES

Crocodiles are the ultimate survivors. Having arisen some two hundred million years ago, crocodiles have outlived dinosaurs by sixty-five million years, and all twenty-three species have avoided extinction at the hands of human poachers. The word "crocodile" comes from the ancient Greek phrase *ho krokódilos tou potamoú*, "the lizard of the river." Extraordinarily hardy animals, crocodiles endure violent lives but manage to live decades even with debilitating injuries, including missing limbs, tails, and mangled jaws suffered from territorial disputes. Crocodiles mostly live in freshwater habitats like rivers, lakes, and wetlands, with a notable exception being saltwater crocodiles, the largest reptiles on Earth, who prefer brackish environments such as swamps, estuaries, deltas, and lagoons. Adults also vary greatly in size, from just five feet long and 40 pounds (dwarf crocodiles) to twenty-three feet long and 2,200 pounds (saltwater crocodiles). And unlike sharks, who almost never attack human swimmers, Nile and saltwater crocodiles are responsible for hundreds of fatal attacks on humans every year. (Other species are less dangerous. For instance, American crocodiles, found mostly in Central and South America, are more timid; fatal attacks are rare.)

Since crocodiles are so different than most animals—biologically, they are more closely related to dinosaurs than to most other reptiles—and because they are so fierce, play wouldn't seem to be a part of their life. So, when the zoologist Vladimir Dinets heard that a Cuban crocodile at an Ohio zoo was playing with an inflatable ball, he was skeptical. But after spending more than three thousand hours observing crocodiles in the wild and in captivity, Dinets concluded that crocs engage in a wide variety of play.

Among animals, locomotor play means any kind of playful activity involving intense movement, such as wrestling or tag. As it relates to crocodilians—an order that includes crocodiles and their close relatives alligators, caimans, and gharial—Dinets observed particularly daring water sports, including repeatedly bodysurfing ocean waves and sliding down muddy slopes into rivers. As the zookeepers witnessed in Ohio, crocs also love playing with objects. They are routinely spotted nibbling on their favored wooden toys, not to mention tossing their dead prey into the air before consuming it. They also seem especially attracted to pink flowers, often clutching them delicately in their mouths while stalking the riverbanks. Dinets also documented how crocodiles, alligators, and caimans play tag, give each other piggyback rides, and engage in mock fight.

Crocodiles vs. Alligators

If you're staring into the eyes of an eight-hundred-pound semiaquatic reptile with armored scales and eighty razor-sharp teeth, the last thing on your mind is identifying whether he's an alligator or crocodile. But in case you're curious (and in the safety of your own home), here are the basic differences.

- *Snout.* Compared to crocodiles, alligators have wider, U-shaped snouts. Crocodiles have pointier, V-shaped snouts.
- *Grin.* Alligators have a wide upper jaw and a narrow lower jaw, meaning nearly all their teeth are hidden when they close their mouth. However, when a crocodile closes his snout, you'll spot several snaggleteeth protruding over his lip.
- *Born in the USA.* There are only two extant species of alligator. The larger of the two, *Alligator mississippiensis,* is found exclusively in the southeastern United States, while the critically endangered *Alligator sinensis* is found in eastern China. Anywhere else in the world, you're looking at a crocodile.
- *Speed.* If you aren't fleet of foot, you better hope you are running from a crocodile. Alligators are smaller, nimbler, and faster on land. In water they are downright deadly, able to swim at speeds approaching 20 mph.

Why do animals play? Do they play to learn survival skills? Do they play to become better hunters? Do they play to become statesmen who are adept at navigating complex social hierarchies? Or do they play because it's fun?

No one really knows. Some animals do indeed play to learn skills that are useful later in life. Others seem to play in ways that boldly challenge the basic rules of evolution. What possible evolutionary purpose can snowboarding crows, wrestling meerkats, or tag-playing gorillas actually serve? Perhaps the Earth's animals have managed to evolve and persist in spite of their passion for what some biologists might deride as "purposeless activities." Play may not be a survival skill or a social skill or any skill at all. The pursuit of fun may simply be hardwired, rooted in the most ancient parts of the brain that even the tiniest insect and the most mammoth predator share.

As the naturalist John Muir once said, "Surely all God's people, however serious and savage, great or small, like to play. Whales and elephants, dancing, humming gnats, and invisibly small mischievous microbes, all are warm with divine radium and must have lots of fun in them."[64]

SECTION II:

Revolutionary New Ways to Show Them Compassion

As you have now seen, over the last few decades we have uncovered a staggering amount of new knowledge about the animals who share this planet with us. Still, there is an enormous amount left to learn about their incredible abilities, extraordinary talents, and fascinating lives. In the meantime, while the effort to understand our fellow animals continues, sharp people are coming up with truly extraordinary advances in science, technology, medicine, and manufacturing—advances that have allowed us to stop using and harming animals and, instead, to swap them out for usage of superior clothing materials, research methods, foodstuffs, and entertainment. We have made great strides, but are far from having exhausted all that can be done. Many more impressive innovations await us and the other animals.

In the following section we will examine how animals have been exploited in four specific areas of human life—science, clothing, entertainment, and food. And we will show how humankind has learned to find innovative and 100 percent humane methods to advance human interests without abusing animals. Consider scientific research. Forty years ago, the standard pregnancy test consisted of sending a urine sample to a laboratory, injecting it into a frog, rabbit, or mouse, and checking to see if the animal died. Today, you can pick up an over-the-counter test kit and know within minutes whether or not you have a new family member. Forty years ago, there were only a handful of cosmetics companies in the world that refused to test a new product by smearing it into the eyes of live rabbits, on their shaved skin, or pouring it down their throats. Today, few cosmetics companies test on animals—in fact, that kind of animal testing is now illegal in Europe and much of Asia, and most products no longer contain animal-derived ingredients such as mink oil, musk, and placenta.

Two generations ago, pigs were blow-torched to study the treatment of burns. Today, doctors can order sheets of cloned human skin in the morning, have them air-couriered to a hospital, and graft them onto a patient by the afternoon, saving far more lives. During the 1990s, scientists injected hundreds of chimpanzees with the AIDS virus, hoping to model the disease. Today, we have a cocktail of HIV/AIDS drugs developed by a high-speed computer, all without the patter of little feet or the angry thump of a chimpanzee's head banging against the cage walls. We also have synthetic vaccines that, unlike the old animal-based ones, cause no side effects or fatalities. The list of improvements is long, but what's ahead, from exoskeletons that allow people with disabilities to walk and lift heavy objects, to organs grown in a laboratory, is as promising for human health as it is vital for animal well-being.

As for clothing, *Gone with the Wind*'s Scarlett O'Hara sewed up curtains to make a dress—the norm at the time, as a scant choice of materials existed from which to choose. The grandest options, such as a fur coat, cost more than many people earned in a year. But fur was fashionable, even though it was not always a practical choice. Getting wet while wearing fur meant a soggy, smelly carpet on your back. But back then warmer synthetics weren't for sale in the shops; there was no faux fur or fleece, let alone vegan leather. Today, a host of nonanimal choices is creating a fantastic future of clothing as young designers employ cutting-edge materials that do not involve or harm animals.

Entertainment has also come a long way. For many years, fun was reserved for humans, not for animals (who can indeed have fun, as detailed in Section I). In an era when video games were only science-fiction fantasies, circus wagons rolled into town and children bubbled over with excitement to see "wild" animals—that is, elephants and tigers so demoralized that they did whatever the man with the whip commanded them to do. Today, at the touch of a button (or with a voice command), children can watch animals at play in their natural habitats instead of living in cages and wearing absurd headdresses or trying to balance on rubber balls. Virtual-reality headsets allow us to observe bears and panthers at close range, even enter their dens, without interfering. Few movies nowadays feature wild animals that were actually hurt or, as was often the case, killed. Computer-generated tech lets animals perform amazing feats without shedding a drop of blood (or requiring anyone to clean up afterward).

Finally, there's food. Not that long ago, a man wasn't a man without a steak dinner prepared by the "little woman," an image that today sounds like a cartoon rather than real life. People in the West ate meat, eggs, meat, milk, more meat, and, occasionally, potatoes. Now most people are too conscious of their health to eat a diet entirely composed of dead animals. They are also knowledgeable about the environment, i.e.: the harmful effects of animal agriculture on our waterways, oceans, and forests (not to mention knowledgeable about the primitive and cruel conditions of factory farming and transport).

Where once soy milk came only in powder form at a food co-op and had to be mixed by hand, today's supermarkets display soy, almond, coconut, oat, hemp, hazelnut, and other milks, enough to make you giddy. Vegetable and fruit selections no longer depend on seasons; you can eat a mango in December and asparagus when there's no *r* in the month. Bookstores are filled with vegan cookbooks authored by everyone from chefs to celebrities to professional athletes.

Coming soon is "clean meat": actual flesh grown from animal cells in a laboratory under conditions that eliminate *E. coli* and other dangerous bacteria, conserve water, and eliminate slaughterhouses once and for all. Ever more "taste-alikes," from shrimp to sausages to chick'n, are rolling off the production line—foods that could fool your grandfather into thinking nothing has changed when, actually, everything has! We are entering a new age of animal-free living.

Just imagine an entire world without misusing animals.

What a wonderful world that will be.

Scientific Research

*There is no research more valuable than our own integrity
and ethical coherence, and our treatment of animals is a
direct reflection of our values toward life and one another.*

—John P. Gluck, PhD, emeritus professor of
psychology at the University of New Mexico

Thanks to a rat named Ratsky, Dr. Neal Barnard, founder of Physicians
Committee for Responsible Medicine (PCRM) and author of *Your
Body in Balance* and *The Cheese Trap*, changed the way medical schools
in the US and Canada use animals.

While in college, Barnard, interested in how the human mind
works, enrolled in a psychology course that included placing rats in
boxes and depriving them of food and water so they would press levers
or do whatever the experimenters wished them to do. One day Barnard was conducting a test in which he had to drill holes into a rat's
head and insert electrodes inside the brain. To steady the skull, the rats
had to be placed in a stereotaxic device that held them in place by way
of bars in their ears. Barnard's professor walked by and told Barnard
that his stereotactic was too loose; when Barnard tightened it, he could
feel it pierce the rat's eardrums. He reported this to the professor, who
shot back: "Well, I guess he won't be able to listen to his stereo in the
morning."[65]

Barnard was taken aback. The professor had always struck him as
a kind man but, Barnard says, "this callous remark, this disregard for

the suffering of animals, was something very different." Troubled by this attitude, Barnard took one of the rats, doomed to death, home. He began to see, even in that tiny body, a sentient being who loathed pain, bonded with others, had a wide range of complicated emotions. He named her Ratsky.

Ratsky lived for some months in a cage in his bedroom. And in her cage, she behaved the way Barnard assumed rats behave. But when he started leaving the cage door open so she could scurry around, he began to see actions he hadn't anticipated. After several days of cautious sniffing at the cage door, Ratsky began to investigate the world outside. "As she explored my apartment (under my watchful eye), she became more and more friendly. If I was lying on my back reading, she would come and stand on my chest," Barnard says. "She would wait to be petted, and if I didn't pay her enough attention, she would lightly nip my nose and run away. I knew that her sharp teeth could have gone right through my skin, but she was always playfully careful."[66]

Shortly afterward, when Barnard was attending the George Washington University School of Medicine, an instructor announced that an upcoming laboratory exercise would involve giving numerous human heart drugs to a dog to record any reactions. All the dogs would be killed at the end of the exercise. Barnard refused to participate. Apart from the obvious cruelty involved, he also felt that medical students could sufficiently grasp the concepts of pharmacology without a graphic (and fatal) demonstration with a dog. Instead, Barnard and one other student turned in reports of the expected physiological effects of these drugs. Both passed the course.

Years later, Barnard founded PCRM, whose first focus was to eliminate the use of animals in medical education. PCRM set about strategically producing information on talking with faculty and students, offering alternatives. In some cases, Barnard says "it was quite easy, but other times it was a knock-down, dragged-out fight." Some schools agreed quickly; others fought to the bitter end. Yet in the end, PCRM won. Today, no medical school in the United States or Canada uses animals to teach medicine. As fate would have it, Barnard today is on the adjunct faculty at the George Washington University School of Medicine.

Dr. Barnard's experience at medical school was not atypical. Animals have been used for experimental purposes for as long as medicine has been part of human civilization. Physicians in ancient Greece dissected animals for anatomical studies (partly because animals were plentiful, partly because of taboos regarding human autopsy). And this wasn't just to train doctors; animals have been used for countless medical procedures as well. Today, however, animal testing and experimentation are slouching toward obsolescence throughout the medical world, thanks to new methods and innovative technologies that are faster, cheaper, more accurate, and don't involve animals at all. In fact, Francis Collins, director of the National Institutes of Health, has predicted that within a decade, researchers may not be using animals at all.

Yet many excruciating and wasteful old ways continue, often merely to satisfy curiosity rather than to discover new treatments. Millions of animals—mostly mice and rats, but also rabbits, monkeys, cats, dogs, birds, fish, horses, sheep, reptiles, octopuses, and apes—are harmed and killed to study toxic chemicals, drugs, or diseases. Just a few examples:

- In April 2018, four clever baboons kept in an outdoor corral at the Texas Biomedical Research Institute in San Antonio rolled a fifty-five-gallon drum up to the wall, pushed it up on end, and used it as a ladder to escape the enclosure. Then they did what anyone whose life consists of being experimented on would do: They ran for their lives, fleeing through street traffic. The facility, which holds some 1,100 baboons, has been cited and fined multiple times for the harm or death through negligence of animals in their care. Additionally, Texas Biomedical runs a biohazard lab that infects the nearly three thousand primates it holds there with contagious diseases for which there is no known treatment or cure. While the human scientists wear extensive protective gear, monkeys suffer all the effects of deadly viruses. An estimated seventy thousand nonhuman primates are used in research each year in the United States alone—most kept in banks of small, lonely, indoor cages.

• For decades, Joseph Kornegay, a scientist at Texas A&M University, conducted experiments on dogs bred to suffer from a form of muscular dystrophy (MD) as a means to study the disease in humans. Because of the illness, the dogs could not walk and could barely eat—yet still no cure has been found for the disease in either species, and dogs have been dismissed as a model of the human form of MD. Across the country dogs are also used to test pesticides and other chemicals in federally required toxicity tests, where they may be injected with, force-fed, or placed in box-like rooms and blasted with noxious substances. Some sixty thousand dogs were used in experiments throughout the US during 2015 alone.

• Mice feel as much pain as any dog, yet mice used in studies at the University of Pittsburgh had their intestines intentionally punctured so feces and other bacteria would leak into their bodies, causing them to go into sepsis, a life-threatening reaction to infection. To study this reaction, which science has already shown is different in mice than in humans, the animals endured excruciating misery until they died. It's estimated that tens of millions of mice are used in research annually.

Public support for vivisection— the practice of performing operations on live animals—has declined steadily over the past few years, yet more animals than ever before are being used in laboratories. An analysis published in the *Journal of Medical Ethics* in 2015 found there was a nearly 73 percent increase in animal use in US government–funded research over a fifteen-year period.

You may be thinking, *Well, we don't need to eat or wear animals or put them in circuses. But don't we have to use animals if science is to advance and medicine is to cure disease and save lives?*

No, we don't.

HOW DID WE GET HERE?

Ever since the formal practice of Western medicine began around 3000 BCE in ancient Egypt, humans have been dissecting, poking, prodding, and operating on live animals in hopes of better understanding their anatomy, physiology, and the diseases we share. These early scientists put animals under the knife because dissecting human corpses (much less living people) was considered taboo.

Vivisection was championed by the respected thinker-physicians of ancient Greece and Rome, including Aristotle and, especially, Galen of Pergamon, who used animal research to generate a body of medical knowledge (some of it accurate, some not) that was accepted for more than a thousand years. As far as we know, few questioned the morality of harming animals in the pursuit of science. As discussed in Section I, many human societies believed in a fixed hierarchy of nature, with humans at the top (under God or gods) and beasts at the bottom. This notion was reinforced as Christianity came to thrive, by the biblical teaching that animals, lacking souls, were here solely to serve mankind.

For many centuries after the fall of the Roman Empire, religion and superstition pushed scientific research to the margins, and animal experiments fell from favor. Using animals in medical research and training wasn't resurrected until the development of the scientific method—the standardized process of observing, measuring, experimenting, and forming a hypothesis.

Philosopher-scientists of the Enlightenment era, including British statesman Francis Bacon and Frenchman René Descartes, rationalized that vivisection was ethically acceptable. Descartes went a step further. He saw animals as akin to clocks: mere machines. (Descartes's contempt for animals was so legendary that he supposedly once nailed his wife's live dog to a wall and sliced the poor soul open to examine her organs.) Other thinkers granted that animals can feel pain, but as the seventeenth-century Dutch philosopher Baruch Spinoza put it in his famous treatise *Ethics,* humans should feel free to "use them as we please, treating them in a way which best suits us, for their nature is not like ours."[67]

Still, animal experiments didn't start to provide answers until the seventeenth century, when William Harvey, physician to the English kings James I and Charles I, published a detailed description of blood circulation and heart function based in part on animal studies that disproved many of Galen's ideas. In the eighteenth century, the first modern medical schools, or *académies*, opened in France, and animal experiments became a standard part of the curriculum. The situation worsened in the nineteenth century when French researcher Claude Bernard—"the father of physiology"—stated, "Experiments on animals are entirely conclusive for the toxicology and hygiene of man. The effects of these substances are the same on man as on animals, save for differences in degree."[68]

That belief spread during the late nineteenth century after the discoverer of the rabies vaccine, Louis Pasteur, infected hundreds of animal species to prove the then revolutionary idea that germs cause disease. This success led to the suffering of exponentially more animals in research, including primates, who were killed by the thousands in the development of the first, disastrous polio vaccine.

Not everyone felt similarly. Nineteenth-century scientists, including the animal advocates Charles Darwin and physician Joseph Lister (who introduced sterile surgery), believed that animals should only be used for scientific research when absolutely necessary, and that their pain should be minimized as much as possible.

THE ANTI-VIVISECTION MOVEMENT

For as long as vivisection has existed, there have been those who fought against it. It took many centuries for organized opposition to arise, however, even as vivisection grew more grisly, and more public. For instance, the seventeenth-century physician Robert Boyle, as part of his research on respiration, repeatedly performed "Experiment 41":

imprisoning a bird, mouse, or snail in a chamber and allowing the public to observe as the animal went into convulsions and eventually dropped dead. Likewise, in the nineteenth century, the French physiologist François Magendie appalled the public with his sadistic science presentations, such as dissecting the face of a live dog crucified on a board or cutting nerves in the brains of live rabbits.

Claude Bernard became notorious for heating live creatures in ovens to study how the body maintains its core temperature (his wife divorced him over it). These extreme experiments caught the attention of influential public figures, including Queen Victoria, whose opposition to vivisection helped make it one of the most passionately debated topics of the time. Compassion for animals helped lead to the passage of the Cruelty to Animals Act by the British Parliament in 1835. Originally created to prevent bearbaiting and cockfighting, the act was amended in 1876 to regulate the use of animals for scientific purposes—the first law of its kind in the world. Among other restrictions, the act required vivisection facilities to be licensed and set limits as to when and how live dissections were performed. Just the previous year, Irish suffragist Frances Power Cobbe founded the Victoria Street Society for the Protection of Animals Liable to Vivisection, the first animal protection society aiming to end all animal experiments. Opposition to animal research was also on the rise in the United States, leading to the founding of the American Anti-Vivisection Society (AAVS) in 1883.

The use of anesthesia during human surgery, introduced in 1846, led to a renewed interest in vivisection, with scientists divining that since animals could be rendered numb or unconscious during experiments, there was no limit to the number and types of uses to which the creatures could be put. By the 1920s, the anti-vivisection movement had fallen out of favor.

VIVISECTION BECOMES LAW

Vivisection once again became standard practice, with surveys at the time showing that large majorities of Americans supported it. One possible reason was the growing use since 1900 of specially bred mice and other small and docile rodents who had long been stigmatized as disposable vermin.

Eventually, *allowing* animals to be experimented upon evolved into governments *requiring* them to be. In the US, this precedent was set in 1937, when the pharmaceutical firm S. E. Massengill Company marketed an elixir made with a solvent called diethylene glycol (DEG). Unknown to the company's chemists, DEG is highly poisonous. After more than one hundred people died from using the product, Congress passed the 1938 Federal Food, Drug, and Cosmetic Act, overseen by the Food and Drug Administration (FDA). The act was the first law requiring product safety testing, eventually stipulating that drugs and industrial chemicals first be crudely tested on animals before they can be sold to humans, creating a false sense of security, as time would tell.

Animal testing of cosmetics is no longer required under US law, but the FDA continues to accept the results of animal research trials submitted by companies to get their products approved. Meanwhile, China still requires animal testing for cosmetics, although the European Union and many other nations no longer do.

Today, animal studies remain a prerequisite for human clinical drug trials, under the intention of ensuring that medical discoveries and treatments are safe and effective, and for determining which chemical compounds are toxic in various species—even when that does not always predict the effect on humans. The same is true for many other countries, which require toxicity testing on animals for the sale or import of chemicals and products. (Megadoses of the substance are typically force-fed to animals via a feeding tube, or they are restrained and forced to inhale it in liquid or gaseous form.) While humans still endure side effects, some quite serious, from this reliance on animal tests, animals still pay the biggest price.

FEW PROTECTIONS FOR ANIMALS

While animal testing rules were created to try to protect public health, for many years few guidelines existed to protect the animals exploited for scientific research. The exception was Britain, whose Cruelty to Animals Act was the only legislation of its type in Western countries for decades, although it was basically unenforced and was largely inadequate.

Eventually, in the 1950s, the UK's Universities Federation for Animal Welfare recruited two scientists, William Russell and Rex Burch, to develop a set of more humane animal research principles known as the 3Rs. The Rs stand for *replacement* (avoiding animals and using something else); *reduction* (using the fewest number of animals to obtain the data needed); and *refinement* (using techniques that reduce pain and stress in any animals). However, the 3Rs didn't catch on until the late 1970s, with the rise of the modern animal rights movement ignited by books like Peter Singer's *Animal Liberation* and later Tom Regan's *The Case for Animal Rights*. These bestsellers urged people to consider what the biologist Nuno Enrique Franco called "the central idea that there are absolute and non-negotiable limits to what can be done to animals."[69] The 3Rs were adopted worldwide in word if not always in deed, as countless exposés show, and they became enshrined in international agreements like the 3Rs Declaration of Bologna of 1999 and the Basel Declaration of 2011. However, less harm is still harm: The Basel Declaration concedes that "the undersigned scientists expect society to recognize that animal experiments are essential for medical progress both now and in future."

There are two main US regulations currently governing some but not all aspects of animal research. The Animal Welfare Act of 1966 (AWA) is a federal "housekeeping" law setting bare-minimum standards for caging, feeding, handling, and veterinary care for live animals used in research, testing, teaching, and other areas. But it does not require pain relief or establish means to prevent any experiment, no matter how frivolous, from being carried out. "Animals" means dogs, cats, guinea pigs, hamsters, rabbits, and nonhuman primates. The remaining 99 percent of animals—including chickens, turkeys, rats, mice, cows, horses, pigs, and most invertebrate animals like octopuses—are not covered at all.

Businesses using these animals in federally funded research must be registered with the US Department of Agriculture (USDA), and facilities with regulated animals must be inspected by the government, but inspections are rare, often a cursory "pop in" every three years even if the facility houses thousands of animals. Penalties are rarer still. The USDA is responsible for enforcing the AWA but is much criticized, even by the US Congress, for failing in its duties.

Where inspections are required, budgets are limited. As of 2016, there were only 112 animal care inspectors and veterinary medical officers responsible for performing the bulk of inspections at more than 7,400 registered facilities. Catching abuse and neglect is often left to activists and whistle-blowers. When problems are identified, the penalties are usually to create what the USDA calls "a teaching moment." In the extremely rare case of a hearing, the result is little more than a slap on the wrist: The maximum fine per violation is $10,000.

The second set of rules, simple recommendations, are contained in the US Public Health Service Policy on the Humane Care and Use of Laboratory Animals, and cover facilities performing animal research funded by a health service agency. Overseen, in theory, by the National Institutes of Health's Office of Laboratory Animal Welfare (OLAW), the policy comes without the force of law. Because inspections aren't mandated, enforcement is based primarily on self-reporting. The penalty for violators is loss of federal funding, but for obvious reasons this is almost unheard of.

Organizations applying to sell drugs and medical products must also follow the animal husbandry guidelines in the FDA's Good Laboratory Practice for Nonclinical Laboratory Studies, and facilities must allow inspections but, again, as whistle-blowers and undercover investigations have repeatedly shown, enforcement is almost nonexistent.

Vivisection Isn't Worth It

Some argue that animal testing is a necessary evil to protect the public health. However, many of the loudest objections to this belief are coming from within the scientific community itself. Here are just a few reasons why:

- Our fellow beings can never be reliable stand-ins for human research subjects; while they certainly feel pain and fear as we do, other species' anatomy, physiology, and biochemistry are just not similar enough to ours. Even chimpanzees and bonobos, who share about 99 percent of our DNA, differ in important ways. Think about it: How much sense does it make to place different species in artificial environments under severe stress? Studies show that animals' adrenaline, pulse, and heart rate increase when they see the laboratory doorknob turn.
- More than 90 percent of scientific discoveries from animal experiments fail to lead to human treatments, according to a report published in the *Journal of the American Medical Association*. The authors cautioned: "Poor replication of even high-quality animal studies should be expected by those who conduct clinical research."[70]
- Animal research is extremely wasteful. Repeated experiments crippling dogs to mimic human muscular dystrophy have brought us no closer to a cure for the disease. Scores of potential AIDS vaccines that worked on primates, and thousands of experimental cancer drugs effective in ani-

mals, turned out not to protect or cure humans—wasting years of time in reaching a cure. As Richard Klausner, the former director of the National Cancer Institute, put it, "The history of cancer research has been a history of curing cancer in the mouse. We have cured mice of cancer for decades and it simply didn't work in humans."[71]

- Drug testing on animals can end up harming people as well. The painkiller Vioxx had to be pulled from the market even after extensive animal tests because it increased the risk of heart attack and stroke in humans.

Human clinical trials have led to the most important health advances, including the links between smoking and cancer and between cholesterol and heart disease. We'll never know how many new medicines that failed in billion-dollar animal studies might have worked for us.

SCIENTIFIC RESEARCH WITHOUT ANIMALS

As scientific understanding has grown concerning the lives, health, and wonderful complexity of animals (see Section I of this book), vivisection is becoming obsolete. That's why there has been an effort to focus on the "replacement" leg of the 3Rs.

In the United States, a government body called the Interagency Coordinating Committee on the Validation of Alternative Methods (ICCVAM), composed of representatives from sixteen federal agencies, was established in 1993 and made permanent in 2000. Its mission: to identify and promote scientifically sound methods of toxicity and safety testing and medical research that use fewer or no animals, and then share the information across agencies.

Also since 1993, scientists and policymakers from academia, the corporate world, and animal welfare groups from around the globe have met every two or three years for the World Congress on Alternatives and Animal Use in the Life Sciences. These meetings are for sharing developments in fields such as biomedical engineering and computer science, along with new ways of looking at old scientific problems, that can spare animals in research and testing. And, in 2007, the US National Academies of Sciences published its *Toxicity Testing in the 21st Century: A Vision and a Strategy* report, at the request of the EPA, which explicitly called for revamping the system away from "time consuming and resource intensive" animal "models" toward high-tech methods using cells and data from humans.

CUTTING-EDGE, CRUELTY-FREE TECHNIQUES

While some government agencies have been slow to act, and others helpful, public and private research institutes and tech firms have been developing new, noninvasive, cruelty-free methods to study how chemicals and drugs affect our body, to better understand diseases, and to explore more effective—even personalized—treatments. Most of them employ machines or actual humans—their tissues, data about them, and even their bodies—without harming them. This is much more efficient than breeding, housing, and feeding animals for each test or experiment. Researchers can now use the same samples multiple times, crunch numbers many different ways, and so on, and do it in minutes not years. And that can save them—and taxpayers—millions of dollars.

Some of these cutting-edge practices have been in use for a while; others are still being perfected and developed—many of which are just as good as or even better than traditional practices that involve animals.

Perhaps the most important lesson we've learned from thousands of years of animal testing: No living being should ever have to endure cruel experimentation. That's why scientists are developing new techniques that can safely and more accurately test chemicals and medications without endangering human life. Here are just a few:

IN VITRO TECHNIQUES

When you hear the term "in vitro," you might picture a couple conceiving their baby in a lab at a fertility clinic. Just as scientists can grow an embryo outside a woman's body by uniting egg and sperm in a petri dish, they can also culture human cells in a precisely controlled environment. (Culturing means providing nutrients and other conditions that nudge an individual cell to start dividing, replicating identical copies of itself over and over.) These cultured human cells can then be studied and manipulated for research purposes. Labs use existing "cell lines" with the same known genetic heritage or new cells extracted from sterilized tissues donated by volunteers or left over from surgeries or biopsies.

Besides cells derived from a specific organ or tissue, researchers use stem cells, which are capable of dividing indefinitely and developing into many different cell types in the body. Induced pluripotent stem cells (iPSCs) are adult stem cells with a superpower: They can be "reprogrammed" to revert to an embryonic state and then become whichever cell type is needed. Scientists can grow cell samples from human skin, hearts, lungs, stomachs, and so on to study disease processes and the effects of drugs and chemicals—all without causing pain or expending animal lives. Among other things, in vitro research has already led to major advances in understanding and treating cancer.

ORGANOIDS

Another sophisticated in vitro technique uses clusters of programmed stem cells to generate organelles (also called organoids). These are miniature versions of the human intestines, liver, breast, lung, and more, made by growing cells in a special gel under conditions similar to how they develop inside the human body. These tiny organs can even be built using a 3-D printer, as Wake Forest Institute for Regenerative Medicine did to create a beating heart in 2015. Organoids are structured and function like real organs, but on a much simpler level, and can last for months. They can be used to study diseases, drugs, and to test chemicals for safety. They also hold promise for medical research, in which a mini kidney crafted from a sick person's kidney cells can be compared with one made from a healthy person's kidney cells. Organoids may soon be used for personalized medicine, to test how an individual would respond to a certain treatment.

Three-dimensional tissues can even be made from human cells left over from surgeries or from cadavers. Companies such as the Mat-Tek Corporation (which is funded by the PETA International Science Consortium) and Epithelix Sàrl sell these tissues, which include dermal, ocular, respiratory, intestinal, oral, and vaginal models from healthy or deceased donors. These tissues can be used for basic research, product development, or to meet regulatory testing requirements of government agencies. For example, the skin and eye tissue models can be used internationally instead of regulatory tests that previously required the use of rabbits. These models have also been used to study drug delivery and metabolism, inflammation, and fibrosis among other applications.

ORGANS-ON-A-CHIP

Scientists have been engineering organ-on-a-chip models that more closely mimic those inside humans and allow us to study how we're likely to respond in a real-world environment. These flexible plastic chips, about the size of a matchbox, contain channels filled with a circulating, blood-like fluid and are lined with living cells that simulate the behavior of actual tissues and organ function. In this way, an organ-on-a-chip can mimic the chemical and physical reactions scientists would see in the human body in response to a germ, a nutrient, a drug, or a gene. Organs-on-a-chip even allow researchers to re-create disease states. There are organs-on-a-chip for the kidney, bone, eye, brain, and more.

HUMAN-ON-A-CHIP

The most ambitious tool yet is now under development. The Food and Drug Administration, the National Institutes of Health, and the Defense Advanced Research Projects agency are collaborating on the human-on-a-chip, more of a "living" machine than a cyborg. The idea is to integrate ten different, 3-D-printed organoids with digital hardware to create a linked system that would operate similarly to the human body, mimicking circulation, digestion, respiration, and so on. (So far other scientists have been able to link several mini organs at a time.) The human-on-a-chip could revolutionize the study of disease, toxicity testing, and other health research.

USING MACHINES AND BIG DATA MATH

Computer simulations. Just as today's sophisticated, multiplayer video games can re-create worlds online, computer simulations let scientists experiment on digital visualizations and other representations of human biology. Researchers can then ask "what if" questions and test them under different conditions without ever leaving the room. Computer simulations have been used to model the effects of drugs on cancer cells, study heart function, and analyze how diseases like hepatitis C act on the body.

Bioinformatics. Bioinformatics is a scientific field that integrates techniques from computer science, math, and engineering to gather or study biological data. Scientists can create big databases (or use existing ones) of huge numbers of records on chemicals, drugs, and patients and store them in centralized computers. Using powerful programs, they can retrieve and crunch information that helps them spot patterns to identify drug and chemical risks and side effects, responses to treatments, and so on.

USING (BUT NOT HARMING) HUMAN VOLUNTEERS

Noninvasive Medical Imagery. Devices typically found in doctors' offices, from ultrasound machines to MRIs to CAT, PET, and SPECT scanners, can safely and quickly "see" inside the bodies and functions of sick and healthy people and permanently record that information. Using sound waves, magnets, dyes, gamma rays, and other tools, scientists can study how our brains work, drug effects, and disease processes, among other things.

Full Clinical Studies. These are the gold standard for medical research, in which people with ordinary and serious illnesses, along with healthy "control" participants, volunteer for short- or long-term studies of drugs, treatments, or other types of experiments or surveys for the benefit of helping others, and possibly themselves. (Animals, on the other hand, never get a say.) Clearly, clinical studies are one of the most accurate ways to gather information on human health. The Yerkes National Primate Research Center, one of seven such labs funded by the NIH, still uses monkeys for research, including for Alzheimer's disease. Yet studies involving seniors with Alzheimer's allow scientists to observe, talk to, and assist actual human beings—a much more realistic approach.

Microdosing. Microdosing is basically the world's tiniest clinical study of drug effectiveness, usually involving only a handful of human volunteers. (It's actually considered a Phase Zero clinical study.) Here, people are given an extremely low dose of a drug—too small to affect their whole body or cause symptoms, but high enough that researchers can observe how their cells process it. This type of test helps rule out new drugs early on if they don't have the desired effects.

Epidemiology. The study of health and disease across human populations, epidemiology is big-picture research. It helps researchers understand patterns of risk from information collected on where, when, how, and in whom illnesses occur. Some epidemiological studies involve volunteers who answer surveys and are tracked over time; others involve parsing existing data.

One of the most famous examples of epidemiology took place during the summer of 1854 in the Soho district of London. The city was in the midst of a terrible outbreak of cholera, an infectious bacterial disease that had killed tens of thousands of residents since the early 1830s. The prevailing theory was that cholera was caused by inhaling a "miasma in the atmosphere," but an obstetrician named John Snow suspected the cause was more terrestrial: polluted drinking water. Snow noticed that the most recent outbreak was clustered around a single water pump. His theory was that the drinking water was contaminated with sewage, but the town officials did not believe him; a local minister attempted to disprove Snow's theory by claiming that divine intervention was to blame. But after tracking nearly every case of cholera in Soho back to the single water pump, Snow eventually discovered that a local woman had washed the diapers of her baby, who had contracted cholera, at a nearby cesspool, contaminating the water and triggering the outbreak.

This type of deductive reasoning also helped establish the link between smoking and lung cancer, and exposure to industrial chemicals and workers' illnesses. One of the longest such studies ever, the ongoing Framingham Heart Study, a project of the National Heart, Lung and Blood Institute and Boston University, began in 1948. It has revealed much of what we now know about the risks for heart disease, including high blood pressure, cholesterol, obesity, social factors, and more.

Autopsies and Postmortem Organ Studies. Medicine has learned much from dissecting human cadavers. Autopsies examine tissues and organs to identify underlying illnesses or cause of death. Many previously unknown ailments were discovered based on autopsy research, including Legionnaires' disease and the blood disease aplastic anemia. Autopsies of combat casualties from the Korean War helped medical researchers realize that atherosclerosis—the buildup of plaque in arteries, which leads to heart disease—begins very early in life, decades before the first signs of coronary distress (the result, we know now, of a diet rich in animal products).

While bodies used in autopsies are usually returned to the deceased's family, people who choose to donate their organs (and medical records) to science, such as to an organ bank, allow them to be studied far into the future. The Harvard Brain Tissue Resource Center in Massachusetts, for example, collects and distributes samples of human brain tissues that researchers use to study neurological diseases such as Parkinson's, epilepsy, Tourette's syndrome, and many others.

In recent years, a spate of suicides by former National Football League players led researchers to believe that repeated head trauma could damage the brain and cause severe mood swings, depression, and early-onset dementia. The disease, chronic traumatic encephalopathy (CTE), can only be diagnosed at autopsy. These findings have led to multimillion-dollar lawsuits against the NFL by former players claiming the league failed to disclose the risks of football, as well as improvements in helmet technology that have reduced instances of concussions.

Cosmetics and Product Testing Without Animals

For decades, the standard way to test whether a personal care product such as makeup or shampoo was an eye irritant was the dreaded Draize test. Caustic substances would be put into a restrained animal's eyes without anesthesia or even a painkiller, potentially causing afflictions from redness and swelling to hemorrhaging and blindness. Even now, some cosmetics or products used on human skin are tested for skin irritation and allergy on rabbits: lab techs shave a bare patch on animals' bodies and apply potentially harmful compounds onto the skin, leaving it there sometimes for weeks to see whether the chemicals eat through to organs, among other effects.

In the US, the Federal Food, Drug, and Cosmetic Act doesn't require animal testing for cosmetics. Many skin care brands have taken steps toward becoming cruelty-free, but at the time of this writing, some major brands, including Maybelline, Clinique, Avon, Estée Lauder, and others, still sell their makeup in China, which continues to conduct these tests in its own laboratories.

For a constantly updated list of approved animal-free testing methods for everything from personal lubricants to antitoxins, check out the PETA International Science Consortium website at http://www.piscltd.org.uk.

THE NEW WAYS

Now, thanks to in vitro techniques, cells from actual human skin—sterilized surgical waste donated by hospitals from patients who've had a tummy tuck, biopsy, circumcision, or other procedure—can be coaxed to grow in a lab dish to form dime-size, transparent disks to which myriad products from makeup to moisturizers to shampoos and more can be applied to test for their effects. In this way, companies can spot a bad reaction before the formulation is marketed and develop better ones.

These hairless, nerveless human skin substitutes are produced en masse and shipped to company and government labs under brand names including EpiDerm (made by MatTek) and SkinEthic (made by EpiSkin), becoming the industry go-tos. Product-sensitivity tests can also be run on cell-cultured tissues from many other parts of the human body, including the eye, lung, intestine, vagina, and mouth.

Other types of in vitro–based advances are being developed. Researchers at cosmetics giant L'Oréal have developed two new animal-free assessment methods to test product formulas for potential allergic reactions.

U-SENS uses cultured skin cells that carry specific "immunity marker" molecules, which signal our immune system that an invader is in our body. Their Human Corneal Epithelium Eye Irritation Test (HCE EIT) reproduces a 3-D model of the epithelial tissue from the human cornea (which mimics the behavior of the real thing) to test for eye irritation. These methods have been approved by the Organization for Economic Cooperation and Development, and are available for use across the world.

The Boston-based company Genoskin, meanwhile, has invented a way to keep donated human skin alive for several days using a patented method of "recycling" it using a special biological material in a testing well. It can be used to test the effects of cosmetics, pharmaceuticals, and other chemicals on human skin.

Toxicity Testing Without Animals

Understandably, the US government—including the USDA, FDA, EPA, National Toxicology Program, and Department of Transportation—requires known human poisons used around the home, such as weed killers, paint strippers, and industrial chemicals, to be studied so that "safe" and deadly exposure levels can be set to protect the public. As one example of a toxicity test, for years the LD50 (lethal dose 50 percent) test has been the standard, in which rats and mice are force-fed, injected, or sprayed with chemicals to find the amount that kills half of them outright. Some such tests kill thousands of animals each time they are conducted.

THE NEW WAYS

Scientists at Cedars-Sinai Hospital in Los Angeles have developed an in vitro technique using human pluripotent stem cells (which can be tweaked in the lab to become any type of cell in the body) to test the effects of man-made chemicals called endocrine disruptors. Endocrine disruptors mimic hormones and are known to cause disease. Endocrine disruptors BHT, PFOA, and TBT, synthetic chemicals found in common household items including cereal, cookware, and paint, have been linked with obesity, but previous tests on animals were inconclusive.

Researchers Dhruv Sareen and Uthra Rajamani took cells from the blood of human volunteers and used their stem cells to grow hormone-producing epithelial tissues (which line the gut) and hypothalamus tissues (from a brain region that controls appetite and metabolism). They then exposed the tissues to the chemicals. After examining the effects on tissue cells, the researchers found that the chemicals damage the hormones our digestive system uses to "talk" to our brain while we eat and let us know we are full. That helps explain why people with regular exposure to BHA, PFOA, and TBT tend to overeat and gain weight.

This one discovery, published in the journal *Nature Communications* in 2017, opens the door for safety-testing old and new endocrine disruptors and other chemicals relatively quickly in the lab. There are tens of thousands of these compounds on the market, but we know little about their health effects because until now there has been no safe way to test them.

ToxCast. The US Environmental Protection Agency uses bioinformatics and automated high-throughput screening—a technique often used in the pharmaceutical industry in which robots or computers test the properties of huge numbers of different chemical combinations—to gather information on the behavior and safety of known chemicals. By compiling this data into a database called ToxCast, the agency can predict whether a new chemical is likely to be toxic, based on its similarity to existing chemicals. ToxCast is designed to replace certain animal studies on endocrine disruptors and will someday be used to assess other types of chemicals as well.

Glow Lights. Research by EPA toxicologist Elizabeth Medlock Kakaley and her team, published in the journal *Environmental Science and Technology,* discovered a way to use bioluminescence and high-throughput screening to test for chemicals that may harm the human reproductive system and fetal development. They altered certain proteins in reproductive cells to emit light when exposed to chemicals that may be toxic to them. Most toxicology tests take at least a day to show results, but this "instant glow" technique provides answers in seconds. It can also be adapted to identify chemicals that may be toxic to other human body processes.

Liver-on-a-Chip. Emulate, a biotech company in Boston, produces a liver-on-a-chip designed to test drugs. The small, plastic rectangle is engineered to hold several types of human liver cells kept alive in a liquid similar to blood. In early 2017, the FDA became the first agency in the world to start using the liver-on-a-chip to test whether new food additives, dietary supplements, and cosmetics are toxic to people. They even examined how germs contracted through food affect the liver (which plays many roles in our body, especially in digestion and removing waste). The FDA scientists also plan to experiment with kidneys-, lungs-, and intestines-on-a-chip to test these substances. The hope is that companies will be allowed to use safety data obtained with the chips instead of animal tests when they apply for FDA approval of a new compound.

DRUG TESTING WITHOUT ANIMALS

By law, makers of most pharmaceutical drugs and vaccines (and some medical devices) must test them on animals. Considering that every new medicine must be tested against many different criteria in animal trials, and that scores or even hundreds of animals are used for each type of test, the amount of suffering and death endured by animals every day is staggering. For example, a test on whether a compound causes birth defects typically requires 900 rabbits and 1,300 rats. That's *before* the drugs are even tested on humans. When human tests fail, then it's back to the drawing board and the cycle repeats.

THE NEW WAYS

Clinical Trial in a Test Tube. The Modular IMmune In vitro Construct (MIMIC©) system by Sanofi Pasteur VaxDesign creates a dime-size faux human immune system out of donated human cells. It's being used to test flu and other vaccines for effectiveness, and its various modules can be used to test immune-system reactions to other drugs, chemicals, and even cosmetics.

Heart in a Jar. Novoheart, a Vancouver-based company, is growing miniature, beating hearts for drug testing. The company takes human blood cells engineered into pluripotent stem cells and then manipulates them into heart cells, forming a gelatin-like solution that can be molded into a "heart" that mimics cardiac functions. The MyHeart Platform is already making strides: A fall 2017 study by Novoheart researchers uncovered why some FDA-approved drugs that help regulate heartbeat actually caused fatal arrhythmias in some patients. The heart-in-a-jar could help companies predict which new drugs are (or aren't) safe early on, without harming animals.

Gut-on-a-Chip. The human gut-on-a-chip produced by the Netherlands-based company Mimetas is used extensively in experiments by Leiden University researchers. In one trial, drug researcher Sebastiaan J. Trietsch and his team exposed more than three hundred of the devices to aspirin over long periods and found that, just as with live people, the medicine has a potential side effect of causing serious gastrointestinal issues. That finding helps demonstrate that model organs respond like the real thing.

Medical Research Without Animals

In order to understand human health and disease and develop treatments, researchers literally make animals sick. Experiments infect with deadly and debilitating diseases all species of animals, from rodents to kittens and monkeys; they blind, deafen, or paralyze them; burn them, withhold food or water; induce seizures; or place them under conditions that cause mental illness.

When studies are completed, the animals are killed and thrown in the garbage with other so-called medical waste. If researchers tell regulators it's necessary, they even inflict pain and suffering without anesthesia or analgesia, and as countless investigations have documented, humane guidelines for animal treatment are ignored and not enforced, even at major, respected universities and research centers.

THE NEW WAYS

Drug Development. Cancer researcher Masamitsu Konno of Osaka University in Japan and his team have developed a mathematical formula to speedily evaluate chemotherapy drugs for effectiveness and evaluate new "targets" in the body to study for future cancer treatments. Using human gastrointestinal tumor stem cells and computer software, they converted big data about how genes behave into an easier-to-analyze equation to identify key genes related to cancer development and drug resistance. In a paper published in *Scientific Reports* in 2016, they reported that the method allowed them to discover a new drug target for human gastrointestinal cancers that had already been studied in mice. In the future, the math may replace the mouse.

Custom Tumors. Two biotech companies, Cellink in Sweden and CTI Biotech in France, have teamed up to create tumor organelles made with tumor cells from individual patients and then 3-D-print them using "living ink," a blend of sugar-containing gels and bacteria. The custom tumors are designed for use in cancer research, including studying how specific types of cancer progress and what types of drugs could best treat them. One goal is personalized medicine:

finding alternatives to chemotherapy and radiation with treatments tailored to one's own cells. No more injecting human cancer cells into animals!

Breast Cancer Risk–on-a-Chip. Scientists at Purdue University in Indiana have created a device to identify breast cancer risks. "We want to be able to understand how cancer starts so that we can prevent it,"[72] according to researcher Sophie Lelièvre. It's of course dangerous to expose people to potentially cancer-causing substances, but animal genes are too different from ours to be worth studying. The breast cancer risk–on-a-chip device creates a microenvironment filled with fluids and equipped with sensors on a small plastic rectangle. Researchers add human breast tissue, then introduce possible carcinogens to observe how the cells respond at the genetic level. Since there are many different types of breast cancer and risk is different for women of different ethnicities, the device can be adapted to study multiple cell types.

Education and Training Without Animals

About ten million live and killed frogs, cats, fetal pigs, turtles, and more are still dissected in high school and tortured in college classrooms— all so students can learn that animal's particular anatomy, no matter what their future career plans. PETA's investigations into major biological supply companies, which buy animals and their bodies, then sell them on to schools, have uncovered grotesquely cruel treatment of animals, including the drowning of rabbits and pigeons, and the injection of live crayfish with latex. Countless amphibians are captured in their wild homes, and both companion and feral cats are taken from shelters, barns, and the streets.

THE NEW WAYS

Computer software simulations (often animated, with explanatory voice-overs) are being heralded by biology teachers and students as an alternative to dissection. These digital solutions allow students to virtually dissect, in great detail and an unlimited number of times, an animal that exists only in pixels. They also remove the gross-out factor that can get in the way of learning, and exposure to preservatives used on animals' bodies.

Froguts Dissection Simulator by Froguts Inc. is a set of online software modules that let K–12 and college students dissect a frog, squid, sea star, cow eye, and fetal pig. Each unit is organized by body system and uses audio narration, text, and interactive visual simulations like virtual scalpels. Froguts will soon debut 3-D versions of its simulators, complete with augmented reality that can even be used on a mobile device. Digital Frog by Digital Frog International is similar, but the software package also includes mini movie demos of animal anatomy and physiology and even a unit on ecology. This helps students understand how animals actually *live* in their habitats (something they can't learn from dissecting corpses).

Medical Education & Military School Training

As noted earlier, American and Canadian medical schools no longer use animals to teach medical students. But other types of medical programs, such as those for EMTs, still train human health professionals using invasive and even deadly procedures on animals, including slicing the throats of or stabbing dogs, pigs, sheep, and goats.

Meanwhile, the US Department of Defense is still conducting trauma training exercises in which animals including pigs and goats are horribly injured and then killed in crude exercises loosely designed to teach military recruits how to treat wounded soldiers. They've been shot, stabbed, set on fire, and had their bones broken or amputated in the field. Aside from encouraging barbarity, these methods can endanger the soldiers involved. As Iraq War veteran and Indiana University School of Medicine surgeon Michael P. Murphy put it: "No animal model can duplicate the anatomy and physiology of injuries inflicted upon the human body in war."[73]

THE NEW WAYS

For years, doctors and emergency medical technicians practiced operating on live animals. These practices are, however, being phased out. In 2017, for instance, the US Coast Guard became the first military branch to stop using animals entirely in trauma training drills. A smart solution for both schools and barracks is TraumaMan, a surgical simulator made by Simulab Corporation that is widely used the world over for basic and advanced surgical training. Resembling a mannequin, TraumaMan is a portable, anatomically correct head and torso constructed of synthetic material (and *no* animal tissue!). It's outfitted with many different types of replaceable "tissues" and even "bleeds" faux blood. The system allows trainees to not only cut open a human-like body, but practice procedures such as chest tube, catheter, drain insertion, cricothyroidotomy (surgical airway opening), and venous cutdown (to prevent shock).

Given all these advances, there's no need to use animals in medical testing—which is why there is a growing movement across the US government and industry to integrate new approach methodologies, or NAMs, into standard practices. In 2017, the US Congress passed the Frank R. Lautenberg Chemical Safety for the 21st Century Act, requiring the Environmental Protection Agency, which regulates toxic chemicals and assesses their risks, to prioritize information gathered using the cutting-edge methods discussed above before demanding any animal tests. It also called for the EPA to create a strategic plan to promote and develop these alternatives by June 22, 2018. The law explicitly mentions the "quality and relevance" of nonanimal testing methods, which might help ease the backlog of evaluating the more than eighty thousand existing compounds whose safety has yet to be proven.

On January 30, 2018, the NIH's National Toxicology Program announced its own strategic plan to *replace animal use in toxicity testing* of drugs and chemicals with methods more relevant to humans. Developed by ICCVAM with input from the Physicians Committee for Responsible Medicine and PETA's International Science Consortium, a team of nineteen scientists, the *Strategic Roadmap for Establishing New Approaches to Evaluate the Safety of Chemicals and Medical Products in the United States* is intended to encourage the application of new technologies by helping connect developers of new study methods with those who can best use them across government and industry. The plan stipulates what government, scientists, industries, and others need to do to achieve these goals. As Warren Casey, PhD, director of the NTP's Interagency Center for the Evaluation of Alternative Toxicological Methods, put it, "If actionable progress in this area is going to happen, the agencies need to take the lead."

In 2018, the EPA took two important steps to help animals. First, the agency released a draft document outlining a process to identify alternative testing methods and encourage their use in the chemical industry and in regulatory decision-making. Then, the EPA announced it had begun accepting nonanimal methods for detecting skin sensitivity and allergenic potential of pesticides and other chemicals.

Meanwhile, in Europe and across dozens of countries, testing cosmetics on animals has been outlawed. Under the European Union's Registration, Evaluation, Authorisation and Restriction of Chemicals (REACH) program, animal testing of toxic chemicals is allowed only as a last resort, and those who perform the research must share the results with others so the tests need not be repeated. And in China, whose government has required animal testing on cosmetics made or sold domestically, regulators agreed last fall to accept data from a nonanimal test method to evaluate a product's safety. The government has also opened a nonanimal testing laboratory near Shanghai, where it will partner with the nonprofit Institute for In Vitro Sciences to increase the use of cutting-edge techniques.

What You Can Do

Progress is being made but much more can be done—but only if people speak up and take action. Become a part of this change. Those who harm animals for science and profit are learning that their practices create bad publicity and tarnish their brands. Keep up the pressure. Those who are doing the right thing need your support so others will follow in their footsteps.

SHOP RIGHT

Buy only cruelty-free personal care and household products.

There are more than three thousand big and small companies to choose from. A few go-to options include Nature's Gate, 365 (Whole Foods), The Body Shop, and Aubrey Organics. Not sure about your favorite brands? Give them a call, send an email, or check one of these searchable databases:

- PETA's Beauty Without Bunnies (http://features.peta.org/cruelty -free-company-search/) lets you search for companies that test on animals; cruelty-free companies by product type; companies working on regulatory change; cruelty-free products by country; and companion animal food manufacturers. There's also a helpful PETA app you can use: https://www.peta.org/action/bunny -free-app.
- Cruelty Free International has a globally recognized certification program for cosmetics, personal care products, and household products called Leaping Bunny. You can look for their logo at the store or search their database at: https://www.crueltyfreeinterna tional.org/LeapingBunny.

Boycott brands that do test on animals. Contact these companies and let them know you won't be buying their products until they stop. Not sure who's who? Check one of the lists above. Some of the more well-known companies to avoid until they change include Shiseido, Johnson & Johnson, and Estée Lauder. Write, call, or use social media to reach the CEO, corporate accountability officer, or brand managers. Be polite and make your request specific. Names and contact information can often be found on the company's website.

PUT YOUR MONEY WHERE YOUR VALUES ARE

Give only to health-related charities that don't support research using animals.

Many charities including the March of Dimes, American Cancer Society, and the National Multiple Sclerosis Society, use a portion of donations to fund cruel animal experiments, when others do not. Hard to believe? In just one example, researchers funded by the March of Dimes blinded kittens by sewing their eyes shut, injecting chemicals into their skulls for weeks to study brain development, before then killing them. In contrast, Easterseals, a nonprofit organization that provides services for people with disabilities or others in need, does not fund any animal experiments at all.

While medical research to end diseases is vital, there are more relevant and cost-effective approaches to studying them. Your contributions are best directed to groups that support cruelty-free studies and are making real progress.

Visit http://www.peta.org to find out which charities do and do not fund research on animals. Among the latter: Avon Foundation for Women, Children's Oncology Group, and the Spina Bifida Association of America. Is the organization you wish to help not on the list? Just ask about their policies. If they do bankroll animal experiments, tell them why they won't be receiving your check.

Do you donate to your alma mater? Contact your college or university's alumni association and tell them you won't contribute to fund-raising campaigns as long as animal experiments are being conducted on campus. College and university websites and alumni bulletins often boast about their research projects and major grants; life sciences and social sciences departments or centers will highlight them on their landing pages or professors' web pages. If you know or discover that animals are being used in these studies, let them know it's a source of shame, not pride.

University-based animal experiments are common. To date, here are just a few of the schools involved: Wayne State University (inducing heart failure in dogs); University of Utah (many types of experiments, often on animals bought from shelters, along with repeatedly violating animal welfare laws); and each of the Ivy League universities: Brown, Columbia, Cornell, Dartmouth, Harvard, Princeton, University of Pennsylvania, and Yale. All of them have received millions and even billions in government research funding despite multiple and repeat animal cruelty violations.

Donate to nonprofit organizations and think tanks working on alternatives to animal research:

- PETA International Science Consortium:
  https://www.piscltd.org.uk
- Physicians Committee for Responsible Medicine:
  http://www.pcrm.org/
- Wyss Institute for Biologically Inspired Engineering:
  https://wyss.harvard.edu/

SPREAD THE WORD

There are many different ways to educate people about the mistreatment of animals for research and testing and the alternatives that are better for us all. The simplest actions can be done from wherever you have an internet connection.

Share videos from laboratories on Instagram, Facebook, Twitter, and more to help educate people who otherwise might not be exposed to the realities of systemic animal cruelty. Be sure to describe what's shown fully and accurately: Include who, what, when, and where, and tell people what actions they can take to help stop it. Since most of these images are disturbing, include a warning that the footage may be difficult to watch, but is important to see.

Be bold! Gather some friends or set off alone and head for storefronts, public parks, or your college campus. Create or get prepared leaflets on cruelty-free issues and vivisection. Hand them out to passersby. Be prepared to answer people's questions and maintain a civil discussion. Suggest alternatives to products they may be using and other actions they can take (such as those in this book).

HOLD GOVERNMENTS ACCOUNTABLE

Lobby, write, or sign petitions directed at government decision-makers on laws and policies related to animal welfare.

Historically, major improvements have come when they have the power of law behind them. For all their flaws, policies like the European Union's REACH law, the US Animal Welfare Act, and Britain's Cruelty to Animals Act have made a difference, and our representatives won't know that we want better laws unless we tell them.

The Friends Committee on National Legislation offers a primer on how to lobby a US representative here: https://www.fcnl.org/up dates/how-to-meet-with-congress-19. In a nutshell: Know your "ask," choose your team, schedule an appointment, prepare your statements, communicate respectfully, and always follow up. The same principles apply when meeting with state and local leaders.

Cruelty-free personal care company The Body Shop is running a campaign to call on the United Nations to adopt an international convention to outlaw animal testing of cosmetics and their ingredients throughout the world. You can sign a petition specific to your country here: https://foreveragainstanimaltesting.com/page/9583/petition/1

Call, write, or sign petitions directed at the US National Institutes of Health, which funds government agency, university, and other research involving animals. Nearly half of NIH-funded research uses animals, paid for with billions of taxpayer dollars. Tell them politely that animal experimentation is unethical and that you don't want to underwrite animal experiments for any reason. Instead, ask them to redirect the funding into the use of epidemiological, clinical, in vitro, organ-on-chip, and computer-modeling studies.

Send all correspondence to:

Francis S. Collins, MD, PhD,
Director, National Institutes of Health,
Shannon Bldg., Rm. 126,
1 Center Dr., Bethesda, MD 20892

Or email him at francis.collins@nih.gov.

If you want to dig a little deeper, it's easy to find out which facilities are receiving NIH funding. Visit NIH's Research Portfolio Online Reporting Tools (RePORT) page at https://report.nih.gov/ and search using the forms provided. Among other things, it tracks awards by location, organization, and researcher.

COMPLAIN DIRECTLY

Write or call university and government centers and companies (such as pharmaceutical makers) and let them know you object to animal research and testing. Do not let them get away with form replies and platitudes. Keep writing back if you receive one until you get the response you want.

Urge scientists to invest in nonanimal methods, pointing out that they are falling behind the growing number of scientists who are adopting cutting-edge techniques that are cheaper, faster, and more accurate than using animals. The PETA website lists the latest campaigns addressing specific issues, and can help you find out if there's a lab that experiments on animals near you.

Registered animal research facilities must submit annual reports about their work. To discover the type of animal testing companies and institutions are performing, and to find USDA inspection reports on these facilities (which include any violations found and actions recommended), visit: https://www.aphis.usda.gov. Be aware that this may take years due to attempts that started in 2017 to make it difficult even to obtain the information required by law to be disclosed.

Become a whistle-blower by reporting animal cruelty you discover at a lab or research center. If you are working at or just visiting a scientific research facility, be on the lookout for animal test subjects. Stay alert to what you see, hear, and even smell—for any indication that animals are being neglected or abused, or that rules for their health and safety aren't being observed. If you see something, say something to a supervisor and report it to an anti-vivisection group. Try to document what you witness as much as possible using video, photos, or audio recordings.

If no action is taken, always notify an animal protection organization. You can contact PETA by emailing whistleblower@peta.org, calling 757-962-8383, or using this form: https://www.peta.org/issues /animals-used-for-experimentation/hero-animals-labs. You may also contact the US Department of Agriculture, which is in charge of making and enforcing regulations on animal welfare. Find the USDA's Animal and Plant Health Inspection Service regional office closest to you here: https://www.aphis.usda.gov, and follow up or nothing may be done.

Some of the most successful anti-vivisection campaigns and legal cases have been built through the courage of people who document and publicize cruelty in animal research. Shocking, real-world footage is devastating to view and cannot be ignored.

SET AN EXAMPLE

If you are a scientist, veterinarian, or human healthcare professional—or aspire to be one—don't design or participate in any live animal experiments or training sessions.

Explain your stance to your colleagues or professors and educate them on the suffering (and scientific weaknesses) involved in using animal models. Share information in this book and beyond about newer, nonanimal methods that aren't just more humane, but more effective. Use these techniques in your research and help develop new innovations! And don't be afraid to hold a strong ethical position.

Besides keeping abreast of the professional journals in your field, you can sign up for email updates on the latest discoveries through Physicians Committee for Responsible Medicine: http://www.pcrm .org/. If you're a student, exercise your right to opt out of dissections in science class and insist on a software simulation instead. If your school isn't in one of the thirty-eight states that provide that right, ask administrators to purchase virtual dissection software and to pursue alternatives to dissection.

BECOME AN ACTIVIST

Being an animal rights activist can be as simple as educating others, signing a letter, distributing materials, posting videos on social media, making a phone call, or sending an email to those in a position to effect change. Better yet, be on standby to take collective action when egregious animal experiments come to light or a new campaign begins. You can also join an activist list and be ready to peacefully protest when needed.

Clothing

Born in 1896 in Lancashire, England, Dorothy Gladys "Dodie" Smith grew up with her mother and other relatives after her father died when she was just two. These uncles, aunts, and grandparents were avid theater-lovers. They suggested Smith become an actress, a career that did not pan out, and then encouraged her to become a playwright, a career that did. By the 1940s, after meeting her husband, Alec Macbeth Beesley, in the furniture store where she worked to support herself while writing, she'd written several modestly successful plays.

When World War II began, Beesley was in danger of being imprisoned for being a conscientious objector, so the couple moved to the United States. There, the couple took in a handsome Dalmatian named Pongo, who eventually sired a litter of his own—one of whom, seemingly stillborn, was miraculously revived by Beesley. Over the following decades, Smith and Beesley integrated nine more Dalmatians into their family. In photos, the couple can be seen posing happily on a beach with a collection of beaming, spotted dogs. One day, a friend of Smith, admiring Pongo's beautiful spotted fur, suggested the dog would make a beautiful coat. Smith was horrified, and rather than letting the comment slide, she turned her friend's comment into the inspiration for a children's story that eventually taught generations of Americans about the horrors of the fur industry.

The Hundred and One Dalmatians, published in 1956, introduced the world to Cruella de Vil, a woman driven so mad by her love of fur coats that she abducts dozens of Dalmatian puppies so she can turn them all into exactly the kind of black-spotted fur coat that Smith's friend had envisioned for Pongo. With the release of Disney's animated movie version in 1961, the book's window into the fur industry was dramatized for an even wider audience.

But while it's easy to deride a cartoon character like Cruella de Vil, many people make daily fashion choices that inadvertently support cruelty to animals just as severe as, if not worse than, the cruelty that would have awaited Pongo and those Dalmatian puppies, had Cruella gotten her way.

Cruelty to animals in the name of fashion comes in many forms, many unsuspected. For example, while it is obvious that animals have to be killed to produce a fur coat, a leather handbag, or a pair of suede shoes, it's less obvious that materials such as wool, silk, or the down feathers that fill winter coats are taken from animals using stressful, torturous, and even lethal means.

Fortunately, today it is easy to dress yourself stylishly and/or practically in materials that aren't taken from animals. Plant-based fabrics like cotton and linen, which have been used for millennia, are being joined by innovative materials like rPET, Lyocell, and "skin-free skin." Top fashion designers such as Stella McCartney and Diane von Furstenberg are embracing choices that leave materials made from the suffering of animals off the runway. Thanks to advances in technology, and the growing popular awareness of the harm caused by wearing clothing literally stolen right off the animals' backs, people are dressing themselves fashionably, functionally, responsibly, and compassionately.

But it hasn't always been so easy.

We don't know exactly what the earliest clothing looked like but anthropologists generally agree we've been wearing animal hides, furs, and leathers for as long as the concept of clothes first occurred to humans. Early sewing needles made of bone have been found in caves in places like Slovenia, Siberia, and South Africa, suggesting that humans began working with hide and leather sometime between forty-seven and sixty thousand years ago.

It's likely, however, that the invention of clothing happened even farther back than that, before early humans left Africa between fifty and one hundred thousand years ago. As we pushed out of Africa and into the Mediterranean—and, eventually, into the colder climates of Europe, Scandinavia, Russia, China, Siberia, and, via the Bering Strait, into North America—early humans likely had no choice but to wear materials made from animals to survive in the harsh environments they encountered, as the population of our species spread across the planet.

Nonetheless, in some of the earliest human civilizations, especially those in warmer climes such as Egypt, Mexico, and India, people found innovative alternatives to wearing animals' skin. The cultivation of cotton, for example, developed independently in the ancient world in both America (in Mexico) and South Asia (in India). And in Egypt, the fertile waters of the Nile made the ancient Egyptians into masters of the cultivation of the flax plant, from which we get linen. In ancient India, some tribes specifically avoided using animal products of any kind, feeling a religious kinship with other living beings, and some chose instead to make clothing from the grassy wetland plant sedge.

Leather, hide, grasses, and flax were all important parts of humans' gradual expansion throughout the world. But for much of history, choosing the kind of clothing to wear was a decision based on survival, not fashion. The story of how, when, and why this changed is in many ways the story of fur: Not only did early humans want the warmth provided by furs to push into the coldest regions of the planet, over time the growth of the fur trade became so ravenous that it lured Europeans into exploring the vast, unknown continent of North America.

FUR

For centuries, especially in Europe, clothing was a necessity worn more for its practical qualities than to signify social class. From noblemen to lowly servants, the men and women of early Europe wore simple wool tunics and linen undergarments that varied only slightly, in length or cut, between class and sex. While expensive, fur was still obtainable by the poor, and was deemed essential to survive the chill of winter. A fur coat might cost a commoner a few weeks' worth of wages, so few families could afford more than one or two, whereas the rich might have a wardrobe full. But for much of European history, these coats were likely worn with the fur facing inward to maximize comfort and fur's natural insulating capabilities, rather than to convey wealth or status. And that's how it stayed for centuries: From the early Middle Ages until the mid-1300s, clothing styles in Europe barely changed.

How did we get from there to here, from fur worn as a necessity to the status obsession of Cruella de Vil? According to the fashion historian James Laver, a profound shift occurred in Europe in the early 1300s that forever changed how people thought about clothing. According to Laver, these years marked the beginning of *fashion*—and the world of clothing in Western civilization has never been the same.

What brought about this change? Most likely, the Black Death. The plague hit Europe in 1347, and within just a few years reduced Europe's population by 30 to 60 percent. Those lucky enough to survive found an unexpected silver lining: Fewer people meant more land, money, and food to go around. Individual wealth grew, and for the first time many commoners could put money toward a few luxuries. This in turn led to an explosion in varieties of dress.

This new economic surplus wasn't a blessing for animals. A sudden interest in fashion meant a surge in the ways people exploited animals. Demand for fur became so great that in 1363, the English Parliament passed the sumptuary law. A Statute Concerning Diet and Apparel, decreeing that certain nobles could wear exotic furs like ermine, lynx, sable, beaver, and the Baltic squirrel, while everyone else was restricted to local furs such as lamb, rabbit, cat, and fox. Laws like these were ostensibly passed to protect the poor from dangerously high expenses, but in reality these restrictions were likely devised to keep the classes separate.

As the French essayist Michel de Montaigne observed years later in 1580, laws like these often backfired:

> The way by which our laws attempt to regulate idle and vain expenses in meat and clothes, seems to be quite contrary to the end designed . . . For to enact that none but princes shall eat turbot, shall wear velvet or gold lace, and interdict these things to the people, what is it but to bring them into a greater esteem, and to set every one more agog to eat and wear them?

In other words, restricting commoners from wearing the finest furs only heightened the perceived value of these furs, spurring even more demand. By the late fourteenth century, the strain on Europe's beaver population was beginning to show. Within a century, beavers had all but disappeared from the Old World except in Scandinavia and Siberia, and by the twentieth century, the Eurasian Beaver, which for millennia had existed all the way from Europe to Asia in vast numbers, was reduced to a population of only 1,200.

With the discovery of the vast, pristine forests of North America teeming with beavers, the pelt trade was given a new head of steam. Over the course of three hundred years the beaver trade pushed explorers into the west, facilitated commercial contact with the Native American population, and otherwise transformed North America. The fur trade spread throughout the world. Over the centuries, animals from every continent—chinchillas, foxes, rabbits, and even dogs and cats—have been hunted, trapped, and, more recently, as with other forms of farming, raised specifically to be killed for their fur.

In the twenty-first century, China emerged as the world's largest exporter of fur. Mink, above all, became the fur of choice, and accounts for 85 percent of today's fur industry. In 2015, eighty-four million mink pelts were sold.

The fur industry continues to operate on a massive scale in China and North America, and cruelty to the animals farmed for their fur has never been worse. On one typical mink farm in Wisconsin, for example, an investigation into farming practices found that the animals lived in tiny, barren cages, their waste accumulating beneath them in piles a foot high. Workers pressure-washed these cages while the animals were still inside them, so their pelts remained as pristine as possible. Minks became so frightened they tried to chew their way out of their cages, bloodying their own faces.

In these animals' last moments, workers grabbed them by their sensitive tails and crammed them, screaming and struggling, into metal drums pumped full of carbon monoxide gas from a running engine. Called "kill boxes," these chambers ostensibly asphyxiate the minks—but, as the carbon is unfiltered and the engine gets hot, death is not swift or painless. When a mink is found to have survived, the unlucky animal is either slammed against the metal drum in an attempt to break his or her neck, stuck back into the kill box for another round, or simply left to die over the course of as much as twenty minutes.

Conditions are worse in China. There, investigators have seen foxes electrocuted, dogs bludgeoned to death, and rabbits and raccoon dogs skinned alive. Dogs and cats are routinely killed and skinned for their fur, only to be sold to unsuspecting Westerners who have no idea the fur they bought was made from animals just like those they keep and love in their homes.

LEATHER

China is also the world's leading exporter of leather—and its record in this industry is as appalling as its record on fur. In fact, many leather accessories sold in the Western world—including work and fashion gloves, belts, leather trim on jackets, even cat toys and other accessories—actually come from the hides of domestic dogs, although you will of course never find them labeled "dog leather." These dogs are treated in ways that might make Cruella de Vil wince: An investigation of a Chinese tannery revealed workers trying to corral dogs by grabbing their necks with metal pincers and then bashing their heads with wooden poles. This knocked some of the dogs out, but others remained awake, crying out in agony. Some of these dogs remained conscious even after their throats had been cut, and took their last breaths only moments before their skins were ripped off their bodies. This facility skinned and bludgeoned up to two hundred dogs a day, making thirty thousand pieces of dog leather to be sold all over the world in everyday products.

Tanning and drying the hides of animals and turning their skins into leather has occurred since the dawn of human existence. The first leather was likely harvested from the leftover hides of animals killed for meat. From primitive shoes, to clothing, to material for tepees and other forms of shelter, to drum skins, to parchment used for writing, to early boats and waterskins, leather played a crucial role in early human societies. The oldest known pair of leather shoes, found in a cave in Armenia, dates back 5,500 years and was made from a single piece of leather shaped to fit the wearer's size-seven feet. Even the shoelaces survive to this day.

Today, leather is produced and sold on such a massive scale that extreme cruelty to animals has become ubiquitous. In 2015, JBS, the largest producer of leather in the world with twenty-six factories on three continents, produced ten million hides from cows, calves, and cattle, supplying the most exclusive car manufacturers with their interior leather. However, an investigation of JBS's Brazilian cattle ranches by a Brazilian nongovernmental organization revealed cows and bulls branded with hot irons on their faces without pain relief, cows jabbed in their anuses with metal-tipped sticks and electric-shock prods, calves dragged away from their mothers, and animals trampling each other in tight chutes. Cows were so poorly cared for that bloody and gaping wounds and maggot infestations went untreated.

While many of these cows would be killed anyway for their meat, that's not the case for ostriches or alligators, who are raised and killed solely for their skin even if the meat is also eaten. A 2015 investigation of a South African ostrich slaughterhouse that provides skins to brands such as Hermès, Prada, and Louis Vuitton revealed feathers being ripped straight out of the skins of fully conscious birds, who were then spun upside down in a machine and electrically stunned before having their throats slit. These intelligent and curious birds, who can live to be as old as forty, rarely make it past their first birthday when raised for their skins.

Crocodiles and alligators, slaughtered for leather used in so-called exotic watchbands, bags, boots, wallets, and belts, are treated just as poorly. It takes two or three small crocodiles just to make a single handbag, which, absurdly, can retail for $50,000 or much more. These animals spend their lives crowded into dank concrete pens, awash in their own waste, awaiting a painful death. In Vietnam, Texas, and Africa, workers kill crocodiles by slitting open their upper back with a knife and ramming a steel rod down their spine; many remain conscious for up to an hour after their spinal cords have been crushed.

The unfortunate surprise to most people who aren't interested in a crocodile skin handbag is that they're supporting cruelty to animals even when they buy a seemingly innocent wool sweater.

WOOL

On a bright sunny day in September 2015, a hiker outside Canberra, Australia, spotted something unusual in the brush: "It was as if a cloud had fallen from the heavens, or a cotton ball had taken steroids,"[74] the *Washington Post* reported a few days later. Upon closer inspection, the hiker realized this cotton ball on steroids was actually a living thing, nonchalantly chewing, seemingly entombed inside a big ball of off-white puff. It was a sheep who, it later turned out, had somehow been separated from his flock a few years before. He was trapped inside his enormous wool coat, which had gone many years without a shearing.

The hiker immediately understood the danger: with the Australian summer fast approaching, this sheep could overheat and die if someone didn't take action. It was hard to believe the sheep was still alive at all; a coat of that density could easily have been a breeding ground for skin diseases. It was also a miracle he was still able to walk or eat, or hadn't become food for some marauding predator. If the sheep had fallen over, there was a good chance he would never have been able to stand up again.

Named Chris by the hiker who found him, the sheep was immediately taken in by Australia's Royal Society for the Prevention of Cruelty to Animals, who put out a call on Twitter for an expert shearer. It took forty-five minutes to remove eighty-nine pounds of wool from Chris who, lying among the remains of his former coat, looked as though he had just been birthed from a woolly cocoon. Under all that hair, Chris clocked in at only ninety-seven pounds—barely half what he'd weighed hours earlier. According to some reports, the wool removed from Chris would have been enough to make thirty men's suits, or eight times what an average annual shearing of a normal merino sheep would produce.

It surprises most people to learn that sheep weren't always so woolly, but have been deliberately bred to maximize wool production, often to their own detriment. Consider the endangered mouflon, a wild sheep found in Iraq, Iran, and Turkey believed to be a primary ancestor of domesticated sheep. Colored a rich brown, rather than a woolly white, with thick hair instead of the kinked and curled hair of sheep bred for wool, mouflons show us what the earliest sheep probably looked like ten thousand years ago. Those ancient sheep likely had thick, long hair in the summer, but would grow a downy undercoat every winter to keep warm. Over time, early humans selectively bred sheep with especially thick undercoats, producing ever fluffier descendants. In Australia, sheep farmers imported the merino from Spain, a breed ill-suited for the Australian climate, compounding their misery in the hot, dry summers by inbreeding those with the thickest coats of all.

Chris's record-setting unshorn coat might have been the largest ever, but he certainly wasn't the first sheep to avoid shearing. Before Chris there was Shrek, a merino who grew up on a sheep farm in New Zealand and gained some celebrity when a then world-record sixty pounds of wool were shorn off of him in 2005. Every year, sheep are rounded up to be shorn, but Shrek had cleverly hidden inside a nearby cave, unknown to his owner, for six straight years.

Why did Shrek and Chris go to such life-threatening extremes to avoid getting a haircut? Most shearers are paid by the number of sheep they shear. Being gentle means taking more time, and therefore earning less money, so shearing is normally a violent and horrifying ritual for sheep. With so many sheep—in 2013 alone, 3.7 million sheep were shorn in the US, and in New Zealand sheep outnumber humans six to one—cruelty is rampant. For example, one seven-person shearing crew on a ranch in Utah boasted to undercover investigators that they could "pump out, like, a thousand a day."[75] To shear that many sheep that quickly, each worker would have to spend fewer than three and a half minutes on any one individual sheep. In practice, this speed encourages fast and impatient work that can leave sheep with gaping, bloody wounds—even cutting off teats, parts of ears, and, in at least one case seen by investigators, ripping open a sheep's penis.

Sheep are starved of food and water before shearing to make them easier to control and so that they do not lose bladder control when they panic. And, being prey animals for whom being held fast means death, they do panic. When this happens, videos shot inside shearing sheds on every continent but Antarctica show that shearers stomp or stand on the heads and necks of sheep, kick them, and slam them against wooden floors. Investigators have seen workers punch and bludgeon sheep in the face with fists, with sharp metal clippers, and even with hammers. In one videotaped case, a shearer twisted a sheep's neck until she died, and even picked up a live sheep by the skin on her back and used her body to wipe her own urine off the floor.

Another cruel practice, mulesing, was invented in 1920 and continues today. To understand, you need to know that flies like to lay their eggs in a sheep's wool, usually in soiled places near the sheep's hindquarters, where maggots then burrow into the animals' skin. Called fly-strike, this condition can be fatal to sheep. The result is wool that is greenish, smelly, and itches so badly that sheep will often try to eat their own skin. To prevent this threat to their income, farmers often use a pair of garden clippers to cut a strip of skin from each side of a lamb's hindquarters, forming scar tissue when healed so that wool no longer grows there, thereby crudely reducing the risk of fly-strike. But this extremely painful process is usually done without pain relief, meaning that millions of lambs a year have their hindquarters painfully mutilated. Most lambs cannot walk for days afterward and their adrenaline levels are elevated due to extreme stress—even though more humane methods of preventing fly-strike exist. In 2018, the Australian wool producers declared that, despite earlier pledges to phase out mulesing, which were made in response to animal welfare groups' and retailers' complaints, they had no intention of doing so.

These kinds of abusive treatments are widespread: An undercover investigation first reported by NBC found that in nineteen shearing sheds in Victoria and New South Wales, Australia, seventy workers employed by nine shearing contractors were all guilty of abusing sheep. It wasn't any better in the United States, where investigators visited fourteen ranches across Wyoming, Colorado, and Nebraska, meticulously documenting abuse and neglect of sheep in each location. In the United Kingdom, the abuse documented in English and Scottish shearing sheds in 2018 proved identical, if not worse.

We set these beautiful animals up for a lifetime of pain. Either we mistreat them so their wool can be sold to clothing companies, or—like Chris and Shrek—they're in danger from their own unnaturally thick coats.

DOWN

Down—the layer of soft, insulating feathers found underneath the thicker layer of exterior feathers on most birds—is another thermal substance upon which humans have relied to keep themselves warm for thousands of years. Ducks and geese shed their down naturally every year during molting season, and these feathers were traditionally collected afterward. Eagle and crow down even constituted important parts of religious ceremonies conducted by the Plains Indians, the Hopi, the Zuni, and other Native American tribes. But today, winter jackets, pillows, and comforters hide a cruelty to birds as injurious as the torments sheep suffer for their wool.

Nowadays, with rare exceptions, workers don't wait until a duck or goose has molted; feathers are "live-plucked," or torn right out of a living bird's body while the terrified bird is held between the worker's knees. The plucking rips their flesh and creates bloody wounds. Sometimes injured birds are left to die. Those who survive are given stitches without analgesic if their wounds are severe, or they're left shivering in fear and pain. Once their feathers have grown back, the process is repeated. Farms might produce as many as fifteen tons of live-plucked down in a year, and since one goose produces just two ounces of down feathers, that comes out to 250,000 live-pluckings annually on a single farm.

While some retailers, such as Canada Goose, may claim that they're devoted to "ethically sourcing all animal materials" in the production of their down coats, they refuse to divulge any details. The reality is grim for birds even if, as the company claims, they are plucked after slaughter. At one farm from which Canada Goose sources birds, investigators witnessed birds being crushed to death, left overnight without water or food, carried upside down by a single leg, and sent to slaughter on a long journey in open-sided trucks in the bitter cold.

As tempting as it might be to purchase a down coat, sink into a down pillow, or take a nap under a down comforter, it is almost impossible to buy down that is truly ethically sourced, and alternatives abound.

SILK

Perhaps you find it easy to sympathize with the plight of animals like raccoons, cows, dogs, sheep, geese, and ducks. How do you feel about worms?

Silkworms have been cultivated for their lustrous silk for thousands of years. According to the Chinese philosopher Confucius, silk was first discovered in the twenty-seventh century BCE by a young empress named Lei Zu, when a silk cocoon fell out of a tree into her cup of tea. The process remained a closely guarded secret in China for the next three thousand years, so much so that Byzantine emperor Justinian sent two monks to China to smuggle silkworms back to Europe by hiding them inside bamboo canes.

Silk is a delicate fabric, and to cultivate it distributors must boil silkworms alive inside their own cocoons to kill the worms and spool the silk yarn. Since the silkworm is actually just the larval stage of a delicate and beautiful adult moth, this means that the vast majority of insects raised by the silk industry don't live past the pupal stage; they are either steamed or gassed alive inside their cocoons when they are still adolescents. Because it takes as many as three thousand silkworms to make just a single pound of silk, and fifty thousand silkworms to make a single Indian sari, the number of insects killed every year by the silk industry is truly staggering.

Silkworms might not be as easy to love as a cuddly sheep, but perhaps all living organisms deserve better treatment. Fortunately, whether it's worms or sheep, dogs or cows, it's easy nowadays to dress yourself without supporting cruelty to animals, and easy to look good doing it.

Clothing Without Animals

Daughter of Beatles singer Paul, fashion designer Stella McCartney, long a staunch animal rights activist, never uses leather, silk, or fur in her designs. So if you weren't in the know, it might have come as a shock when, in March 2015, elegant models strode out onto a catwalk in Paris during fashion week wearing sumptuous-looking fur coats and chic suede and leather trousers and jackets, all designed by McCartney. It was a star-studded show featuring celebrities who care about animals, yet no one objected.

What was going on?

McCartney took a leap forward by using innovative, animal-free materials that looked impossibly like fur and leather. These beautiful and elegant designs were indistinguishable from the genuine article: The fur in the "fur-free fur" coats was actually made from materials like polyester and acrylic, and McCartney's "skin-free skin" was a form of vegan leather, which is usually made from materials like polyurethane.

In the past McCartney had generally resisted using materials like these in her designs because she wanted to convince people it was possible to be stylish without even the appearance of fur or leather. "I've avoided it for many years but I wanted to show the customer and the fashion industry that you really don't need to use fur anymore," she said. "You can't tell the difference with it on the runway. Modern fake fur looks so much like real fur, that the moment it leaves the atelier no one can tell it's not the real thing. And I've struggled with that. But I've been speaking to younger women about it recently and they don't even want real fur. So I feel like maybe things have moved on, and it's time, and we can do fabrics which look like fur, if we take them somewhere else."[76]

Most other major fashion designers have also taken a stand against real fur. Michael Kors, Gucci, BCBG, Furla, Donna Karan, John Galliano, Tom Ford, and Givenchy have all issued antifur statements, promising to adopt cruelty-free faux fur materials. Ralph Lauren,

Giorgio Armani, Tommy Hilfiger, Calvin Klein, Net-a-Porter, Burberry, and Selfridges have rejected fur in their designs as well. And in March 2018, Donatella Versace—the Italian designer who has made animal skins an essential part of her work for decades—told *Vogue* magazine that she was done with fur: "Fur? I'm out of that," she said. "I don't want to kill animals to make fashion. It doesn't feel right."[77]

Ditto for many aspiring young designers. In 2016, Cathryn Wills, creative director of the Australian leather accessories brand Mimco, watched *Cowspiracy,* a documentary about the environmental impact of animal agriculture, and soon afterward quit her job. "The fact that I was heading up a large leather accessories business progressively became incongruous for me," she told *The Australian Financial Review* in 2018. "When I walked away in mid 2016 I needed to take some time out to think about what was next—but I knew that it had to be creative and it had to be non-leather."[78]

Her new company, Sans Beast, joins an exploding market full of stylish and affordable alternatives to leather, which is projected to become an $85 billion market by 2025. Offering chic totes in bold colors and fashionably chunky shapes, Willis is joining designers like Matt & Nat and LaBante who are pairing affordable style with humane ethics. Even luxury car companies such as BMW, Mercedes-Benz, Lexus, and Ferrari now offer vegan leather seating options. As Stella McCartney said after debuting her skin-free-skin collection, "I . . . genuinely pose a question to the industry about why anyone needs to use leather anymore."[79]

McCartney and Wills are just the latest in a long and illustrious line of smart people fascinated by alternatives to animal-based clothing. To find the very first, you have to go all the way back to the beginning of history.

A BRIEF HISTORY OF CRUELTY-FREE CLOTHING

The ancient Greek writer Herodotus is considered to be the first historian, hence the nickname "Father of History." His *Histories,* written in the fifth century BCE, was the first known attempt to organize events and human knowledge into a chronology, and is one of our most important works for understanding life in the ancient world. *Histories* contains the first recorded account of a society that prized animals so highly its citizens refused to hurt them for any purpose, including clothing. Residents of ancient India, Herodotus wrote, "refuse to put any live animal to death . . . Vegetables are their only food." Herodotus was describing the first known vegans. He also described a marsh-dwelling tribe who "wear a dress of sedge, which they cut in the river and bruise; afterwards they weave it into mats, and wear it as we wear a breast-plate."

Even more remarkable than this tribe that clothed itself in grass were the special trees that Herodotus tells us grew in India. Herodotus wrote: "And further, there are trees which grow wild there, the fruit whereof is a wool exceeding in beauty and goodness that of sheep. The natives make their clothes of this tree-wool." This was cotton—the fluffy white fiber that grows naturally in bolls around the seeds of the cotton plant, and which modern-day evidence indicates has been cultivated on the Indian subcontinent for eight thousand years. In a sign that a good idea is universal, the cultivation of cotton developed around the same time, completely independently, half a world away in ancient Mexico.

Cotton is still an excellent alternative to wool that not only avoids the cruelties associated with raising, keeping, and shearing sheep but is also entirely natural. Derived from the fibers of the cotton boll, this "tree-wool" is softer than wool, but its cellulose gives it a remarkable strength, durability, and ability to absorb moisture. In fact, it is stronger wet than dry. And while it might seem hard to beat wool if you need to layer up to keep warm, it isn't. Cotton canvas and cotton flannel are actually excellent alternatives. Not only is flannel thick and more insulated than many other fabrics, it's durable while remaining breathable.

The cultivation of plant-based fabrics goes back even farther than

Herodotus and his tree-wool. A cloth wrapped around the skeleton of an infant found in a Neolithic archaeological site in modern-day Turkey reveals that people were weaving linen and hemp together into fine fabrics, and likely trading those fabrics across the ancient world, nine thousand years ago.

The ancient Egyptians later elevated the production of plant-based textiles into an artform. Flax—made into linen through a process of threshing, retting, scutching, heckling, and weaving—grew easily and plentifully along banks of the Nile, making Egypt famous throughout the ancient world for the beauty of its linen. Ancient inscriptions and wall paintings, awash in images of women in sheer white linen dresses, celebrated the skill and dexterity of Egyptian linen production. Because of the care ancient Egyptians took with their dead, some samples of this linen survive today, preserved inside tombs that remained sealed for millennia. The Metropolitan Museum of Art has in its collection one such fragment: At two hundred by one hundred threads per square inch, it might be coarse by modern standards, but represents a remarkable achievement for the time.

Linen is still a superb alternative to animal-based materials. Like cotton, it becomes stronger the more it is used, but also softer, and remains cool and dry to the touch even in humid conditions. Linen is recyclable, is one of the strongest natural fabrics with twice the strength of cotton, and is comfortable both in summer and winter. From crisp summer suits to blankets and pajamas that make use of its natural insulating capabilities, linen is one of the most comfortable, stylish, and versatile fabrics out there. Anyone can walk like an Egyptian by choosing a pair of linen slacks.

Cotton and linen aren't the only great natural alternatives to wool. Today, comfortable and durable fabrics are produced from disparate sources like bamboo, hemp, wood, soybeans, and even seaweed. Bamboo fiber, for instance, is often compared to the texture of merino wool while being stronger, softer, more breathable, less smelly, and cheaper.

Spun either by itself or blended with cotton, hemp, or synthetics like polyester and spandex, clothing made from bamboo is comfortable, fashionable, and eco-friendly.

Hemp, too, can be easily grown without the need for either pesticides or chemical fertilizers, and has the advantage of being environmentally friendly: When its roots plunge into the ground, they extend down as far as three feet, anchoring the soil and protecting the ground from erosion. Hemp feels similar to linen, but is three times as strong as cotton and is even resistant to ultraviolet light and mold. Its fibers are naturally hollow, making it a cooling fiber in hot weather and a thermal fiber in cold weather.

Even more diverse in its ability to replace animal-based products is Lyocell. Made from wood fiber, Lyocell mimics moleskin, suede, leather, silk, or wool depending on how it's processed. Many prefer it for travel clothing due to its lightness, durability, and resilience to wrinkles. Another excellent option is modal. While not quite classified as a natural fiber due to the processing involved in its production, modal is nonetheless derived from the renewable fiber of beech trees. And modal is not only 50 percent more water-absorbent than cotton, it dyes easily, drapes well, and retains its shape even after frequent washing.

Clothing can even be made from soy, too: Manufacturers take the residue from tofu production and turn it into a fabric that has the comfort of cashmere, the draping qualities and durability of cotton, and the softness and lustrousness of silk. Clothing made from soy is biodegradable, and stronger than wool or cotton.

Soybeans aren't the oddest natural alternative to wool: SeaCell is a fabric that combines cellulose with crushed and ground seaweed. Retailers claim this material activates cell regeneration, limits inflammation, soothes itches, and even detoxifies the body. Wearing seaweed will put you in the company of the sedge-wearing tribe Herodotus described in ancient India. Some fashions are indeed timeless.

There are also excellent synthetic alternatives to wool. Acrylic, polar fleece, polyester, spandex, and nylon are all good options, especially in athletic situations when warmth is necessary. One such material is especially eco-friendly: recycled polyethylene terephthalate, or "rPET." rPET is a polyester material made out of recycled plastic. When you throw away a plastic bottle labeled with the recycle symbol No. 1, it might come back as a bottle, or it might come back as a stylish fleece. rPET fabrics are durable, affordable, breathable, comfortable, and have a 90 percent lower carbon footprint than nylon, a 75 percent lower carbon footprint than virgin polyester, and even a 50 percent lower carbon footprint than organic cotton.

What about down manufacturers who claim they "responsibly and ethically" obtain down? Surprise. It's a myth. If you're buying down of any kind, it's likely you're buying a product from a company that has an unethical live-pluck operation somewhere in its supply chain, or at the least, supports the factory farming and slaughter of geese. Most companies who make grand claims refuse transparency. The only way to know for sure you are not inadvertently supporting cruelty to animals is to avoid down entirely.

Luckily, synthetic alternatives to down are affordable and effective. For example, in 2013 The North Face introduced its Thermoball technology, which mimics down with small, round, lightweight clusters of a synthetic fiber called PrimaLoft. Thermoball displays the same insulating qualities as 600 fill goose down—and, better than down, it retains its thermal capabilities even when wet. Patagonia recently entered the synthetic down market with its PlumaFill insulation for jackets and sleeping bags, which the company boasts is the best warmth-to-weight ratio it has "ever achieved—down or synthetic." Marmot's Featherless insulation is also (as described by Marmot) "better than down." A growing number of sports apparel brands have decided to eliminate down altogether, including Big 5 Sporting Goods, Baum's Sporting Goods, and The Coleman Company, which is the world's leading outdoor gear manufacturer.

For those who would rather take an afternoon nap on a cozy

comforter than weather a blizzard in an insulated sleeping bag, in December 2017 an American company called Buffy unveiled their Buffy Comforter, which rejects live-plucked down for a combination of eucalyptus and mineral-infused microfiber technology. The company claims that for every comforter it produces with this technology, twelve geese are protected from being live-plucked.

What You Can Do

The innovations in alternatives to animal-derived clothing are constantly expanding, making it easy to completely eliminate animal skins, fleece, and feathers from your wardrobe.

DRESS CRUELTY-FREE

Don't wear fur, coats with fur trim, or hats with fur pom-poms or tassels. Consider faux fur alternatives, which are usually more affordable than the genuine article.

Don't wear leather and don't use leather accessories and furniture, like briefcases, suitcases, couches, or chairs. Choose one of the myriad faux leather alternatives. Fibers from coconut water, pineapple, soy, fruit waste, apples, paper, wood, cork, mushrooms, and even substances derived from kombucha tea and grape leaves are all being used to make vegan leather. The pioneer vegan shoe company is Vegetarian Shoes, started in Brighton, England, and is patronized by Sir Paul McCartney among others. It ships shoes worldwide, so visit https:// www.vegetarian-shoes.co.uk. But vegan shoe companies are springing up everywhere, including New York and Los Angeles, where MooShoes has outlets (and sells online: https://mooshoes.myshopify .com). Even Yves Saint Laurent and Steve Madden offer vegan men's shoe selections.

Avoid silk. Plenty of more affordable, more durable, and super-comfortable and luxurious-feeling options exist. Consider Lyocell or modal. Don't trust silk suppliers selling ahimsa silk, also known as "peace silk." Ahimsa silk is supposedly produced by a method that allows moths to go through their natural life cycles and emerge from their cocoons as fully fledged moths before the cocoons are collected and turned into silk. The reality is that there is no authority to adjudicate these standards, and traditional silk harvested using cruel practices is sometimes sold as "peace silk."

Shun wool. There are wonderful, stylish alternatives to wearing wool, and thanks to advances in technology, many of the uses for which wool was long prized (for example, keeping warm in wet, cold weather or while exercising heavily and perspiring) can now be better accomplished through synthetic fabrics like polar fleece. Even companies that claim to farm wool responsibly, such as Patagonia, have been revealed to use suppliers guilty of horrendous cruelty to sheep.

Don't buy down-filled Canada Goose coats, or any other down coats or comforters. Don't trust labels claiming that a coat's down has been sourced responsibly, as there is no definition of "responsible" and usually no transparency in the supply chain. Restoration Hardware, Williams Sonoma, Pottery Barn, and West Elm all offer a synthetic option for nearly every down item they sell. In fact, Williams Sonoma recently committed to increasing their offerings with synthetic fill by 1,230 percent. Crate and Barrel and CB2 both offer synthetic down inserts for their decorative pillows—and the sleepwear-focused Land of Nod offers a synthetic insert called Natural Harmony. Some UK retailers have banned down entirely, including: Adolfo Domínguez, ASOS private label, Boohoo (the parent company of Nasty Gal), Dr. Martens, Fat Face, Hobbs, Jigsaw, Monsoon Accessorize

Ltd., Nigel Hall Menswear, Reiss, Topshop, Primark, Warehouse, Whistles, and White Stuff.

TRAVEL CRUELTY-FREE

If you're heading into the backcountry, select brands like Marmot and The North Face, both of which offer thermal insulating alternatives to down that will keep you warm and safe wherever your adventures take you. There are dozens of alternatives to wool and down that every active person should be aware of: Using technologies like Polartec, Thermogreen, Omni-Heat, PrimaLoft, rPET, Gore-Tex, ThermoBall, Plumtech, modal, Thermafill, and ThermaCheck, adventure brands everywhere are bringing cruelty-free products to the harshest conditions Mother Nature can throw at you.

If you prefer driving over walking, make good decisions when shopping for a new car. Tell the salesperson that you don't want to look at any models with leather interior trim. Not only can this knock a few thousand dollars off the asking price, three to eight animals are killed to produce the typical leather interior. Choosing a vegan interior helps send a message to the world's leather producers that the cruelty they cause animals is now unacceptable.

TURN HEADS

Want to go one step further? Wear clothes that proclaim your anti-cruelty stance loudly and proudly through eye-catching slogans sure to get you—and your values—noticed. Brands like Vegan Police, Veganized World, In The Soulshine, Wholesome Culture, Alba Paris Art, Viva la Riva, Barefoot Bones, Vegetaryn, Wear Bare Bones, Crazies and Weirdos, The Tree Kisser, and RAW Apparel all make T-shirts and accessories emblazoned with slogans like: "Meat Sucks," or "Talk Vegan to Me." Many of these brands also sell cruelty-free versions of accessories like wallets, belts, bags, and other items that are typically made from leather. The Herbivore Clothing Company in Portland, Oregon, for instance, not only offers stylish T-shirts with phrases like "Eat Like You Give a Damn," they also offer a range of vegan leather belts, wallets, and handbags. The outerwear company Save The Duck makes cozy coats with a happy duck emblem on the sleeve.

Alternatively, don't wear clothes at all. Join Gillian Anderson, Tommy Lee, Khloe Kardashian, Eva Mendes, and Pink by taking a stand and saying you'd rather go naked than wear clothes taken from an animal.

MAKE YOUR CONSUMER DOLLARS COUNT

Don't keep your activism in the closet. Write a letter or tweet to brands that continue to exploit animals. Tell them why you've stopped buying their products. Be polite, but be specific and firm. Writing to a big brand might feel insignificant, but never doubt the power of your voice. If a CEO realizes that many consumers are actively choosing other brands because of the company's stance on animal welfare, that brand is that much more likely to change its business practices, identify a new supplier, or discontinue a line of products altogether.

Phoning or sending a letter to your local legislators can have an impact. So can getting involved in local politics by attending local committee meetings, rallies, and other community events. You will find more people in your community who share your values than you realize.

For instance, in spring 2018, San Francisco voted to ban the sale of fur outright, becoming the first major American city to do so (Los Angeles quickly followed). This victory came on the heels of weeks of appeals by animal rights activists to the San Francisco Board of Supervisors. These citizens debated local fur retailers in committee meetings, rallied at City Hall, and kept the pressure on their legislators so much that the Board of Supervisors voted to approve the ban on fur sales unanimously. And actress Alicia Silverstone wrote a letter to the board explaining that the ban would make her "even more proud to call San Francisco home." However, you don't have to be famous for your letters to make a difference. Legislators estimate that for every letter they receive on an issue, there are a thousand more constituents who care just as deeply. Make writing letters to your state and federal representatives a regular part of your routine and ask others to join you. The San Francisco fur ban and other landmark achievements would never have occurred without compassionate citizens choosing to make their voices heard.

CHANGE THE GAME

Do you care deeply about animals and have a knack for fashion? You could be part of a growing wave of designers who are committed to bringing cruelty-free materials into the rarefied world of high fashion. Manhattan's Fashion Institute of Technology (FIT) graduates thousands of students every year who go on to become some of the biggest names in the business. In recent years, FIT has added an annual Sustainability Awareness Week to its curriculum. One panel, "How to Make It in (Vegan) Fashion" includes a specially curated panel of top vegan designers. The message is clear: Vegan fabrics are the industry's future, and so is vegan design. If you want to design clothes that do not cause animals to be harmed and killed, now is the time to consider a career in fashion design.

JUST MAKE A START

What if you've only recently started taking steps to make your wardrobe cruelty-free? What should you do with the wool sweaters, leather jackets and accessories, or old fur coats you used to wear? Now that you've made the decision to dress yourself compassionately, it might feel strange—or even downright wrong—to keep your old animal-derived clothing around. It might seem expensive to replace your clothing unless you are a trendy or practical thrift shopper.

Don't worry: if you don't want to do it all in one go, consider replacing old items with cruelty-free alternatives as they age or when you decide you no longer have a use for them. Consider donating anything made from an animal to charity. Goodwill, Salvation Army, and homeless shelters could all make good use of your old clothing for people who cannot afford to choose. Any fur items may be welcome at a local wildlife center where they might help keep an orphaned baby animal warm and safe until she is healthy enough to walk or fly on her own. Animal protection groups will give you a tax deduction for your furs, too, and use them in educational displays or send them to refugee centers overseas.

For more ideas on how to recycle your old clothing, check out www.veganrabbit.com.

IT'S NEVER TOO LATE

Maybe you're someone who eats vegan, donates to the right organizations, has never considered wearing a fur coat, and proudly owns a collection of T-shirts with spunky and clever pro-vegan phrases—but your closet is home to a row of shiny leather shoes or wool suits.

You're not alone. Be proud of the changes you have made up to this point. More important, it's never too late to make yet another change.

In the 1990s, actress and animal rights advocate Pamela Anderson started wearing sheepskin Uggs with her now iconic red swimsuit to keep warm on the set of *Baywatch*, catapulting the Australian-inspired American boot brand into prominence and an association with sexy, comfortable luxury. It wasn't until years later, in 2007, that Anderson realized that Uggs were made from real sheepskin: "I feel so guilty for that craze being started around *Baywatch* days—I used to wear them with my red swimsuit to keep warm—never realizing that they were SKIN!"[80] she wrote in an online diary. Now Anderson has her own line of vegan clothing, selling eco-fur products and lingerie, and has traded her Uggs for Stella McCartney's shoes, and vegan boots from Juicy Couture. Anderson unintentionally inspired a craze that caused boots made from sheepskin to become massively popular. But that didn't stop her from swapping those boots for humane ones, nor from speaking up honestly about her regrets.

Not sure where to begin? PETA's Cruelty-Free Shopping Guide includes a monthly e-newsletter, pocket guides for cruelty-free living, coupons and special offers from cruelty-free companies, and more information on supporting cruelty-free companies and charities. Learn more at: https://www.peta.org/living/personal-care-fashion/order-cruelty-free-shopping-guide/.

Entertainment

Starring Rene Russo and Alan Cumming, the 1997 movie *Buddy* told the real-life story of an eccentric woman (Russo) who brings home a young gorilla named Buddy to live with her family, which consisted of roguish chimpanzees, a kitten, a horse, geese, a raccoon, and a cheeky parrot among other motley creatures. After a promising start, life for Buddy doesn't go well in the woman's home, and eventually she is forced to bring him to a sanctuary where he lives happily ever after.

But life didn't go as well for a real-life chimpanzee named Tonka who starred alongside Russo and Cumming. Two decades after the film was released, Cumming wrote a letter to the president of the Missouri Primate Foundation:

> I worked closely with [Tonka] on the 1997 film *Buddy*. My character had many scenes with him, and we developed a very close camaraderie during the months when we filmed. By the end of the shoot, his trainers let him groom me. It was a special friendship—one I'll always treasure. I hoped to see Tonka the following year at the film's premiere but was told that he was no longer manageable and had been "retired to Palm Springs." Over the past 20 years, I imagined him living out his post-Hollywood years on a sprawling sanctuary.[81]

Cumming had discovered, however, that while he had been promised Buddy would end up at a sanctuary in Palm Springs, the animal had actually been imprisoned in a small cage at a facility in Festus, Missouri—one that has been repeatedly cited by the US government for violations of federal animal welfare regulations.

While it's true that animals can be thoroughly entertaining, as millions of YouTube videos have proven, they are often abused in the process. Cumming is doing what he can to help his costar—but a great deal more happens to many other animals who are used for human enjoyment.

Humans have been using animals for their own entertainment purposes for as long as we have historical records of such things—and perhaps even before that. Archaeological digs in Macedonia reveal that at least as far back as 2000 BCE, lions and other wild animals were kept in cages to entertain their captors. Other ancient civilizations—Egyptian, Chinese, Babylonian, Assyrian—also trapped and caged wild animals, including elephants, giraffes, and bears. Domesticated animals were used, too: For example, the ancient Romans created elaborate chariot races that often ended in death, sometimes for the humans, more frequently for the horses. Ancient circuses in which animals were tortured and often barbarically killed were enormously popular. Often spectacles involved nothing but killing: In 13 BCE, an ancient Roman circus massacred at least six hundred "exotic" animals brought there from Africa.

Some people noticed this heartlessness, like the Roman scientist and historian Pliny, who wrote about how intelligent the animals were. In his *Natural History,* he says: "It is known that one elephant which was rather slow-witted in understanding instructions given to it and had been punished with repeated beatings, was found at night practicing the same."

In many cases these ancient entertainments involved humans using animals for racing, or for dueling one-on-one, but animals were also captured and set up to fight each other, as in dogfighting, which was popular in ancient Rome; cockfighting, which is at least six thousand years old; bearbaiting, a popular European sport; and bullfighting, which may date even farther back in history and still exists today.

With the collapse of the Roman Empire, animal entertainment became scarce, as did all forms of mass entertainment. However, within a few centuries, new kingdoms and empires began to rise, and so rose the return of animals used for amusement. By the end of the eighth century, the Holy Roman emperor Charlemagne possessed three menageries, housing the first elephants held captive in Europe since Roman times, as well as other exotic animals captured from the wild or presented as gifts by the leaders of other countries. (The practice of government leaders gifting wild animals continues into the twenty-first century. For instance, former Zimbabwe president Robert Mugabe sent many giraffes, zebras, and baby elephants, some of whom died in transport, to both North Korea and China. Russian president Vladimir Putin collects numerous wild animals, including Persian leopards and pure-bred Arabian horses, from world leaders.)

In the late eleventh century, William the Conqueror established his own menagerie, including lynxes, camels, and, apparently, one porcupine. Two English kings later, Henry I created Britain's royal menagerie in the town of Woodstock. Later, this collection, enhanced by King John, was moved to the Tower of London, where it remained for several hundred years, and featured many exotic animals captured from their wild environs or presented as gifts by other countries' rulers. At various times these animals included African elephants, leopards, lions, camels, and even a polar bear, no doubt lonely and a long way away from home.

The English royal menagerie eventually became the longest continuously running animal exhibit in the world, but it was rivaled by royal collections throughout Europe. For instance, by the 1660s, Louis XIV's palace of Versailles housed one of the most exotic animal collections in the world. Menageries also turned into traveling shows—by the early 1700s, animal collections featuring spectacularly large or fierce animals such as elephants and tigers were hauled from city to city across Europe and America.

While royals and aristocrats could afford to maintain exotic animals, and eventually opened these collections up for public view—the price of admission in England was three half-pence or a live cat or dog to be fed to the lions—zoos and circuses became the most common place where the public could see such animals. Archaeologists have found remnants of circus detritus hailing back to and beyond 1200 BCE, but later style animal circuses didn't begin until the mid-eighteenth century when English trick rider Philip Astley learned how to balance himself on a horse while standing. With the hiring of a clown and a ring for the horse to travel within (the "one-ring circus"), the circus became a staple of family entertainment.

Unusual acts became popular in these shows of the 1800s. The American Isaac Van Amburgh allegedly was the first person to entertain a crowd by placing his head inside a lion's mouth—or, at least the first one who lived afterward. His act also included a lion and lamb lying peacefully side by side. The most famous of these circus entrepreneurs was American P. T. Barnum who, in 1841, opened his first so-called museum that contained not just strange beasts, but humans—including a four-legged woman, a lion-faced man, and Siamese twins. Circus audiences preferred the wild animals over the freakish humans. The latter became less prominent as animal-based circuses grew in popularity throughout the twentieth century. Today, however, the largest circus in America, Ringling Bros. and Barnum & Bailey Circus, has folded its tents after receiving the largest fine in circus history for animal care violations stemming from animal deaths caused by negligence. Fewer than thirty traveling shows with animals remain in North America. This is partly due to the high costs of circus maintenance, partly due to the emergence of other forms of entertainment (including circuses such as Circus Vargas, which features only human acrobats and aerialists), and partly due to the work of animal protectionists revealing to the public how poorly these animals are treated.

As a result of all these various transgressions, as of 2018, nineteen countries, including Sweden, Austria, Costa Rica, India, Finland, and Singapore, have restricted the use of wild animals in circuses. The Welsh and Scottish parliaments recently banned certain wild animals in traveling shows. In America, laws to ban the bullhook used on elephants, as well as laws to ban traveling wild animal shows, are now gaining momentum.

ROADSIDE ZOOS, AQUARIUMS, AND MARINE AMUSEMENT PARKS

Most people who go to zoos assume that, unlike animals in circuses, these animals are well treated. That is not always the case, particularly with the almost universally horrific roadside zoo. Even under the best of circumstances, captivity cannot replicate wild animals' habitats, something even large zoos are admitting as they are increasingly making the ethical decision to phase out elephant exhibits.

Animals kept in captivity cannot run freely, forage, choose a partner of their own liking, or, often, raise their own young, who are seen as assets to sell or swap. Cute young animals draw crowds, but "surplus" offspring and those who are not needed for breeding are sold, sometimes to circuses, research labs, or other outlets. Zoos have even sold animals to game farms to be confined within a fenced area and shot as a trophy kill, for a fee. In some of the bear park attractions, bears have been killed for meat. Animals can and do die from the treatment they receive from the viewing public, as when people throw objects into their enclosures, causing the animals to ingest toxic substances. Sometimes the animals are killed trying to escape, as a gorilla did in a Dallas zoo in 2004. And, contrary to conventional wisdom that captive animals live longer than their free-roaming counterparts, a survey of 4,500 elephants both in the wild and in captivity found that the median life span for a captive African elephant was not even seventeen years; African elephants on a nature preserve died of natural causes at a median age of fifty-six.

Finally, sometimes zoos simply cull—a euphemism for kill—animals when they run out of room. In 2017, for instance, a Swedish zoo admitted that it had euthanized nine healthy lion cubs over several years simply because there was no place to put them.

Just as important, the hidden message of zoos is that it's acceptable to force animals into captivity, far from their natural homes and normal lives. Not so. Virginia McKenna, who starred in the classic movie *Born Free* and received an Order of the British Empire in 2004 for her work on behalf of captive animals, says that her participation in *Born Free* made her realize that "Wild animals belonged in the wild, not imprisoned in zoos. . . . Freedom is a precious concept, and wild animals suffer physically and mentally from the lack of freedom captivity imposes."[82]

Aquariums and marine amusement parks impose similar constraints. They also date back to ancient times: The Romans often created tanks with a glass wall allowing people to view unusual water creatures. But the aquarium as we now know it didn't take hold until the mid-nineteenth century. The term was coined by Englishman Philip Henry Gosse, who in 1853 created the first aquarium at the London Zoo, known simply as the "fish house." Today, American marine amusement parks like SeaWorld, subject of the damning documentary *Blackfish*, are part of a billion-dollar industry. Ric O'Barry, who was a dolphin trainer for the popular 1960s *Flipper* television series but has since become an ardent activist for dolphin freedom, has said that no one would support such places if they knew what happened behind the scenes. For example, dolphins are forced to learn tricks through merciless training methods such as food deprivation and isolation; family pods are broken up; and the tiny tanks in which the animals are kept are cleaned with chemicals that can have dangerous side effects on the animals. Some trainers have reported dolphins repeatedly banging their heads against the side of their pool cells or simply not emerging for air—which marine biologist Jacques Cousteau believed to be an attempt to commit suicide.

Richard Donner, coproducer of the film *Free Willy*, has said, "Removal of these majestic mammals from the wild for commercial purposes is obscene. . . . These horrendous captures absolutely must become a thing of the past."[83] It isn't only dolphins who are endangered—all animals, from octopuses to sharks, all snatched from their natural environment and reduced to living amusements for passing humans, deserve better.

OTHER ANIMAL ENTERTAINMENTS

Animal displays are passive entertainments for attendees, who simply watch. Many more entertainments involve animals in which humans are active participants—for instance, rodeos, in which electric prods, spurs, and "bucking straps" are used to irritate and enrage animals. The wild bucking that audiences see does not happen because the animals are having fun; a tightly cinched rope around the abdomen causes them to work vigorously to rid themselves of the torment and a "hot shot" jabbed into their flank is often what sends them flying out of the gate and into the arenas. The animals commonly suffer from bruises, torn ligaments, broken bones, and ruptured discs, and when they are too injured to be suitable for rodeo use, they are sold for slaughter.

Another active form of animal entertainment, dog racing, might seem less harmful. It's not. Alaska's Iditarod course is the equivalent of racing your dog from Orlando to New York, depriving him or her of sleep to complete the course as quickly as possible while hauling roughly four hundred pounds. About 1,500 dogs start the Iditarod, but more than one-third become sick, injured, or exhausted from being forced to run for hours over mountain ranges, over frozen rivers, and through desolate tundra in biting winds, blinding snowstorms, and extreme temperature fluctuations. Some of them die on the trail; many are kicked, beaten, and killed for not being strong or fast enough. *Orlando Sentinel* columnist George Diaz has written that the Iditarod "is nothing more than a barbaric ritual that gives Alaskan cowboys a license to kill."[84]

Then there is bullfighting, one of the most famous of the human–animal active entertainments. Every year thousands of bulls die in these fights, which still continue in Spain today, despite a recent Ipsos MORI survey that showed fewer than 30 percent of Spaniards support such bloody spectacles. Already, more than one hundred towns in Spain have banned bullfighting. Nevertheless, there are still more than 1,200 government-funded bull races and dozens of state-sponsored bullfighting schools in Spain. France, Mexico, and Portugal also still hold bullfights—some bloodless, some not.

Also still popular for the last six thousand years: dogfighting. Here humans breed so-called fighting dogs, pit two of them against each other, and then watch them tear each other apart, all the while betting on who will emerge the victor. Losing dogs are frequently found abandoned, bloody, and dying in alleyways or along highways. Dogfighting is illegal in the United States, as in most countries, and participating in dogfighting is considered a felony offense in every state. So is cockfighting, in which two or more roosters are placed in a ring and forced to fight to the death, usually with razor spurs attached to their feet. Yet, like dogfighting, it goes on.

Among the deadliest spectacles is one of the least known and perhaps most innocuous-seeming: pigeon racing. Races vary, but they usually involve releasing "homing" pigeons who race back to their loft from sometimes hundreds of miles away. Taken from their life mates and their offspring, whom these devoted parents know they must feed with the milk both males and females make in their crops, they race their hearts out to get home. They succumb not only to predators, power lines, hunters, and exhaustion, but in many races more than 80 percent of the birds get lost or, in races that require them to cross from one land mass to another, fall into the sea and drown. Races that are particularly fatal—where only a minuscule percentage of birds makes it home—are referred to as "smash races": In one such race in Queens, New York, only 4 out of 213 birds returned home. The final blow is when a bird arrives back to the loft last or late, or is found collapsed, identified by the band on his or her foot, and turned in by a well-meaning person. As one racer told an investigator, "The first thing you have to learn in pigeon racing is how to kill the losers,"[85] which means wringing their necks.

Horse racing is a multibillion-dollar business throughout the world involving the maltreatment of horses from birth to death. Horses are raced so young that their bones have not even matured and right from the start they are drugged—often legally—to keep them running when their bodies should be allowed to rest and recuperate from injury and strain. This leads to broken bones and death. At least three horses die on the track every day in North America, and hundreds of racehorses are injured and killed every year in training. Those who survive are often too injured to race past the age of five. The end of the line for these horses is usually the "kill auction," from which they are sent on a grueling multiday journey to Mexican or Canadian slaughterhouses to become horse meat. Live horses are also shipped to Japan and South Korea, sometimes to be bred first, perhaps to be raced, but often to end up as ground meat. Before PETA persuaded the racing industry to implement a decent retirement program in 2012, as many as ten thousand thoroughbreds were trucked out of the US for slaughter.

FILM AND TELEVISION

"Hi-ho, Silver!" "Lassie, come home." "That'll do, pig." "A horse is a horse, of course, of course." "Yo, Rinny!"

What would film and television be without animals?

In the old days, the answer was: a lot less entertaining and a lot less successful. Filming animals came along as soon as film began—in fact, the first motion-picture films on record date back to 1878, when English photographer Eadweard Muybridge used high-speed stop-motion photography to film a galloping horse. According to legend, he won $25,000 from the American businessman and university founder

Leland Stanford by proving that when a horse ran, at one point all four legs were off the ground.

The film business quickly understood the benefits of exploiting animals. For instance, the Edison film company's 1903 short *Electrocuting an Elephant* was the first known attempt to attract a paying movie audience via the killing of an animal. In 1902, an elephant named Topsy allegedly crushed to death a drunk circus spectator who burned her with a lit cigar. After she was sold to Coney Island's Sea Lion Park, her handler (also drunk) stabbed her with a pitchfork and set her loose on the streets of Brooklyn. After firing her handler, the zoo attempted to sell Topsy. When no one would take her, the zoo staged a publicity stunt by "sentencing" her to death by electrocution, which the Edison film company agreed to film.

Films featuring animals were immediately popular, with bag-punching kangaroos or elephants forced to dance, not unlike circus acts. Also popular were sheep, bears, donkeys, and monkeys, although soon the films were often using the animals as involuntary actors of sorts rather than circus performers. The most famous of these was a German shepherd named Rin Tin Tin, who appeared in twenty-seven movies and received more than ten thousand letters a week from fans. Rin Tin Tin died in 1932, just as a horse named Black Beauty became a national movie star. Still another dog then became a national hero, a collie named Lassie, who starred in the 1943 movie *Lassie Come Home*. The film spawned a radio show, which in turn spawned a television program that ran for seventeen years. At least nine different dogs played the role, all of them male, who tend to be heavier than females (although some of Lassie's stunt doubles were female).

Despite how much audiences loved these animals, Hollywood didn't. Instead, its four-legged stars were often maltreated, abused, or killed.

For instance, in *Hollywood Hoofbeats: Trails Blazed Across the Silver Screen*, author Petrine Day Mitchum discusses the trip wire, a device used to simulate horses being shot or otherwise stopped. "Wires attached to the horse's forelegs were threaded through a ring on the cinch and secured to buried dead weights," Mitchum explains, so that "when the horse ran to the end of the wires, his forelegs were yanked out from under him."[86] This might have thrilled audiences, but it usually crippled or killed the horses, as it did in the movies *Stagecoach* (1939) and *Jesse James* (1939). Likewise, four horses were killed on the set of *Heaven's Gate* (1980), two horses were killed on HBO's *Luck* (2011–12), and in the 2006 film *Flicka*, one horse broke her neck after reportedly becoming entangled in a rope, and a second horse was euthanized after breaking his leg in a similar incident. According to film historians, five horses were killed during the filming of 1925's *Ben-Hur*, and many more in the 1959 version.

Few of us have any idea what goes on behind the scenes. The sweet grin that we see chimps make on the screen is what Dr. Jane Goodall calls "a fear grimace," as chimpanzees do not bare their teeth out of joy. It comes in response to a command. These young chimps are often beaten with blackjacks or pool cues or are electroshocked into submission. Some have their teeth removed. When primatologist Sarah Baeckler conducted a fourteen-month undercover investigation of a prominent Hollywood training facility, she "saw a lot of physical violence. A lot of punching and kicking, and the use of the 'ugly stick,' a sawed-off broom handle, to beat the chimps," and "all kinds of physical abuse to keep them paying attention and in line with the trainer."[87]

Dogs and cats don't fare much better. For example, in 2007, Disney faced calls to drop distribution plans for its film *Snow Buddies* when fifteen puppies used in the production became ill, some fatally. Many of the dozens of puppies were shipped to the Canadian production company from a commercial breeder in New York—these pups were only six weeks old, rather than eight weeks as required by federal law. According to a 2013 article in *The Hollywood Reporter*, the tiger in *Life of Pi* almost drowned. During the filming of *The Hobbit: An Unexpected Journey*, whistle-blowers on the set reported that twenty-seven animals perished, including sheep and goats who died of dehydration and exhaustion or drowned in gullies.

More often than audiences realize, animals die during filming. Fatalities also take place during housing, training, and traveling. A 2018 exposé published in The Dodo revealed that Sidney Yost, a Hollywood animal trainer and owner of Amazing Animal Productions, has hit animals with sticks, kicked them in the head, and kept them in filthy enclosures among other physical abuse. In a three-year period, the USDA issued Yost approximately forty animal welfare violations. Yet Yost continued to train animals for blockbuster films including *The Hunger Games*, *The Butler*, and *12 Years a Slave*. The USDA eventually fined Yost $30,000 and revoked his license, barring him from handling, supplying, or exhibiting animals.

Nearly every moviegoer has seen the phrase "No Animals Were Harmed in the Making of This Film" in the ending credits. However, like much of Hollywood, the truth is not quite what it seems. The group that provides this endorsement is American Humane (AH), a Los Angeles–based association formed after a horse was deliberately thrown to his death for the 1939 film *Days of Jesse James*.

Unfortunately, AH does not have the authority to enforce its own standards: It is only able to grant any of six ratings, which range from "Outstanding" to "Special Circumstances" to "Not Monitored." Moreover, AH is funded by the Screen Actors Guild, meaning it is paid by the very industry it monitors. AH bases its ratings only on when animals are onset, but not when they are being trained or boarded. The director of AH's film and television unit, Karen Rosa, told the *Los Angeles Times*, "We're a non-profit. We're not staffed to do that kind of comprehensive oversight. . . . To make the assumption that when they leave the set, they will treat the animals differently is not something we do."[88] In 2013, *The Hollywood Reporter* ran an in-depth story implicating American Humane of underreporting incidents of animal abuse on television and movie sets.

Besides not monitoring preproduction training or living conditions, AH does not take into account a trainer's animal-related of-fenses or violations of the federal Animal Welfare Act. For example, a group called Predators in Action was hired to provide the grizzly bear for the movie *Semi-Pro*, even though the company had been previously cited by the USDA for animal welfare violations including failing to maintain the animal quarters in good repair, keeping a lion in a tiny shelter box in the snow, and failing to provide animals with drinking water. AH also did not criticize *Evan Almighty* producers for using Birds & Animals Unlimited, an animal supplier warned repeatedly by the USDA for its failure to comply with veterinary care, housing, and caging requirements. Furthermore, no agency monitors the separation of babies from their mothers, and AH doesn't take into consideration living conditions or the disposal of animals after they are no longer of use to the exhibitor.

Entertainment Without Animals

In the winter of 2018, a group of female British soldiers did something to deserve their nickname of Ice Maidens: they crossed Antarctica using just human strength and endurance. In a record-breaking sixty-two days, the women traveled more than a thousand miles of treacher-ous landscape in temperatures as low as 40 degrees below zero, using just skis while dragging sledges with equipment weighing roughly 176 pounds per woman. The Iditarod may be cruel, but who needs dogs when humans can voluntarily get out there on their own, prove their mettle, make international news, and never hurt a single animal along the way.

There's an entire world, from the North Pole to the South Pole, of entertainment possibilities now available. For one, if you prefer to visit wild animals near your home, but you don't want animals to inhabit zoos, no problem. Aside from videos of every animal under the sun or sea, new tech such as Oculus Rift and other virtual-reality headsets are replacing miserable animals with interactive scenes of wild animals so realistic you can all but feel their breath on your face and their fur or feathers. There are also replicas that have heartbeats, that can yawn, and that can even sport realistic-looking wounds for those who want to learn how to care for animals safely and effectively.

ANIMALS WHO AREN'T THERE

The London Zoo is among the leaders in the charge, having created a lion so realistic people find it difficult to distinguish replica from reality—a creature molded out of clay and cast in layers of latex before synthetic fur was hand-stitched onto his body. His eyes—made of glass. His claws—plastic. His whiskers—blades of dried glass. The verdict from those who have been scared by it: He looks just like a real lion.

An animal found neither in the jungle nor in the zoo was created in the early 2000s by the Royal de Luxe, a French marionette street theater company. One of its premier attractions is a twelve-meter-high, eight-meter-wide mechanical elephant, made from forty-five tons of wood and steel, that can take up to forty-nine passengers for a forty-five-minute walk. Likewise, the company's Heron Tree is a steel structure forty-five meters across and twenty-eight meters high, and topped with two herons—visitors can climb on the back or the wings of either bird for an aerial view of the company's hanging gardens.

Another way to interact with animals without exploiting them: holographic theater. The world's first opened up in Los Angeles in the fall of 2017, created by Alki David, founder of the internet-based TV provider FilmOn and owner of Hologram USA. All of the theater's performances, whether human or animal, are holographic. (The entire food selection is vegan as well.) David has plans to roll out 150 more locations, starting with Chicago. No real animals. No foods made from them.

CIRCUSES WITHOUT ANIMALS

Animal-free circuses are springing up around the globe. Founded in Montreal in 1984, Cirque du Soleil, the world's largest theatrical producer, tells stories through jaw-dropping, seemingly impossible human acrobatics, and through theater, costumes, special effects—and for the most part, no animals (although some shows occasionally use domestic animals). More recently, in India, two artists, Romain Timmers and Sharanya Rao, created a circus that mixes dance, juggling, acrobatics, and dance, also without animals. According to the artists, the Puducherry show differs greatly from "the old-fashioned, dusty image that it still holds here, with all due respect to the tradition and the artists."[89] And in Germany, in 2019, Circus Roncalli changed from an animal circus to one that uses only holograms.

The public approves. Fewer and fewer people are attending animal-based entertainments. After months of discussions and productive meetings with PETA, TripAdvisor—the world's largest travel site—announced in 2016 that it will no longer sell tickets to activities where wild animals are forced to come into contact with the public, including elephant rides, tiger encounters, and "swim with dolphins" excursions. In 2017, Virgin Holidays announced it would not sell or promote any new attractions or hotels featuring captive whales and dolphins for theatrical or other entertainment purposes and will encourage existing partners to "promote the highest welfare standards for the animals in their care, while also evolving their offering away from theatrical performances." In that same year, leading travel agency Thomas Cook dropped SeaWorld and some dolphin and elephant attractions in Thailand, India, Cuba, Turkey, and Dominican Republic after a report showed they did not meet official welfare standards. After countless campaigns by animal rights groups, more than 160 travel companies have stopped offering elephant tourism programs and one-off elephant attractions, according to World Animal Protection, which is also putting pressure on cruise lines to reconsider shore excursions that force donkeys, ponies, camels, and elephants to take passengers up the sides of mountains, and otherwise cause animals to suffer.

If you want to see real elephants, the Elephant Sanctuary in Tennessee offers a webcam that allows you to observe what their charges, many rescued from a hard circus life, are up to. Check out https://www.elephants.com/elecam.

And if you would like to see a terrific elephant who isn't a real elephant, track down companies like Circus 1903, an American circus that travels with elephants brought to life by the same puppeteers who also created the extraordinary animals in the award-winning play *War Horse*. See them at https://circus1903.com/.

ANIMATRONICS

The confluence of fewer animal "attractions" with improving technology is resulting in new kinds of companies springing to life. One of the most innovative is Creature Technology Co., which produces "technologically sophisticated, creatively inspired, and lifelike animatronics for arena spectaculars, theme parks, exhibitions, stage shows and events." Founded in 2006 in Melbourne, Australia, Creature Technology has won many awards creating the animatronics for the arena shows *Walking with Dinosaurs* and *How to Train Your Dragon*, and the stage show *King Kong*. Creature Technology Co. also created the animatronic dinosaurs that star in *Jurassic World: The Exhibition*, based on the movie.

Likewise, Animal Makers Inc., headquartered in Moorpark, California, builds and animates realistic beasts and creatures for movies, television, internet videos, zoos, hotels, restaurants, and even for luxury personal collections (taking the place of the royal menagerie). The company offers more than three thousand individual products. The company's founder, Jim Boulden, began by selling original animal art for store displays and personal collections in 1979. He then went into film and television work, starting off in 1986 with *The World's Richest*

Cat (1986). Since then, Boulden's creatures have appeared in many other productions, including *Dances with Wolves, A River Runs Through It,* and *Pirates of the Caribbean: At World's End.* Meanwhile, Feld Entertainment, along with Universal Brand Development, announced in early 2018 that they were creating a touring show based on the movie *Jurassic World;* it will feature a herd of life-size dinosaurs up to forty feet long.

VIRTUAL ANIMALS

Virtual reality is also creating a stage for animal-free animal entertainment. For instance, rather than going to the zoo to witness a live birth, VR can give you a much better view. You can watch and even feel what it's like to be a cow born on a dairy farm through "I, Calf," a virtual-reality experience that employs a combination of filmed footage and computer animation. The viewer is virtually placed in the body of a young calf whose mother (voiced by actress Alicia Silverstone, herself a vegan) secretly gave birth to twins and, remembering that farmers took her previous babies away, hid one of the newborns to protect him.

Another virtual- and augmented-reality program is PETA's "I, Orca," which uses wireless Google virtual-reality goggles to immerse participants in a world where they can swim freely in the ocean with their orca family. They meet an orca mother (voiced by *Nurse Jackie* star Edie Falco) who still mourns the baby who was abducted from her decades ago and sent to SeaWorld, where he has been sentenced to a miserable life in captivity.

Fish, too, no longer need to be captured to be entertaining. *National Geographic,* long at the forefront of photographic imagery, offers an exhibit in New York's Times Square that allows visitors to journey to the depths of the Pacific Ocean, interacting with enormous schools of fish, giant squids, humpback whales, and dolphins. The imagery for the show, called *Encounter: Ocean Odyssey,* was created by SPE Partners, the animators responsible for the visual effects in HBO's *Game of Thrones.* Audiences can interact with the fish, walk underwater, play with a seal, touch coral reefs, or relax in darkness to the sound of whale song.

Another aquarium of the future is LightAnimal, a Japanese digital software system that creates a virtual underwater environment without causing animals harm. LightAnimal, which proved enormously popular in Japan, is now appearing in China and South Korea as well.

If you prefer your reality virtual, consider that the winner of the 2017 Webby Award in "VR: Gaming, Interactive, or Real-time" was Oculus Rift's Virry VR, a virtual safari filmed at Kenya's Lewa Wildlife Conservancy, home of some of Africa's most endangered animals, including black and white rhinos, lions, and elephants. With Virry you feel you're right next to these large creatures as they run, feed, and play. You'll meet other animals as well, including zebras, leopards, and vervet monkeys.

COMPUTER-GENERATED IMAGERY

Perhaps some of the biggest changes in the nonanimal entertainment world come out of Hollywood through CGI, or computer-generated imagery.

CGI is the usage of computer graphics to create images, whether for film, video games, or any other application. In use as far back as the 1982 film *Tron* (the first movie to extensively use 3-D CGI), sometimes CGI is used to create animals (or anything else) that don't exist in real life, such as Gollum in the Lord of the Rings film series (2001–2003), the extraordinary creatures in *Avatar* (2009), or perhaps most famously, the dinosaurs in *Jurassic Park* (1993). Increasingly, CGI is used to create animals so that no real animals have to be used: for example, the bear in the Leonardo DiCaprio film *The Revenant* (2015), or nearly all the animals in the movie *Noah* (2014).

When actor/producer Jon Favreau set out to direct Disney's live-action *The Jungle Book,* he was tasked with bringing to life some of the most iconic animal characters in literature, from Baloo the bear to Shere Khan the tiger. Favreau opted to employ CGI, explaining, "It's amazing what they can do with [creating the appearance of] fur and live-flesh animals, and so every day I go into work it's astounding what these visual effects artists accomplish."[90] The result is a realistic yet mythical world filled with larger-than-life, anthropomorphic animals who live, breathe, fight, and flee amid lively, lush scenery. Meanwhile, the hit zombie show *The Walking Dead* uses CGI and animatronics to create the stunningly realistic tigress Shiva.

Given the long history of animals and the world of entertainment, given how entertaining humans have found animals, given how many ways we've employed them to make us laugh . . . is it possible to be equally or even more entertained without them? The answer is clearly yes.

What You Can Do

The most important step to take: Do not patronize any entertainment that uses animals. Here are more specific actions to consider:

If you see a film, television show, or advertisement that exploits any animal, contact the producers, the studio, or the company advertising their product and tell them why you object. Be articulate, be thoughtful, be polite. Tell the theater manager that you refuse to support the abuse of animals. (You can also ask for a refund.) Write to your local newspaper's film critics and request that they mention in reviews whether or not a film uses animals.

If your school or local sports team still exploits an animal as a mascot, start a campaign to switch to a costumed human mascot.

If you suspect that dogfighting is taking place in your neighborhood, contact local law-enforcement authorities. Dogfighters typically keep their dogs chained, so you can deter dogfights by trying to pass an anti-chaining ordinance in your community.

Cockfighting is a felony almost everywhere. Even attending a cockfight is illegal in most states, as is possessing roosters for the purpose of fighting. In 2002, President George W. Bush signed legislation that made the transport of roosters across state lines to engage in fights a federal crime. In 2007, the Animal Welfare Act was amended to make "knowingly buying, selling, or transporting animals across state or international borders for the purpose of fighting" a felony. If you are aware of any cockfighting activity in your neighborhood, contact local law-enforcement authorities.

Don't visit facilities that have captive wild animals of any sort—even domesticated birds. Report poor conditions to the US Department of Agriculture and to animal protection organizations, write letters to the editors of local publications, and support or suggest the introduction of legislation that closes down roadside zoos and marine amusement parks.

Do not patronize the Iditarod or other dogsled races or tourist attractions that include dogsled rides. If you are planning a trip to Alaska, be sure to let your travel agent know that you do not want any packages that include dogsled rides. Let sponsors of dogsled races know that you don't support businesses that involve such cruelty. Instead, support human sled races like the Ice Maidens. For example, Lowell, Massachusetts, hosts the National Human Dogsled Championship in February as part of its annual Winterfest, in which teams of humans dress up in costumes and race for the finish line. In New York City, the "Idiotarod" features some five hundred human racers who push shopping carts over the Brooklyn Bridge into Manhattan.

If a rodeo comes to your town, protest to local authorities, write letters to sponsors, distribute leaflets at the gate, or find out from a local animal protection organization how to hold a demonstration.

Check state and local laws to find out what types of activities involving animals are and are not legal in your area. For example, after a spectator videotaped a bull breaking his leg during a rodeo event, Pittsburgh passed a law prohibiting bucking straps, electric prods, and sharpened or fixed spurs. Because most rodeos use flank straps, the measure effectively banned rodeos altogether. Another successful means of banning rodeos is to institute a state or local ban on calf roping, which many rodeo circuits require. Eliminating it can result in the elimination of all rodeo shows.

Visit an animal sanctuary sanctioned by the Global Federation of Animal Sanctuaries (GFAS). GFAS sanctuaries never breed animals or allow them to be used in commercial activities.

Visit an animal-free circus. These include Circus Vargas in the US and Canada, which once used animals and now only has human performers; Cirque Italia, a traveling water circus with a stage that holds thirty-five thousand gallons of water; Fern Street Circus, which offers many acts to underserved neighborhoods across America; Flying High Circus, which features high-wire, acrobatics, and juggling acts; Imperial Circus, one of the most outstanding of the Chinese circuses that play internationally; and many of the Cirque du Soleil shows.

Go on a virtual field trip. Instead of disrupting animal lives, or patronizing SeaWorld, you can watch animals closely, and less intrusively, through live cams set up in nature allowing you to observe animals in a way that's safe for everyone. You can pick any place from the Arctic tundra to watering holes in Africa to an underwater orca lab or an island off the coast of Scotland where birds nest and raise their young. And, you will learn more about animals than you would at a zoo because you are seeing them in their natural home environment, not in a cage or a tank.

Go snorkeling and scuba diving. Here you can watch fish and other aquatic creatures live in their own homes, on their own terms.

Take a safari at a natural haven for animals, such as Sweden's Glasriket's Moose Park, where you can watch moose in their beautiful natural habitat.

Spend your leisure time at:

Botanical gardens and parks, which are found in most cities, and where you can observe local wildlife from chipmunks to birds in a beautiful, natural setting.

Whale-watching tours. On both American coasts, and elsewhere around the world, approved tours allow you to watch whales from a proper distance. Be sure to research the tour operator's reputation before you book as some have been cited for disturbing whales and their calves.

Natural history museums. One of the best ways to see animals in their natural habitat are the dioramas at these museums that offer not only close-up views of contemporary animals, but animals who have existed throughout the Earth's history.

For a truly intimate time spent with animals, volunteer! Many farmed-animal sanctuaries have volunteer programs, and there are now scores in America alone, others overseas. The odds are good you can find one near you or your travel destination. You can find a comprehensive list at https://www.vegan.com/farm-sanctuaries/ or at http://www.sanctuaries.org.

Travel the World Kindly

Do not go for a ride on an elephant—no matter how friendly the elephants seem to be. These animals have been tortured into submission to obey their trainers. Elephant rides can even be dangerous to you—in 2016, a British tourist was killed in Thailand when his elephant, having been taunted and beaten, snapped and trampled the thirty-six-year-old man to death. Many elephants are infected with the human strain of tuberculosis. Elephants are not built to be chained between rides or to carry large weights on their backs or climb steep hills, as many captive elephants are made to do, from Jaipur's Amer Fort to the jungles of Burma.

Say no to swimming with dolphins. Sure, it sounds like an entertaining way to spend a day, but the animals available for a swim date have usually been captured from their homes and forced to interact with humans in enclosures depriving them of their right to swim great distances, to experience ocean currents, and to raise their young.

Do not take selfies with animals. In 2016, a rare baby dolphin was killed by a group of people handing him around while taking selfies in Argentina (although one witness said the animal was already dead, which is not a good result, either). Other animals recently killed while people were taking selfies include a swan dragged out of a lake, peacocks, sharks, and sea turtles.

Do not attend bullfights. It's intensely cruel to the bull, who may be weakened with laxatives and partially blinded with gel before being sent into the ring.

Avoid animal foods, but particularly look out for delicacies that sound as though they may not come from animals. For example, kopi luwak is a beverage made from the beans of coffee berries that have been eaten and excreted by the Asian palm civet—these animals are often snatched from their forest homes and imprisoned in tiny cages and fed only coffee until their hair falls out, and many die.

Avoid souvenirs that are made from animal parts, such as tortoiseshell ornaments, fur-covered toys or hats, turtle oil, and feather earrings.

For more information, check out:

GigSalad.com, which allows users to search for traveling entertainment by zip code. (Note that not all acts listed on this site are animal-free, but many are.)

PETA's Animal-Friendly Destination list, including visits to animal sanctuaries accredited by the Global Federation of Animal Sanctuaries (GFAS) and many more fun activities.

National Geographic's website (www.nationalgeographic .com), where you can find out how to tell if an animal sanctuary is a true sanctuary, whether a facility allows interaction with wild animals or breeds them, and more.

Global Federation of Animal Sanctuaries "Find a Sanctuary" on Facebook allows you to search GFAS accredited and verified facilities. GFAS upholds rigorous standards of sanctuary management and animal care. Member sanctuaries don't breed or use animals in commercial activities, and they provide excellent lifetime care.

Vegans.UK's Ten Alternatives to Animal "Entertainment" blog (http://vegans.uk/cruelty-free-living/ten-alternatives-to-animal-entertainment/) lists alternatives to cruel activities such as animal circuses, bullfighting, and horse-drawn carriages with animal-free options like human-only circuses, boxing, and bike riding.

Food

Close your eyes. Go back in time. Fifty thousand years back. You're living in the Paleolithic Age. You and your family are returning to your home cave after a long day of foraging in the nearby forests. It's very cold outside, but every day seems more frigid than the last. You enter the cave where you find the other members of your family, the ones too sick or too young to forage, huddled around the fire for warmth. Everyone is hungry and looking forward to a good meal.

What's on the menu?

Forget the popular image of groups of spear-bearing cavemen chasing down gazelle and tigers. The contents of your plate are mostly what you found in the forest: plant foods. Early humans' average meals likely consisted of starch-rich foods like tubers, rhizomes (horizontally growing roots), corns, seeds, fruits, and vegetables. Little—if any—meat was on the plate, mostly because Paleolithic humans weren't strong or fast enough to hunt down other animals. If and when they did eat meat, it was the scavenged leftovers from larger carnivores' kills.

The diets of our closest relatives—chimpanzees—offer insights into our ancestors' primary foods. These primates' diets consist of fruit, leaves, flowers, bark, nuts, and insects. While chimps occasionally eat meat, they do so opportunistically, usually after a leopard or another large carnivore leaves behind the remains of her catch. All told, meat comprises barely 3 percent of wild chimpanzees' diet. Considering we share 99 percent of our DNA with chimps, it makes much more sense to take our dietary cues from our fellow primates rather than from television infomercials.

Like our primate relatives, our intestines are long and winding, which means they are ideal for digesting fruits and vegetables. Chimps and humans also have small stomachs, comprising around a quarter of their digestive tract, making it difficult to eat a great deal of food at once.

Vegan Animals

Think meat makes you big and buff? Consider these giants of the animal kingdom, who mainly eat fruit, shoots, and leaves.

- Gorillas can grow to more than four hundred pounds and stand nearly six feet tall.
- The largest-ever dinosaur was the *Amphicoelias fragillimus*—a dinosaur that weighed up to an estimated 122 tons. How did this dino grow so large? Eating literally tons of plant food.
- Elephants love peanuts, but that's not the only plant food they eat. Indian and African elephants subsist on grass, plants, bushes, fruit, twigs, tree bark, and roots.
- The swift, strong bison, who can run at speeds up to 35 mph, prefers a diet of grass, sedges, berries, and lichen.
- Manatees, a.k.a. the underwater cows of the sea, enjoy a steady diet of sea grass, eating up to 190 pounds per day.
- Wild yak, muscular and powerful, stand seven feet tall and weigh up to 2,200 pounds on a diet fueled by grass, sedges, and herbs.

THE EARLY HUMAN DIET

Our dietary journey through time begins about sixty-five million years ago with a rat-size mammal named *Purgatorius,* widely considered to be the first primate. He was a committed vegan, munching on tropical fruits, seeds, and nuts. For millions of years his descendants maintained a similar diet, consisting mainly of fruits, flowers, and the occasional insect. About fifteen million years ago they mixed in nuts and hard seeds, but the first major change took place six million years ago with *Sahelanthropus,* one of the first primates to walk upright on two legs. He also sported smaller canine teeth and thick tooth enamel, suggesting that he preferred to chew rather than grind his food.

About four million years ago, a critical human ancestor, *Australopithecus,* began roaming the woodlands, riverine forests, and seasonal floodplains of Africa, fueled by a diet of plants. As indicated by their enormous jawbones used to crush plant matter, *Australopithecus*'s diet likely resembled a chimp's. *Australopithecus* may have been opportunistic scavengers who occasionally ate meat, although their digestive tracts were not equipped to do so regularly. Similarly, paleoanthropologist Dr. Richard Leakey believes that humans only sought out animal flesh when supplies of nuts, seeds, and grains were running low. According to Dr. Leakey, "Hominins are considered to be opportunistic scavengers of meat where they could find it, while relying on plant-based diets."[91]

By 2.6 million years ago, meat became more commonplace in the early human diet. Dental studies of *Homo habilis*—a.k.a. Handy Man, or the first maker of stone tools—reveal a diet of tough foods like leaves, woody plants, and some animal tissues. About 1.8 million years ago came *Homo erectus* (known as Upright Man, the first known human to walk on two legs, not four) who lived in hunter-gatherer communities and were also the first to cook food with controlled fire. *Homo erectus* occasionally ate meat, but subsisted primarily on crisp root vegetables like tubers. Finally, about 200,000 years ago, the human species as we know it today—*Homo sapiens*—arrived. Our modern ancestors foraged for grass seeds, roots, sedges, and succulents, while also scavenging for meat from dead animals.

Throughout the twentieth century, most scientists believed the extra protein from scavenged meat was central to our evolution, particularly in relation to the growth of the human brain. However, recent research suggests that other innovations were more important—most notably, the invention of cooking. In his book *Catching Fire*, Dr. Richard Wrangham argues that cooking increased the digestibility of both meat and plants, supplying the brain with more calories and more growth.

About twelve thousand years ago, human life took a revolutionary turn with the introduction of farming. Thanks to changes in climate, greater population density, overhunting, and tool use, by the following seven thousand years humans were growing food on every continent except Australia and Antarctica. This also meant that the animals they used to supplement their diet had to remain in one place, launching the history of animal domestication.

Mouflons may have been the first domesticated farm animals. Ancestors of modern-day sheep, mouflons are small in stature. The males (and some females) have beautiful, curved horns that curl almost into a full circle. Nowadays they inhabit mountainous regions of Iraq, Iran, and Armenia, although their range and population was far greater ten thousand years ago. Humans initially raised these early sheep ancestors for meat, milk, and hide. By 3500 BCE, when mouflons had been selectively bred and more resembled modern-day sheep, they were prized for their wool, which could be woven and spun into clothing.

By about 9000 BCE, the first pigs were domesticated in China from the wild boar (which are still in existence). Boars are a tremendously adaptable species. Despite the destruction of their habitats, boars have actually expanded their territory across all of Asia and even into parts of Europe, Australia, and the US. They live together in herds, known as sounders, and use their muscular snouts to forage through soil for fungi, ferns, roots, leaves, frogs, and insects. No one knows exactly how humans managed to tame these fiercely independent animals, but perhaps generations of boars who were more friendly and less cautious roamed into human habitats and rummaged through food waste, finding so much to eat that they stayed.

Humans domesticated the aurochs approximately 10,500 years ago in Mesopotamia. The ancestor to today's cattle, the auroch was a muscular horned animal that roamed throughout much of Europe, Asia, and North Africa (becoming extinct by the seventeenth century BCE). By 5400 BCE, aurochs had been sufficiently domesticated to be used as work animals in the ancient Sumerian city of Eridu, principally for plowing fields, hauling wagons, and dragging riverboats against the current. Generations of selective breeding eventually gave rise to two meaty species of cattle: zebu cattle, found mainly on the Indian subcontinent; and taurine cattle, found in Eurasia.

Our other major domesticated food source, chickens, are descended from the red jungle fowl, which is still extant in the bamboo forests of Southeast Asia and India. Male jungle fowls have golden feathers and beautiful red combs that adorn their heads like crowns, while females have camouflaged plumage that serves as protection as she cares for her eggs and newborn chicks. Humans most likely domesticated jungle fowls around 2000 BCE in Asia. Millennia of selective breeding have drastically changed the appearance of chickens: While jungle fowls weigh a maximum of about 2.5 pounds as adults, modern-day chickens can reach their five-pound slaughter weight in only five weeks.

Are Humans Carnivores?

Humans have short, soft fingernails and small canine teeth. In contrast, carnivores (such as lions and tigers) all have sharp claws and large canine teeth that are capable of tearing flesh. Carnivores' jaws move only up and down, requiring them to tear chunks of flesh from their prey and swallow them whole. Humans and other herbivores can move their jaws up and down and from side to side, allowing them to grind up fruit and vegetables with their back teeth. Like other herbivores' teeth, humans' back molars are flat for grinding fibrous plant foods. As Dr. Richard Leakey summarizes, "You can't tear flesh by hand, you can't tear hide by hand. Our anterior teeth are not suited for tearing flesh or hide. We don't have large canine teeth, and we wouldn't have been able to deal with food sources that require those large canines."[92]

Carnivorous animals swallow their food whole, relying on extremely acidic stomach juices to break down flesh and kill dangerous bacteria. Human stomach acids are much weaker, as strong acids aren't needed to digest prechewed fruits and vegetables; that's why we generally can't consume meat raw without cooking it first. Carnivores have short intestinal tracts and colons that allow meat to pass through their bodies relatively quickly. The human intestinal tract is much longer, allowing the body more time to break down fiber and absorb the nutrients from plant-based foods. But eating uncooked meat is very risky for us: The bacteria in meat have extra time to multiply during the long trip through the digestive system, increasing the risk of food poisoning. Moreover, meat actually begins to rot as it makes its slow journey through the human intestine, boosting the risk of colon cancer among other intestinal disorders.

Dr. William C. Roberts, editor of the *American Journal of Cardiology,* writes, "Although we think we are, and we act as if we are, human beings are not natural carnivores. When we kill animals to eat them, they end up killing us, because their flesh, which contains cholesterol and saturated fat, was never intended for human beings, who are natural herbivores."[93]

THE MEAT INDUSTRIAL COMPLEX

As late as the 1950s, many farmers were providing a more humane life for their animals, even though their animals were eventually slaughtered and consumed. Farmers largely lived off the crops they grew, and the eggs and milk from animals. Meanwhile, manure from cows and pigs was used to help keep the fields nutrient-rich.

Today, the average American tucks away 222 pounds of red meat and poultry every year—that's compared to 138 pounds in 1950. Before long, small family farms were unable to keep up with Americans' expanding appetite (and waistlines), especially with the explosion of fast-food restaurants beginning in the 1960s. Today, close to ten billion land animals are raised and killed for human consumption in the United States alone. Around the world, that number is closer to fifty billion. As for fish, their deaths are measured by the ton. By the time you finish reading this paragraph, tens of thousands of animals will have been slaughtered.

Killing at this scale requires massive factory farms. The 1930s witnessed new systems of raising chickens with incubators, allowing farmers to operate large-scale operations. In the late 1940s, Tyson Foods introduced vertical integration for raising chickens, enabling the company to wholly own and maintain tight control over their entire supply chain. By consolidating farms, Tyson and other conglomerates could essentially turn animal agriculture into an assembly line.

Meat and Dairy Subsidies

The persistence and growth of factory farms and cheap animal products over the last century is no coincidence; it has been heralded by government subsidies and assistance to dairy farmers throughout the twentieth and twenty-first centuries. While the US Department of Agriculture's (USDA) MyPlate guidelines urge Americans to eat more fruits and vegetables and less meat, the government still spends $38 billion each year on subsidies to the meat and dairy industries. When it comes to actually purchasing the recommended foods, consumers are seduced by inexpensive meat and dairy products.

The relationship between the federal government and the dairy industry is especially problematic. A recent report by Grey, Clark, Shih and Associates found that in 2015, 73 percent of the returns received by American dairy farmers came from taxpayer subsidies. Encouraged in part by these handouts, farmers have been pumping out more dairy products than Americans can eat. In June 2018, the *Washington Post* reported that the US had reached its largest stockpile of cheese in a century—nearly 1.4 billion pounds' worth. That's 4.6 pounds for every man, woman, and child. Yet the industry likely isn't too worried: When the surplus hit more than a billion pounds in 2016, Uncle Sam agreed to bail out the industry by buying $20 million in cheese for distribution to food banks and pantries. These tight relationships even extend to schools: Between 2010 and 2014, Domino's convinced three thousand schools in thirty-eight states to serve its pizza in lunchrooms.

Government subsidies also help fund campaigns to persuade Americans to buy more meat and dairy products. Remember the "Got Milk?" campaigns from the 1990s? How about "The Incredible Edible Egg," "Beef. It's What's for Dinner," and "Pork. The Other White Meat"? Thanks to intense lobbying efforts and agreeable politicians, the meat and dairy industries installed a direct line of influence to the American consumer.

The faster farmed animals reach their slaughter weight, the higher the profit. One common method of making animals gain weight rapidly is to pump them full of antibiotics. In fact, about 70 to 80 percent of all antibiotics in the United States are given not to sick people, but to cattle, pigs, and poultry to make them grow faster. Some of that antibiotic residue persists after the animal is slaughtered and cooked. As a result, human resistance to antibiotics has been rising at an alarming rate, leading to superbugs that are resistant to all medications. Speaking to a reporter at the *New York Times,* Dr. Martin J. Blaser, chairman of the Presidential Advisory Council on Combating Antibiotic-Resistant Bacteria, said, "We've become addicted to antibiotics. We're using them as if there was no biological cost to using them. And there are costs."[94]

To maximize efficiency, factory farms generally specialize in one kind of animal: either cattle, pigs, chickens, or fish.

Cattle. Twenty-nine million cows, steers, and calves are slaughtered in the meat and dairy industries every year in the US alone. Cattle raised for their meat typically spend a year on ranches. While they are granted a small degree of freedom, they are typically branded by ranchers with hot irons or with freezing brands, while males are usually castrated without pain relief. They are left out in storms and floods, and in the winter, many cattle freeze to death in states such as Nebraska, South Dakota, and Wyoming. During the summer, frequently denied shade, they die from the heat in states such as Kansas and Texas. After about a year, cows are shipped to an auction lot and then may be sent hundreds of miles away to feces- and mud-filled holding pens, known as feedlots, where they're crammed together by the thousands, living in their own waste. Many are sick on arrival and die shortly afterward.

You might assume that dairy cows live happier lives. Not so—their lives are worse than cows raised for meat. To meet the demand for milk, yogurt, and cheese, cows are artificially impregnated via a human's hand stuck up inside her to inject sperm, again and again, to keep output and profits high. After a cow gives birth, her beloved calf (for whom the milk was intended) is dragged away right after or within a day or two of birth. Female calves are typically condemned to be dairy cows like their mothers, while males serve a more immediate purpose: they are confined to a tiny crate to restrict their movement and are fed an anemia-inducing gruel to ensure that their flesh remains tender. When they are only a few months old, males are slaughtered and sold as veal. And once a mother's body can no longer produce enough milk at the frenzied pace required by factory farms (by about age four or five), she, too, is sent on the truck to the slaughterhouse, usually to be made into low-grade beef products like dog food or jerky.

For years, the dairy industry has insisted we all drink milk—not because it is good for us, but because it's profitable. The calcium in cow's milk is the least absorbable kind you can eat—green leafy vegetables provide the best source of this bone-strengthening mineral. Contrary to popular belief, dairy milk can actually hurt your bones. A set of studies published by *The British Medical Journal* analyzing one hundred thousand people for about twenty years found that milk may increase the chance of bone or hip fractures. This might explain why some of the highest rates of osteoporosis are found in the countries with the highest rates of milk consumption. Americans take in more calcium from dairy products than any other country. We also have a high incidence of osteoporosis.

Pigs. Pigs have complex communication systems and extensive cognitive abilities. They are social, playful, protective animals who form bonds, recognize their names, learn tricks, and love to show affection to everyone around them. Approximately 115 million of them are killed for chops, bacon, ham, and other pork items each year. Sows are kept in gestation crates—tiny enclosures so small that they cannot even turn around. After barely ten days, their piglets are moved to cramped and overcrowded pens to be raised for meat.

When it's slaughter time, frightened pigs are forced onto transport trucks that travel for many miles through all weather extremes. Many pigs die from heat exhaustion in the summer, or because they have human-like skin with little hair, arrive frozen to the inside of the truck in the winter. According to industry reports, more than one million pigs die in transit each year, and at least forty thousand more sustain injuries by the time they arrive at the slaughterhouse.

Egg-laying and "Broiler" Chickens. Each year in the US, approximately 9 billion chickens are raised and killed for their meat—yes, that's billion with a *b*—and another 305 million hens have their reproductive systems exploited for their eggs. To meet the mass demand for eggs, which are an ingredient in everything from cookies and cake to nog and noodles, hens are kept in wire battery cages. Each cage holds at least five hens in cramped conditions that often lead to respiratory distress from having to inhale the ammonia in their accumulated waste. The quarters are stacked so that chickens must urinate and defecate on hens below them. Egg-laying hens have been genetically engineered for decades to the point where they produce an abnormal three hundred or so eggs per year. In comparison, the ancestor of modern-day chickens, the red jungle fowl, lays between ten and fifteen eggs per year. Male chicks born from laying hens are useless to the industry because they cannot lay eggs. They are immediately killed by mass suffocation, thrown alive into a Dumpster, or tossed into an "eviscerator," which grinds them up alive.

"Broiler chicken" refers to a chicken specifically raised for his or her flesh. These birds have been relentlessly bred to put on as much weight as possible, and reach their full size within just six weeks. Such intense breeding to produce more breast meat, for instance, plus the addition of artificial growth hormones and antibiotics, leads to serious health problems. Many chickens are so breast heavy that they cannot walk, and many suffer heart attacks despite being just weeks old. They are crammed by the thousands into massive, windowless sheds. While chickens can function well in small groups, in which each bird understands his or her spot in the pecking order, it's impossible for them to establish a social structure in such large numbers. The more aggressive, frustrated birds often peck at the more submissive ones, causing injury and even death.

To suggest an air of compassion, the chicken industry often employs labels such as "free-roaming," "free-range," or "pasture-raised" and puts misleading pictures of the farm on the cartons that bear no resemblance to reality. According to the USDA, in order to qualify as a free-range operation, a farm must merely demonstrate that "the poultry has been allowed access to the outside." This language is purposefully vague, and can mean the chickens have no more than a peephole of access to a small patch of dirt outside the shed, if they can fight their way to it through the thousands of other hens. As an undercover investigation of Nellie's Free Range Eggs showed, because the peephole was closed in winter, in the evenings, in bad weather—i.e.: most days—so even those hens right next to the opening never managed to go outside. Meanwhile, the term "cage-free" means that hens are "housed in a building, room, or enclosed area that allows for unlimited access to food, water, and provides the freedom to roam within the area during the laying cycle." In reality, this is usually not the case, with birds still trying to exist in large, massively crowded sheds with sometimes one square foot of space or less, and no way to "roam" at all. Likewise, terminology such as "pasture-raised" implies that the animal has "continuous free access to the outdoors for a minimum of 120 days a year." This raises the question: What happens the other 245 days of the year?

Fish. Factory farms aren't only a terrestrial phenomenon: Nearly half of all fish consumed each year in America are now raised in man-made enclosures called aquafarms, found in rivers, lakes, and oceans. Much like land animals, fish are subjected to severe crowding, injuries, starvation, and contamination. They become infested with lice and receive frequent wounds from brushing up against other trapped fish. Yet aquafarming has not stopped the depletion of the ocean's fish. Fish are caught at such rates that dozens of once-common species may become extinct within decades.

Aquafarms discharge waste, pesticides, and other chemicals directly into ecologically fragile coastal waters, destroying local ecosystems. Aquaculture farms that raise fish directly in fenced-in areas of natural waters also kill off thriving natural habitats by overloading them far beyond their capacity. Waste from excessive fish populations can trigger vast blankets of algae on the water's surface, depleting oxygen and killing much of the life in the water. In Brazil, destruction caused by aquaculture changed the local climate so much that some aquaculture operations have been forced to shut down.

Raising one ton of fish commercially takes eight tons of water. Intensive shrimp production takes up to ten times more water. According to a study published in the journal *Science*, a two-acre salmon farm produces as much waste as a town of ten thousand humans. Salmon farms in British Columbia were even found to be producing as much waste as a city of half a million people.

ORIGINS OF THE ANIMAL PROTECTION MOVEMENT

While our ancestors might not have been able to imagine what happens on today's factory farms, humans have long considered animals little more than tools. French philosopher René Descartes (1596–1650) summed up this relationship succinctly in his *Discours de la méthode*, writing that animals were essentially unthinking, unfeeling machines—or as he called them, "soulless automata." Factory farms, then, would merely represent the logical extreme of the human–animal relationship as it has persisted for generations.

While most humans throughout history have cared for little beyond the taste of their meat, eggs, and milk, some have dedicated themselves to securing a semblance of compassion for farmed animals whose lives are otherwise devoid of it. Among the very first Western thinkers to publicly advocate for animal rights was the French philosopher Michel de Montaigne (1533–1592), who argued that cruelty to animals was wrong. Montaigne also questioned man's supremacy over animals: "By what comparison between them and us does he infer the stupidity he attributes to them?" he asked. "When I play with my cat, who knows if she is making more of a pastime of me than I of her?"

A century later, the famed English philosopher and founder of political liberalism, John Locke (1632–1704), argued that adults should stop children from abusing animals because "the custom of tormenting and killing of beasts will, by degrees, harden their minds even towards men." Locke never denied that animals were inferior to men; rather, he sought to prevent children from growing comfortable with violence because they could one day direct it toward other humans. Echoing this argument, the German philosopher Immanuel Kant (1724–1804) wrote that "cruelty to animals is contrary to man's duty to himself, because it deadens in him the feeling of sympathy for their sufferings, and thus a natural tendency that is very useful to morality in relation to other human beings is weakened."

One of the first philosophers to undeniably advocate for animals was Jeremy Bentham (1748–1832), who is best known as the founder of utilitarianism, which posits actions are just if they promote happiness and well-being amongst a majority of people—and, as he would argue, animals. To Bentham, the relative intelligence of all creatures on Earth did not matter. Who cares that animals cannot talk as humans can? Bentham argued. They are still living things. "The question," he stated in *An Introduction to the Principles of Morals and Legislation*, "is not, Can they reason?, nor Can they talk?, but Can they suffer?"

His words moved only a small minority. Still, by the early nineteenth century, the English House of Commons had begun proposing bills outlawing some forms of animal cruelty. The force behind the legislation was Col. Richard Martin, referred to as "Humanity Dick" by King George IV for his unrelenting support of animals and the poor. One report from the *Times* of London recounted that when Martin "suggested protection should be given to [horses], there were such howls of laughter . . . When the Chairman repeated this proposal, the laughter intensified. Another member said Martin would be legislating for dogs next, which caused a further roar of mirth, and a cry 'And cats!' sent the house into convulsions."

Nevertheless, Martin succeeded in passing the "Ill Treatment of Horses and Cattle Bill," the world's first major piece of animal rights legislation. From then on, to "beat, abuse, or ill-treat any horse, mare, gelding, mule, ass, ox, cow, heifer, steer, sheep or other cattle" was punishable by up to five pounds or two months in prison. Worried that the Act would not be enforced, Martin and other members of Parliament founded the Society for the Prevention of Cruelty to Animals in 1824, tasking it with inspecting slaughterhouses and bringing prosecutions against offenders. Three decades later, France followed with the *Loi Grammont*, which outlawed cruelty against domestic animals. A handful of similar laws followed in numerous states in the US including Maine, New York, Massachusetts, Connecticut, and Wisconsin.

Along with animal rights laws came the first animal rights organizations. The first in the United States was the American Society for the Prevention of Cruelty to Animals (ASPCA), founded in 1866 by a wealthy New Yorker named Henry Bergh. The ASPCA's mission was to care for homeless and abused animals—or "these mute servants of mankind," as Bergh called them. The organization provided animal rights education for the public and worked alongside law enforcement to bring animal abusers to justice. (As mentioned earlier, nine years later Irish writer and social reformer Frances Power Cobbe founded what would become the National Anti-Vivisection Society, the world's first organization devoted to ending animal research.) In 1910, author Rupert Wheldon published what is believed to be the first-ever vegan cookbook, *No Animal Food*, which included essays on abstinence from animal food as well as one hundred recipes.

Still, the notion of swearing off all animal products was rare in the West. Even vegetarians were skeptical of abandoning eggs and dairy. Donald Watson (1910–2005), a British woodworking teacher by trade, had other ideas. While still a child, after witnessing the violent slaughter of a pig on his uncle's farm, Watson gave up meat. By age thirty-two, he realized that imprisoning cows for their milk was no less cruel than slaughtering them, and he gave up all dairy products. He later wrote, "We can see quite plainly that our present civilization is built on the exploitation of animals, just as past civilizations were built on the exploitation of slaves, and we believe the spiritual destiny of man is such that in time he will view with abhorrence the idea that men once fed on the products of animals' bodies."[95]

In 1944, Watson, along with wife, Dorothy, and four friends, founded an organization devoted to ending mankind's dependency on animal products. As for a name, Watson suggested "vegan" because it contained the first three and last two letters of "vegetarian." "Veganism starts with vegetarianism," he later reflected, "and carries it through to its logical extension."[96] They called their new outfit the Vegan Society. It is still in existence today.

No one knows the exact number of vegans in the world, but the numbers are trending exponentially upward. According to a 2017 report, "Top Trends in Prepared Foods," 6 percent of Americans now identify as vegan, up from just 1 percent in 2014. Vegan restaurants and businesses are booming: Data commissioned from Nielsen reveals that the plant-based food industry has grown by 8.1 percent since 2017. The number of excellent animal protection organizations has also grown substantially. There isn't enough room here to mention them all, but just a few worth looking into (besides PETA) are the Animal Legal Defense Fund, Animal Rights Foundation of Florida, Compassion Over Killing, Direct Action Everywhere, Northwest Animal Rights Network (WA), Performing Animal Welfare Society, Physicians Committee for Responsible Medicine, Sea Shepherd Conservation Society, The Save Movement (a.k.a. Pig Save and Cow Save), Vegan Outreach, and ZooCheck (Canada).

Food Without Animals

The single greatest step you can take to end animal suffering is to adopt a plant-based diet. By giving up animal products, you can personally prevent the slaughter of two hundred animals each year. Fortunately, it's much easier to go vegan today than it was for Donald and Dorothy Watson in the 1940s.

Becoming vegan doesn't mean giving up your favorite foods. Whereas a half-century ago it might have required such a sacrifice, today it just means choosing new versions of them. You can find a plant-based adaptation of practically all the foods you grew up eating, from mac and cheese and ice cream cakes to "shrimp" cocktail. By choosing a vegan option, you're having your dairy-free cake and eating it, too, satisfying your taste buds while still helping animals, the environment, and your own health.

Every nutrient your body requires is easily attainable with a vegan diet. The three primary nutrients we eat are carbohydrates, fat, and protein. You need each to live, no exceptions. But animal flesh contains only two—fat and protein—and often in dangerously high amounts. Carbohydrates, which are your body's primary source of energy, are missing entirely. Most whole plant foods are abundant in healthy, unprocessed carbohydrates that provide a slow release of energy all day long. And plant fats are generally rich in omega-3 and omega-6 acids, which are associated with a reduced risk of heart disease, diabetes, and many cancers.

One of the first questions people ask vegans is, "But where do you get your protein?" This stems from a myth that plants don't contain protein. Actually, almost every food, from sirloin steak to broccoli to Twinkies, contains protein. (Broccoli has more protein per calorie than steak does.) In fact, protein malnutrition is such a rare condition that the English language had to borrow a term, *kwashiorkor*, from the Ga language of Ghana, to define it. According to the National Academy of Medicine, we need 0.8 grams of protein per kilogram of body weight. That's about 50 grams for a person who weighs 150 pounds. But on average, American males and females are taking in much more than is necessary: 102 grams and 70 grams of protein per day, respectively.

Purely plant-based diets can be so protein-packed that many highly successful athletes have switched to a plant-based diet to fuel their careers, including ultramarathon champion Scott Jurek, UFC fighter Nate Diaz, mixed martial artist Mac Danzig, tennis superstars Venus and Serena Williams and Novak Djokovic, NBA superstar Kyrie Irving, and Formula One world racing champion Lewis Hamilton.

For the rest of us, a plant-based diet is critical for a long, healthy life. Despite continuing advances in medicine, people are sicker than ever before. In 2017, the life expectancy for Americans declined for the second year in a row. More than seven out of ten Americans take at least one prescription drug, with 50 percent taking more than two and 20 percent taking at least five. From cholesterol-lowering statins to blood pressure drugs to diabetes medication, pharmacists are filling more than four billion prescriptions annually to help America deal with its myriad health problems.

Chief among them is heart disease, claiming more than six hundred thousand lives each year in the US. "There's no question that diet has a huge impact on heart disease," explains Dr. Walter Willett, professor of epidemiology and nutrition at the Harvard T. H. Chan School of Public Health. Dr. Willett points to a 2014 study published in the *Journal of Family Practice,* which followed nearly two hundred people with severe heart disease for several years. The patients were raised on the Standard American Diet—characterized by high intake of processed meat, fried foods, high-fat dairy products, refined grains, eggs, and sugary beverages. In the study, the patients were asked to cut out most animal products while adding in plant foods like whole grains, fruits, vegetables, and legumes. Of the 21 people who didn't stay with the diet, 13 experienced another cardiovascular event such as a heart attack or stroke. But for the other 177 who kept animal food out of their diet for an average of four years, just a single person had an event (a small stroke). As the study concluded: "Though current medical and surgical treatments manage coronary artery disease, they do little to prevent or stop it. Nutritional intervention, as shown in our study and others, has halted and even reversed Coronary Artery Disease."[97]

A plant-based diet can dramatically improve and even reverse type 2 diabetes. In a federally funded research study conducted by the Physicians Committee for Responsible Medicine, men and women with diabetes were randomly assigned either to a conventional "diabetes diet" that cut calories and limited carbohydrates, or to a low-fat vegan diet that included unlimited fruits, vegetables, beans, whole grains, and the myriad foods made from them. The vegan diet turned out to be three times more powerful for blood sugar control, allowing many participants to reduce or eliminate their medications. In a follow-up study, people with long-standing diabetes that was causing nerve damage, called neuropathy, were still able to improve with a vegan diet. Since then, many people have used this approach to reverse diabetes, as well as to lose weight, control cholesterol, and reduce blood pressure.

As for cancer, a joint 2013 study by Loma Linda University and the National Cancer Institute found that vegan women have a 34 percent lower rate of female-specific cancers including breast, cervical, and ovarian cancers. A meta-analysis comprising seven separate studies and nearly 125,000 participants concluded that "vegetarians have a significantly lower ischemic heart disease mortality (29%) and overall cancer incidence (18%) than nonvegetarians."[98] Meanwhile, a study of more than 63,000 participants published in the *American Journal of Clinical Nutrition* found that "the incidence of all cancers combined was lower among vegetarians than among meat eaters."[99]

In some cases, a plant-based diet can even reverse cancer. Around fifteen years ago, Dr. Dean Ornish, president and founder of the nonprofit Preventive Medicine Research Institute, recruited ninety-three men with early-stage "watch-and-wait" prostate cancer. Half the group continued with their typical diet, while the other half adopted a plant-based diet rich in vegetables, fruit, legumes, and whole grains. By the end of the study, the first group's PSA markers—an indicator of prostate cancer growth—shot up by 6 percent. But the group who adopted a plant-based diet saw their PSA markers *fall* by 4 percent, meaning their tumors shrank.

The science is clear: Avoiding animal products is one of the most significant steps you can take to avoid chronic disease later in life. But shaking an unhealthy habit takes resolve. Just as smokers are addicted to nicotine, people raised on the Standard American Diet sometimes have difficulty abstaining from the enormous amounts of salt, sugar, and fat that keep them hooked on unhealthy food.

Fortunately, today's plant-based food selections make it simple to say good-bye to animal products once and for all.

NOT YOUR FATHER'S VEGGIE BURGER

Veggie burgers and meat substitutes have long been a staple of an animal-free diet, with brands like Gardein, Field Roast, Neat Meat, Sweet Earth, Yves, and Amy's Kitchen offering vegan and vegetarian taste-alikes in grocery stores across the US. Today, there is a vegan replacement for nearly every one of your favorite foods from soy "chicken" nuggets to hummus "crab" cakes to grain-based meats. A report from MarketsandMarkets estimates that by 2023, the meat substitutes market will be valued at nearly $7 billion. While these products are tasty and popular, they were not created to replicate meat—they were created to give plant-based eaters a choice.

Enter the Beyond Burger. Debuting in May 2016, this plant-based protein-packed patty (twenty grams, to be precise) is made without gluten, antibiotics, hormones, GMOs, or cruelty. Instead, the team behind the Beyond Burger has developed their meat-y burger using pea protein and other plant-derived ingredients. It even bleeds red, thanks to beet juice. According to the burger's maker, Beyond Meat, it's created using a "proprietary system that applies heating, cooling, and pressure to align plant-proteins in the same fibrous structures that you'd find in animal proteins." In other words, it uses plant-based ingredients to mimic the structure, feel, and taste of meat—a patty that sizzles and browns on the skillet like a burger that comes from animal flesh. The company's mission is to create "mass-market solutions that perfectly replace animal protein with plant protein. We are dedicated to improving human health, positively impacting climate change, conserving natural resources and respecting animal welfare."[100]

Investors in Beyond Meat—which filed for a $100 million initial public offering at the end of 2018—include actor Leonardo DiCaprio; Twitter cofounders Evan Williams and Biz Stone; Microsoft founder Bill Gates; and even a former McDonald's CEO, Don Thompson. Their products are easy to find: Major retailers like Kroger Stores, Whole Foods, Safeway, Stop & Shop, and over five thousand grocery chains across the country already carry the Beyond Burger, and the number is growing. Restaurant chains like TGI Fridays, A&W Restaurants, and Veggie Grill feature Beyond Meat products as well. (Beyond Meat also has a line of Beyond Sausage, Beyond Chicken, and Beyond Beef Crumbles.)

If you prefer buying your plant-based meat from a market, try one of the many vegan butcher shops, including Minneapolis's The Herbivorous Butcher, which offers vegan spins on classic deli slices including hickory bacon, capicola ham, roast beef, pastrami, turkey, rib eye steak, chorizo, sausage, and jerky; or Brooklyn-based Monk's Meats, whose menu includes Seitan Steaks and Meatless Meatballs. Other plant-based butchers include The Butcher's Son (Berkeley, CA); The Very Good Butchers (British Columbia, Canada); No Evil Foods (Asheville, NC); Cena Vegan (Los Angeles, CA); Abbot's Butcher (Costa Mesa, CA); and YamChops (Toronto, Canada).

CRUELTY-FREE MEAT

In his 1932 *Popular Mechanics* essay, "Fifty Years Hence," Winston Churchill predicted, "We shall escape the absurdity of growing a whole chicken in order to eat the breast or wing, by growing these parts separately under a suitable medium."[101] Fifty years may have been too optimistic, but Churchill's prediction may finally be a reality in fewer than ten—in a manner of speaking.

For those who still crave meat but don't want to harm animals, entrepreneurs have been developing lab-produced meat—also known as in vitro, or clean meat—over the past decade. The methods vary, but the basic idea is to "grow" real meat from animal cells through tissue culture. No factory farms, transport trucks, or slaughterhouses. No leveling forests to grow feed for cattle. No pollution as their waste seeps into groundwater and into waterways. And, grown in a laboratory, there will be no *E. coli*, salmonella, or campylobacter outbreaks.

In 2013, Professor Mark Post and researchers at Maastricht University, funded by Google cofounder Sergey Brin, introduced the first lab-grown beef patty by assembling ten thousand strips of cow muscle individually grown in their lab. From this breakthrough came the company MosaMeat, which is working to "develop tissue engineering into a technology that can mass-produce affordable meat."

While that first burger cost $300,000 to produce, MosaMeat is swiftly streamlining its process and hopes to have its patty in high-end restaurants by the early 2020s, and competing with traditional supermarket meat not long after. Other producers may even beat them to the punch. Clean meat is quickly gaining backers: In a $300 million trade agreement, the Chinese government in 2017 invested in three Israeli companies—SuperMeat, Future Meat Technologies, and Meat the Future—to join in on the innovation. Eyeing the profit opportunity in clean meat, venture-capital firms, including New Crop Capital and Stray Dog Capital, have also invested millions in similar companies. As New Crop Capital partner Christopher Kerr explains, "From an investment standpoint, this is potentially a trillion-dollar market opportunity."[102]

Traditional animal food companies know change is on the horizon. In 2018, Tyson Foods, the world's second-largest processor and marketer of chicken, beef, and pork, invested in the start-up Memphis Meats, which produces meat by regenerating animal cells in large steel tanks without the need to feed, breed, and slaughter actual animals. The explosion of lab-grown foods is not limited to land animals—a company called Finless Foods is developing lab-grown fish.

Entrepreneurs are even studying ways to convert traditional animal farms into new-age cellular farms. Yaakov Nahmias, founder and chief scientist of Future Meat Technologies, plans to supply farmers with small collections of cells and the necessary equipment to grow them into chicken breasts, ribs, and ground beef. "These distributive models allow us to grow organically and essentially replace chicken coops with these bioreactors,"[103] he explained to *Fast Company* in 2018.

EGGS

There are now several brands of vegan eggs. Perhaps the best known is Follow Your Heart's VeganEgg, which is perfect for a quick breakfast scramble. Starbucks is introducing a vegan egg sandwich, and vegan egg salad is found in most health food grocery stores with a deli section. And if you want a runny yolk, there's Vegan Egg Yolk from Vegg that is, like all vegan foods, 100 percent cholesterol-free.

For baking, myriad egg replacements exist, from substitutes such as apple sauce, silken tofu, mashed bananas, and flaxseed meal to packaged egg replacements like the VeganEgg, Vegg, and Bob's Red Mill Egg Replacer. Or simply take the aquafaba from a can of chickpeas: From the Latin words *aqua* (water) and *faba* (bean), aquafaba is the leftover liquid found in the can (or from boiling dried chickpeas). Accessible and affordable, aquafaba is perfect for decadent desserts, including lemon meringue pie, pavlova, chocolate mousse, macarons, and vegan brownies.

There are countless new ways to enjoy your favorite vegan, egg-centric meals. Tofu scramble is a staple among plant-based brunch devotees. To make it, crumble up some tofu, add seasoning such as turmeric, nutritional yeast, or Indian black salt and pop it into the skillet. As for mayonnaise, which is made from egg yolks and oil, you can find it in vegan form from many vendors, such as Follow Your Heart's Vegenaise, Trader Joe's store brand, and now from Hellmann's. Or make your own by blending canola oil, soy milk, lemon juice, and ground mustard.

MILK

Plant milks have become so popular that many non-vegans prefer them to the bovine kind. A 2016 study by MarketsandMarkets found that the Dairy Alternatives Market—focusing on almond, soy, coconut, oat, rice, and hemp milks—is projected to be worth more than $14 billion by 2022. Other varieties include cashew, hazelnut, peanut, flax, pea, macadamia, pistachio, and banana. Each nondairy milk has its own particular qualities and benefits. For example, cashew milk is thick, creamy, and an excellent base for sauces; almond milk is ideal for cereal; oat milk goes well in coffee; coconut milk is perfect for curries; and rice milk lends well to desserts and drinks. Recently, environmentally sound oat milk has become so popular that it can be difficult to find, creating grumbles and moans on the internet.

CHEESE

Many people who can get by without meat, eggs, or fish draw the line at omitting cheese from their diet. As researchers have shown, this may well result from cheese containing concentrated casomorphins, the same chemicals that get people hooked on other drugs, including heroin. Luckily, plenty of alternatives can take its place.

Early attempts at faux cheese were usually less than cheesy. Today myriad companies now re-create—and even surpass—dairy-based cheeses. Some of the most widely available ones include Daiya, Follow Your Heart, Chao, Kite Hill, and Miyoko's—all available in Whole Foods and other grocery stores nationwide. For cost-conscious shoppers, many supermarkets also offer generic brand nondairy cheeses.

Whether you're craving pizza, nachos, or grilled cheese, vegan cheese is now so versatile that you can create almost any dish with the same creamy and stretchy texture as dairy cheeses. More remarkable: Newly created artisanal cheeses that rival the consistency and taste of fancier dairy cheeses are now commonplace as well. For example, the Kite Hill brand makes vegan cream cheeses, soft cheeses, and hard cheeses using classic cheese-making methods. Renowned vegan chef Tal Ronnen is one of the cofounders, as is Jean Prevot, who has overseen operations at leading cheese-making facilities in the US and France—where you can get several vegan traditionally French cheeses. Other popular brands include Ste Martaen, Treeline, Dr. Cow, Cheezehound (which makes an extraordinary blue cheese), and Violife. There are even brick-and-mortar stores devoted to vegan cheeses, such as Riverdel in Brooklyn and the legendary Portland, Oregon, vegan cheese outfit Vtopia, which offers everything from goat cheese to mozzarella.

You can also easily create your own vegan cheese at home using simple ingredients you might already have in your pantry, usually raw cashews, nutritional yeast, nondairy milk, and miso. There are countless recipes online. Meanwhile, pizza lovers can find plant-based pies from brands such as Daiya, Amy's, Tofurky, BOLD Organics, and Ian's; many vegan pizzerias are popping up across the country as well. Many traditional pizzerias also offer vegan cheese pizzas, too.

BUTTER

Myriad vegan alternatives to dairy butter are now sold in the refrigerator cases of almost every market. For the most buttery taste, look for brands like Earth Balance and I Can't Believe It's Not Butter!, which recently released an "It's Vegan" product. These buttery spreads are made using a combination of plant-based oils and water, with 40 percent fewer calories and 70 percent less saturated fat than butter. Some specialty options include Miyoko's Creamery European Style Cultured Vegan Butter, made of coconut oil, water, cashews, sunflower oil, and sea salt. Coconut butter can make a wonderful substitute, with brands like Nutiva and Ellyndale Organics found in most health food stores. If you're feeling ambitious, you can even take a stab at making your own out of aquafaba or coconut oil, with recipes widely available online.

YOGURT

For some people, yogurt is the lifeblood of their morning. No need to go back to sleep. There are many flavors of delicious vegan yogurts on offer now, and they contain all the creaminess, and probiotics, of dairy yogurt. For example, Anita's Yogurt, a Brooklyn, NY–based nondairy yogurt brand, uses coconut milk, coconut water, and probiotic cultures to create a thick and rich yogurt. Brands like Kite Hill and Forager employ almonds, cashews, and other nuts to create a decadent texture and taste, while So Delicious brand and Trader Joe's use nuts, coconut milk, as well as soy-based products.

DESSERT

Vegan ice cream options, once rare, are now commonplace, with new brands cropping up constantly. Nondairy-only ice cream companies like NadaMoo!, Coconut Bliss, Tofutti, and So Delicious are staples of the freezer aisle. At the same time, old standbys like Ben & Jerry's, Breyer's, and Häagen-Dazs have introduced their own lines of nondairy ice cream. Artisan ice cream maker Van Leeuwen also has a delicious line of vegan ice creams with flavors including mint chip, cookie crumble strawberry jam, and chocolate chip cookie dough.

Plant-based ice creams typically use different kinds of nondairy milks as bases, such as soy, coconut, cashew, almond, and hemp. If your local ice cream shop doesn't carry nondairy ice cream, ask that they stock it, and meanwhile opt for sorbet, which is almost always dairy-free—just inquire to be on the safe side.

When switching to a plant-based diet, many people often confront the terrifying question: "But . . . is chocolate vegan?" The answer is . . .

often. And some of the most scrumptious dark chocolates and chocolate truffles in the world are vegan as well.

Most milk chocolate contains dairy milk of course, but not all. Milk chocolate can also be plant-based, with many manufacturers opting for coconut and rice milk. Keep a lookout for Charm School's Coconut Milk Chocolate, Ricemilk Chocolate from Enjoy Life, and Raaka Chocolate's Coconut Milk bar. Even international favorites like Nutella can find a vegan counterpart in Nutiva's Organic Dark Hazelnut Spread or Justin's Chocolate Hazelnut Butter Blend.

Check labels for hidden animal products, especially whey and casein. Low-grade chocolate often contains animal by-products such as lecithin and albumin. (Contrary to how it sounds, cocoa butter is vegan, however.) As a general rule of thumb, look for chocolate with a high percentage of cacao—ideally, over 70 percent. The higher the percentage, the purer the bar. Real chocolate comes from the cacao tree and its seeds, which are roasted and ground. (The Latin term *Theobroma cacao* literally means "food of the gods.") Other products such as cane sugar, cocoa butter, vanilla, and soy lecithin are added to create the familiar chocolatey taste. The good news is that most dark chocolate products are already vegan, as well as baking chocolate and cocoa powder. Even semisweet chocolate chips are often vegan. Some excellent, widely available dark chocolate bars: Lindt Excellence Dark Chocolate, Trader Joe's Dark Chocolate Bars, Theo Chocolate, and the Endangered Species Chocolate Bar series. In the UK, it's hard to beat Booja Booja's Gourmet Selection Chocolate Truffles.

Lurking Animal Ingredients

Even the most unsuspecting products may well contain animal products. One common culprit is gelatin, found in products such as most gummies, vitamins, marshmallows, shampoos, yogurts, ice cream, fruit gelatin, Jell-O, puddings, and as a thickener in countless other products. Gelatin is a protein obtained by boiling skin, tendons, ligaments, or even bones, usually from cows or pigs. Fortunately, gelatin can easily be replaced in most recipes with ingredients like fruit pectin, agar-agar, guar gum (vegetable gum), and carrageenan. Many favorite gummy candies are already vegan, including Sour Patch Kids, Swedish Fish, Skittles, Dots Gumdrops, and Annie's Organic Bunny Fruit Snacks. If you can't imagine a campfire without roasted marshmallows, try vegan ones from companies like Dandies and Trader Joe's that offer delicious, gooey marshmallows.

A similarly ubiquitous animal ingredient is isinglass, a pure form of gelatin made from the air bladders of fish, used as a clarifying agent in beers, wine, and other products. Major beer brands such as Guinness, Pabst Blue Ribbon, and Samuel Adams have made the switch to using alternative clarifying methods, but many beers still rely on isinglass. For a list of beer and wine made without the use of animal products, check out www.barnivore.com.

Even sugar can be processed with animal bone char, which acts as a decolorizing filter. Typically, bone char is made from the bones of cattle from Afghanistan, Argentina, India, and Pakistan. The bones are sold to traders in Scotland, Egypt, and Brazil, who then sell them to the US sugar industry. Cane sugar is often processed with bones, but there are many sugars on the market that are not. Turbinado, demerara, and muscovado sugars are never filtered through bone char. Nor are beet and coconut sugars, and certified-organic cane sugar.

Winnie the Pooh loved honey, but that's no reason to eat it. Honey is another product that harms and commodifies animals—in this case, bees, who are fascinating, intelligent, communicative animals. Practices such as cutting off the queen bee's wings, artificial insemination, and mass execution of hives, even burning the hives with the bees in them, are common in the honey industry. Instead of honey, there are countless natural replacements on the market, including maple syrup, agave nectar, coconut nectar, molasses, rice syrup, sorghum, Sucanat, barley malt, brown rice syrup, and date paste. Many companies are developing honey that tastes incredibly close to the real thing, but without taking it from the animals who work so hard to produce it. For example, Bee Free Honee offers honey made from apples. According to the brand, one bottle of Bee Free Honee helps to save 7,500 bees.

RESTAURANTS AND TAKEOUT

Gone are the days when dining out as a vegan meant begging for a salad without cheese or a pasta dish without eggs, as thousands of new vegan restaurants have opened their doors around the world, not that you can't get great vegan food in almost any ethnic restaurant, from Indian to Szechuan, Italian (including pasta e fagioli [if no chicken stock], pasta marinara, pasta arrabbiata), Japanese (avocado, cucumber, and daikon sushi), Korean (vegetable bibimbap), and Mexican (make sure the beans are not cooked with lard). If you like wholesome, fresh market vegetables, properly cooked, perhaps surprisingly, almost any steak house, including Ruth's Chris, will serve you well-selected, steamed, garlicy spinach, baked potatoes, mushrooms, grilled tomatoes, asparagus, and more.

The fast-growing chain Veggie Grill—with no meat, dairy, eggs, cholesterol, or animal fat in their products—operates some thirty restaurants nationwide and has announced plans for national expansion. The fast-casual chain By Chloe has rapidly expanded from its original New York City location, with restaurants in Boston, Providence, Los Angeles, and London and plans for many more. By Chloe's entirely vegan menu features locally sourced ingredients prepared fresh daily.

Vegan food has also made a substantial splash in the culinary world, from Michelin-rated restaurants to James Beard Award–winning plant-based chefs to vegan food trucks. Apps like HappyCow help you discover plant-based restaurants wherever you may travel. Some of the more renowned vegan restaurants include Blossoming Lotus in Portland, Oregon; Bouldin Creek Café, a popular diner and coffeehouse in Austin, Texas; Los Angeles's Bulan Thai, which serves decadent vegetized takes on traditional Thai dishes; Brooklyn's Bunna Cafe, a vegan spin on Ethiopian cuisine; Gracias Madre, the Bay Area's beloved Mexican outpost; and the all-vegan, comfort food–serving Chicago Diner and Ground Control, famous for its portabella-nugget-stuffed po'boys. This list represents only a small fraction of the excellent new restaurants serving vegan food.

These days it's even easy to eat vegan at nationwide chains such as Chipotle (try their sofritas, a sort of vegan "pork"), TGI Fridays, Taco Bell (bean tacos and burritos, hold the cheese), Burger King, White Castle, and Wendy's, which now offer several vegan options at every meal.

In the last several years, a score of vegan meal kits and vegan home delivery services have entered the scene, including Purple Carrot, Veestro, MamaSezz, Healthy Chef Creations, The Vegan Garden, Paleta, Vegin' Out, Kitchen Verde, Takeout Kit, and Sun Basket. Major meal kit services like Blue Apron and Plated also offer vegan options.

Actions You Can Take

Ever more studies confirm that a whole-food, low-oil vegan diet is one of the best ways to improve your health, as well as save animal lives.

Luckily, as noted above, going vegan is a snap. With a wealth of simple, delicious recipes available on the internet and vegan taste-alikes stocked in every grocery store, you can begin making positive changes today. Almost anything can be veganized; for example, at breakfast, swap your bacon and eggs for oatmeal and fruit or scrambled tofu and veggie bacon. Introduce salads at lunch, or choose a hummus wrap or bean tacos, and veggie burgers instead of beef ones. When cooking dinner, you might stick initially to easy recipes like vegan lasagna or hearty veggie stew, even baked potatoes with steamed broccoli and soy cheese toppings, or open a can of vegan soup, pop a vegan pizza into the oven, or put a frozen vegan meal like Thai rice "chicken" or vegan mac and cashew cheese into the microwave.

Don't stop there! You have the opportunity to become an ambassador for the vegan movement. Here are many ways to become that ambassador in your community:

HELP DISPEL MYTHS

Be prepared to dispel some of the most ridiculous, but common, myths about plant-based eating. Here are three:

Vegans don't get enough protein. This is one of the most pervasive myths because many people mistakenly associate protein only with meat. Here are the salient statistics: Every single plant food has protein. Fewer than 3 percent of American adults are protein deficient, most have way too much protein in their diets. On average, even vegans still eat 70 percent more protein than they need. Most official nutrition organizations recommend a modest protein intake, such as 0.8 grams per kilogram of body weight, or 0.36 grams per pound. This amounts to about 56 grams per day for the average sedentary man (that's about 2 ounces), or 53 grams for a woman. To determine your RDA for protein, you can multiply your weight in pounds by 0.36, or try this handy site: https://fnic.nal.usda.gov/fnic/dri-calculator.

Growing children should not be raised vegan. It's pure mythology that children need high amounts of fat and protein to fuel their rapidly expanding bodies. Large-scale studies have shown that children raised on a vegan diet grow to be about an inch taller, on average, than their meat-eating peers. In addition, the latest science reveals that the most deadly diseases begin affecting the body much earlier than previously thought. For example, the beta-amyloid plaques associated with Alzheimer's disease begin tangling brain cells decades before the first memory-loss symptoms appear. Studies have even shown that fatty streaks in blood vessels—the first stage of heart disease—were found in nearly all American children studied under age ten. As the Physicians Committee for Responsible Medicine explains: "Children who acquire a taste for chicken nuggets, roast beef, and French fries today are the cancer patients, heart patients, and diabetes patients of tomorrow."[104]

Eating vegan is expensive. While trendy (and pricey) vegan restaurants are certainly becoming more popular, it's easy as tofu cream pie to eat vegan on a budget. Staples such as rice, potatoes, beans (topped with salsa!), and pasta are cheap and can keep in your pantry for long periods of time. There are numerous ways to prepare them and sauces to put on them that are also not expensive at all. While organic produce is ideal, conventional supermarket produce is inexpensive. (Just be sure to wash all produce thoroughly.) Frozen fruit and vegetables also maintain their nutrients indefinitely and are an excellent choice for budget-conscious shoppers who buy in bulk.

ASK RESTAURANTS FOR VEGAN MENU OPTIONS

The majority of restaurants are responding to customer demand by offering vegan options—nearly every place will try to accommodate their customers. But what happens when there is truly nothing suitable on the menu? More often than not, your server will be happy to help and the cook may feel excited to create something new. Be sure to tip well, thank the restaurant afterward, and show them some love on social media. Ask that they consider including vegan selections on the menu in the future, and even make recommendations. Restaurants are businesses like any other, and more vegan choices will mean more revenue. If you're at any coffee shop, ask for soy or almond milk, even if you know the answer is "no." Always be polite, but help show local businesses what customers want.

FIND A DOCTOR SPECIALIZING IN VEGAN EATING

Doctors used to smoke and appear in TV commercials touting low-tar cigarettes. Today, few still smoke, but many are meat and dairy eaters. Unfortunately, barely a quarter of medical schools offer even one course on nutrition. For those that do, the typical training is just twenty-five hours for the entire four-year program, which means that many doctors, especially those who trained years ago, are not aware of research showing how a vegan diet can help prevent or reverse many of today's leading causes of death.

Be prepared for pushback when you consult with your doctor as you make the switch to a vegan diet. Some people actually say: "I thought about cutting out animal products, but my doctor said it wouldn't help." Today's cutting-edge surgeries and drugs are certainly impressive and can treat conditions once considered a death sentence, but preventing chronic disease through nutrition remains the key and doesn't come with a laundry list of awful side effects. Don't be afraid to ask your doctor questions and then to check his or her answers. Don't be afraid to find a new doctor. If you do look for one, visit www.plantbaseddoctors .org for a list of physicians who incorporate plant-based nutrition in their practice.

SOCIAL MEDIA

Even if you don't consider yourself an activist in the traditional sense, you can help spread the positive message of vegan eating through social media. Emphasize recipes that are quick and easy. Take pictures of your dishes and post them to Facebook, Instagram, and Pinterest. Use high-quality photos that do justice to your dazzling selections and creations. Make sure those brilliant-yellow summer squashes and fire truck–red bell peppers shine.

COOK FOR YOUR FRIENDS, FAMILY, AND COLLEAGUES

Perhaps the best way to become an ambassador for vegan foods is to cook for everyone you know. Prove to them that fruits, vegetables, legumes, and whole grains are more delicious than animal body parts and secretions.

If you are cooking for a particularly skeptical crowd, stick to their old favorites . . . with a plant-based twist. Pizza can be just as delicious with sautéed vegetables, olive oil, and "parmesan" cheese using blended cashews, nutritional yeast, and salt. For Super Bowl parties, think BBQ wings from Gardein, home-style tenders from Beyond Meat, or make your own wings using wheat gluten, tahini, and nutritional yeast. Go out of your way to make plant-based versions of your guests' favorite dishes—for many people, it only takes one meal, like a vegan Wellington or a cheesy macaroni casserole to be hooked on healthy, cruelty-free eating for life.

Afterword

Thank you for reading this book, which could only include a small fraction of the torrent of new studies about animals and their amazing talents, as well as the constantly growing stream of new products that will help you be kind to all of them. Hopefully, it has jump-started your personal journey. Many more discoveries lie ahead, including vegan vacation companies, vegan summer camps, vegan hotels, vegan baby clothes and children's books, vegan chocolate champagne bottles to send as congratulation gifts, and classes in everything from vegan yoga (try www.jivamukti.com) to dating sites like veggieconnection .com—and even vegan remedies for treating the symptoms of menopause. PETA and other groups offer vegan mentors to whom you can turn in a moment of indecision or confusion, perhaps when you are staring at a label and wondering if that "free-range" egg is really humane, or when you want to know where lanolin comes from, or when you've decided how great it would be to buy vegan ballet slippers or work boots.

As you grow into that kind of person who actively respects animals rather than inadvertently hurting them, never think you are alone, even if you haven't joined a vegan meet-up group. Being vegan has never been more effortless and more popular. So now that you know what to do, it's time to get cracking and educate friends and family, the people you work with—actually, everyone you know, from acquaintances in the dog park to the other customers you meet in the grocery store. Most people want to hear about new foods (and certainly to sample them), to share new recipes, learn about new fabrics, hear about great moisturizers and, yes, even things like floor cleaners that are tested on human skin, not in rabbits' eyes.

People are hungry for information on the latest anything. Enhance their lives by introducing them to all things vegan, from shaving and/ or artists' brushes made from synthetics that allow badgers to keep their hair to vegan sportswear that is lighter than real fleece and down, to vegan meals that could add seven or more years to their lives. (And don't feel you have to always announce right away that what you are serving is vegan. Linda McCartney veganized her husband, Paul, by serving him "meaty" dishes like spaghetti Bolognese and vegan tartar sauce–covered "fish" sticks that she didn't tell him weren't made from animals.)

Animals need all the friends they can get. You are one of them. Most people don't realize how much difference they are making by making kind choices, but often those choices can mean the difference between life and death for animals of all types. Once your eyes start to open, and you see what goes on behind the scenes, it is vital not to try to turn away but, as Tolstoy said, to come closer and to try to help. By living a vegan life, by urging others to do the same, you will not only help this dog, and that elephant, and this cricket, and that chicken, but be part of a revolution in human behavior that one day will be the norm. Congratulations on joining the team.

Acknowledgments

Ingrid: To all the animals who have enriched my life and increased my understanding of them, even in passing; and to everyone who has ever lifted a finger, said a word, stepped up, made a donation, or otherwise helped animals who needed someone to care; and to the PETA staff and volunteers whose contributions found their way into this book.

Gene: Thanks go to the four-legged friends, especially Toby, Julia, and Gus; and the two-legged friends, most of all Nick Bromley, as well as Miranda Spencer, Andy Kifer, and Jaime Mishkin.

We are both grateful for the supportive efforts of our agents, John Maas at Park & Fine Literary and Media, and the team at Simon & Schuster, especially our editor, Jonathan Cox, as well as Jonathan Karp, Emily Simonson, Megan Hogan, Sonja Singleton, Carly Loman, Brigid Black, Kimberly Goldstein, Annie Craig, Ryan Raphael, Heidi Meier, and Stephen Bedford.

Selected Sources

Introduction

Jacobson, Rebecca A. "Slime Molds: No Brains, No Feet, No Problem."
PBS News Hour, April 5, 2012. https://www.pbs.org/newshour/science
/the-sublime-slime-mold.

Koerth-Baker, Maggie. "Humans Are Dumb at Figuring Out How Smart
Animals Are." *FiveThirtyEight,* May 18, 2018. https://fivethirtyeight.com
/features/humans-are-dumb-at-figuring-out-how-smart-animals-are/.

SECTION I

The Mysteries of Navigation

Greenwood, Veronique. "How a Kitty Walked 200 Miles Home: The Science of
Your Cat's Inner Compass." *Time,* February 11, 2013. http://science.time
.com/2013/02/11/the-mystery-of-the-geolocating-cat/.

HowStuffWorks. "6 Pets that Traveled Long Distances to Get Home." https://
animals.howstuffworks.com/pets/pet-travel/6-pets-that-traveled-long
-distances-to-get-home2.htm.

Winged Navigation

Avakian, Talia. "This Stork Flies Over 8,000 Miles Every Spring to Visit His
True Love." *Travel + Leisure,* April 23, 2018. https://www.travelandleisure
.com/travel-news/stork-south-africa-klepetan-malena.

https://www.sciencealert.com/birds-see-magnetic-fields-cryptochrome-cry4
-photoreceptor-2018.

"Flight, Food and Echolocation." *Bat Conservation Trust.* http://www.bats.org
.uk/pages/echolocation.html.

Hopkin, Michael. "Homing Pigeons Reveal True Magnetism." *Nature,*
November 24, 2004. https://www.nature.com/news/2004/041122/full
/news041122-7.html.

"How Birds Fly." *Journey North.* http://www.learner.org/jnorth/tm/FlightLesson
.html.

Notopoulos, Katie. "The Heartwarming Story of Cher Ami, The Pigeon Who
Saved 200 American Soldiers." *BuzzFeed,* January 3, 2014. https://www
.buzzfeed.com/katienotopoulos/the-heartwarming-story-of-cher-ami-the
-pigeon-who-saved-200.

https://www.nytimes.com/2018/07/03/science/owls-vision-brain.html.

Pappas, Stephanie. "Are Bats Really Blind?" *Live Science,* September 6, 2016.
https://www.livescience.com/55986-are-bats-really-blind.html.

Braving the Seas

Bergamin, Alessandra. "Why Do Pacific Salmon Die After Spawning?" *Bay
Nature,* November 21, 2013. https://baynature.org/2013/11/21/pacific
-salmon-die-spawning/.

Emerson, Sarah. "We Now Know Why Great White Sharks Gather in a
Mysterious Ocean Void." *Motherboard,* September 18, 2018. https://mother
board.vice.com/en_us/article/7xjbd9/we-now-know-why-great-white
-sharks-visit-the-mysterious-white-shark-cafe.

Geggel, Laura. "Gray Whale Breaks Mammal Migration Record." *Live Science,*
April 14, 2015. https://www.livescience.com/50487-western-gray-whale
-migration.html.

Mott, Cody, and Michael Salmon. "Sun Compass Orientation by Juvenile Green
Sea Turtles (*Chelonia mydas*)." *Chelonian Conservation and Biology* 10: 1
(2011): 73–81.

Osborne, Hannah. "A Fish Just Passed a Test of Self-Awareness by Recognizing
Itself in a Mirror." *Newsweek,* September 4, 2018. https://www.newsweek
.com/fish-passes-self-awareness-test-mirror-recognition-1104273.

"Pacific Salmon, (*Oncorhynchus spp.*)." *U.S. Fish & Wildlife Service.* https://www
.fws.gov/species/species_accounts/bio_salm.html.

Tiny Trips

Anderson, Charles. "Dragonflies That Fly Across Oceans." *TED.* https://www
.ted.com/talks/charles_anderson_discovers_dragonflies_that_cross_oceans
/transcript.

Bittel, Jason. "Monarch Butterflies Migrate 3,000 Miles—Here's How."
National Geographic, October 17, 2017. https://news.nationalgeographic
.com/2017/10/monarch-butterfly-migration/.

Castro, Joseph. "Wow! Dung Beetles Navigate by the Stars." *Live Science,* January
24, 2013. https://www.livescience.com/26557-dung-beetles-navigate-stars.html.

"Cognitive Dissonance." *Economist,* June 12, 2014. https://www.economist.com
/blogs/babbage/2014/06/how-bees-navigate.

Ghosh, Pallab. "Snails 'Have a Homing Instinct.'" *BBC News,* August 3, 2010.
https://www.bbc.com/news/science-environment-10856523.

Smith, Joe. "Dragonfly Migration: A Mystery Citizen Scientists Can Help Solve." *Cool
Green Science,* September 16, 2013. https://blog.nature.org/science/2013/09/16
/dragonfly-migration-a-mystery-citizen-scientists-can-help-solve/.

Williams, Sarah. "Pythons Have Surprising Homing Ability, New Snake
Navigation Study Finds (VIDEO)." *Huffington Post,* March 23, 2014.
https://www.huffingtonpost.com/2014/03/23/python-homing-snake
-navigation-study_n_5017132.html.

Young, Stephen. "Science: How Hoppers Keep Their Bearings on the Beach."
NewScientist, April 29, 1989. https://www.newscientist.com/article/mg1221
6624-600-science-how-hoppers-keep-their-bearings-on-the-beach.

Lumbering on Land

Graham, Sarah. "Internal Compass Helps Blind Mole Rat Find Its Way." *Scientific American,* January 20, 2004. https://www.scientificamerican.com/article
/internal-compass-helps-bl/.

"Great Wildebeest Migration." *Maasai Mar.* http://www.maasaimara.com
/entries/great-wildebeest-migration-maasai-mara.

Helmuth, Laura. "Saving Mali's Migratory Elephants." *Smithsonian Magazine,*
July 2015. https://www.smithsonianmag.com/science-nature/saving-malis
-migratory-elephants-74522858/.

Ishida, Yasuk, Peter Van Coeverden de Groot, Keith Leggett, Andrea Putnam,
Virginia Fox, Jesse Lai, Peter Boag, Nicholas Georgiadis, and Alfred Roca.

"Genetic connectivity across marginal habitats: the elephants of the Namib Desert." *Ecology and Evolution* 6: 17 (2016): 6189–201.

Natural World Safaris. "The Caribou Migration." *Natural World Safaris.* https://www.naturalworldsafaris.com/experiences/natures-great-events/caribou-migration-in-arctic-canada.

The Channels of Communication

Samhita, Laasya, and Hans Gros. "The 'Clever Hans Phenomenon' Revisited." *Communicative & Integrative Biology* 6: 6 (2013): e27122.

Canine Communication

Hare, Brian. "Opinion: We Didn't Domesticate Dogs. They Domesticated Us." *National Geographic,* March 3, 2013. https://news.nationalgeographic.com/news/2013/03/130302-dog-domestic-evolution-science-wolf-wolves-human/.

Hare, Brian, and Vanessa Woods. "What Are Dogs Saying When They Bark? [Excerpt]." *Scientific American,* February 8, 2013. https://www.scientificamerican.com/article/what-are-dogs-saying-when-they-bark/.

International Wolf Center. "How Do Wolves Say Hello?" http://www.wolf.org/wolf-info/basic-wolf-info/biology-and-behavior/communication/.

Animals Who Read

CBS News. https://www.cbsnews.com/news/are-we-smart-enough-to-measure-animal-intelligence/.

Yirka, Bob. "Horses Found Able to Use Symbols to Convey Their Desire for a Blanket." *Phys.org,* September 26, 2016. https://phys.org/news/2016-09-horses-convey-desire-blanket.html?utm_source=nwletter&utm_medium=email&utm_campaign=daily-nwletter.

The Talk of the Farm

Grillo, Robert. "A Revolution in Our Understanding of Chicken Behavior." *Free From Harm,* February 7, 2014. https://freefromharm.org/chicken-behavior-an-overview-of-recent-science/.

Young, Rosamund. *The Secret Life of Cows*. London: Faber & Faber, 2018.
    University of Lincoln. "It's not just a grunt: Pigs really do have something
    to say." *ScienceDaily*, June 29, 2016. www.sciencedaily.com/releases/2016
    /06/160629100349.htm.

Deep-Sea Communication

Herzing, Denise. "Could We Speak the Language of Dolphins?" *TED*. https://
    www.ted.com/talks/denise_herzing_could_we_speak_the_language_of
    _dolphins/transcript.
Manier, Jeremy. "Dolphin Cognition Fuels Discovery." The University of
    Chicago. https://www.uchicago.edu/features/dolphin_cognition_fuels
    _discovery/.
National Geographic. "Blue Whales and Communication." March 26, 2011.
    http://www.nationalgeographic.com.au/science/blue-whales-and-communi
    cation.aspx.
Schneider, Caitlin. "How Scientists Discovered the Song of the Humpback
    Whale." *Mental Floss*, August 11, 2015. http://mentalfloss.com
    /article/67250/how-scientists-discovered-song-humpback-whale.
Weisberger, Mindy. "Frogs 'Talk' Using Complex Signals." *Live Science*, January
    13, 2016. https://www.livescience.com/53358-brazilian-frogs-complex
    -communication.html.

Signing Primates

Gill, Victoria. "Chimpanzee Language: Communication Gestures
    Translated." *BBC*, July 4, 2014. http://www.bbc.com/news/science
    -environment-28023630.
———. "Chimpanzees' 66 Gestures Revealed." *BBC*, May 5, 2011. http://news
    .bbc.co.uk/earth/hi/earth_news/newsid_9475000/9475408.stm.
Hale, Benjamin. "The Sad Story of Nim Chimpsky." *Dissent Magazine*, August
    17, 2011. https://www.dissentmagazine.org/online_articles/the-sad-story-of
    -nim-chimpsky.
Lents, Nathan. "Koko, Washoe, and Kanzi: Three Apes with Human Vocabulary."
    The Human Evolution Blog, July 28, 2015. https://thehumanevolutionblog
    .com/2015/07/28/koko-washoe-and-kanzi-three-apes-with-human-vocab
    ulary/.

A Symphony in the Sky

Callaway, Ewen. "Alex the Parrot's Posthumous Paper Shows his Mathematical Genius." *Scientific American,* February 21, 2012. https://www.scientificam erican.com/article/alex-parrot-posthumous-paper-mathematical-genius/.

Carey, Benedict. "Alex, a Parrot Who Had a Way With Words, Dies." *New York Times,* September 10, 2007. http://www.nytimes.com/2007/09/10 /science/10cnd-parrot.html.

Chandler, David. "Farewell to a Famous Parrot." *Nature,* September 11, 2007. https://www.nature.com/news/2007/070910/full/news070910-4.html.

Feltman, Rachel. "These Birds Use a Linguistic Rule Thought to be Unique to Humans." *Washington Post,* March 8, 2016. https://www.washingtonpost.com /news/speaking-of-science/wp/2016/03/08/these-birds-use-a-linguistic-rule -thought-to-be-unique-to-humans/?utm_term=.484c8b4dd8c2.

McClendon, Russell. "Wild Birds Communicate and Collaborate with Humans, Study Confirms." *Mother Nature Network,* July 22, 2016. https://www.mnn .com/earth-matters/animals/blogs/wild-birds-communicate-and-collab orate-humans-study-confirms.

Mendelson, Zoe. "Traffic Is Changing How City Birds Sing." *Next City,* February 19, 2016. https://nextcity.org/daily/entry/noise-pollution-bird -calls-san-francisco.

PLOS. "Goffin's cockatoos can create and manipulate novel tools: Cockatoos adjust length, but not width, when making their cardboard tools." *ScienceDaily*, November 7, 2018. www.sciencedaily.com/releases /2018/11/181107172905.htm.

University of Zurich. "Bird communication: Chirping with syntax." *ScienceDaily,* March 8, 2016. www.sciencedaily.com/releases/2016/03/160308134748.htm.

Parsing the Language of the Animal Kingdom

BT. "Animals are busy having conversations all around us, say scientists." June 6, 2018. http://home.bt.com/news/science-news/animals-are-busy-having -conversations-all-around-us-say-scientists-11364276341883.

Irish Examiner. "Cheetahs don't roar . . . but the adorable noise they do make will surprise you." April 4, 2018. https://www.irishexaminer.com/breakingnews /discover/cheetahs-dont-roar-but-the-adorable-noises-they-do-make-will -surprise-you-835718.html.

Meeri, Kim. "Chirps, whistles, clicks: Do any animals have a true 'language'?"

Washington Post, August 22, 2014. https://www.washingtonpost.com/news
/speaking-of-science/wp/2014/08/22/chirps-whistles-clicks-do-any
-animals-have-a-true-language/?noredirect=on&utm_term=.3749a1cd837b.

The Intricacies of Love

Economist. "Animals think, therefore . . ." https://www.economist.com/news
/essays/21676961-inner-lives-animals-are-hard-study-there-evidence-they
-may-be-lot-richer-science-once-thought.
Sullivan, Ashley. "Wounda: The Amazing Story of the Chimp Behind the Hug
with Dr. Jane Goodall." *The Jane Goodall Institute,* November 21, 2017.
http://news.janegoodall.org/2017/11/21/tchimpounga-chimpanzee-of-the
-month-wounda/.

Choosing a Mate

Bates, Mary. "What's This Mysterious Circle on the Seafloor?" *National
Geographic,* August 15, 2013. https://blog.nationalgeographic.org
/2013/08/15/whats-this-mysterious-circle-on-the-seafloor/.
Bekoff, Marc. *The Emotional Lives of Animals.* Novato: New World Library, 2007.
Castro, Joseph. "Animal Sex: How Sea Turtles Do It." *Live Science,* May 5, 2014.
https://www.livescience.com/45354-animal-sex-sea-turtles.html.
Gorvett, Zaria. "If you think penguins are cute and cuddly, you're wrong." *BBC,*
December 23, 2015. http://www.bbc.com/earth/story/20151223-if-you
-think-penguins-are-cute-and-cuddly-youre-wrong.
National Audubon Society. "Masked Booby." https://www.audubon.org/field
-guide/bird/masked-booby.
National Ocean Service. "What causes a sea turtle to be born male or female?"
https://oceanservice.noaa.gov/facts/temperature-dependent.html.
Observations of Animal Behaviour. "The Enchanting Pebble," April 11, 2013. http://
blog.nus.edu.sg/lsm1303student2013/2013/04/11/the-enchanting-pebble/.
Pomeroy, Ross. "7 Facts You Didn't Know About Elephant Trunk." *RealClear-
Science,* October 14, 2013. https://www.realclearscience.com/blog/2013/10
/the-most-amazing-appendage-in-the-world.html.
Saad, Gad. "We're just like animals when it comes to finding a date." *Wired,*
March 30, 2016. http://www.wired.co.uk/article/human-animal-behaviour
-courtship-displays-evolutionary-psychology.

Fidelity

Crane, Louise. "The truth about swans." *BBC,* December 4, 2014. http://www
.bbc.com/earth/story/20141204-the-truth-about-swans.

Guzman, Sandra. "Think Pigeons Are a Nuisance? Meet New York City's
Pigeon Whisperer." *NBC News,* October 16, 2015. https://www.nbcnews
.com/news/latino/pigeons-nuisance-meet-new-york-city-s-pigeon
-whisperer-n445506.

Incrediblebirds. "Divorces in Birds." http://incrediblebirds.com/sex-life-birds
-also-have-penises/divorces-in-birds/.

Keim, Brandon. "What Pigeons Teach Us About Love." *Nautilus,* January 4,
2018. http://nautil.us/issue/56/perspective/what-pigeons-teach-us-about
-love-rp.

Krulwich, Robert. "Introducing A Divorce Rate For Birds, And Guess Which
Bird Never, Ever Divorces?" *NPR,* April 22, 2014. https://www.npr.org
/sections/krulwich/2014/04/22/305582368/introducing-a-divorce-rate-for
-birds-and-guess-which-bird-never-ever-divorce.

Strycker, Noah. *The Thing with Feathers.* New York: Riverhead Books, 2014.

Tucker, Abigail. "What Can Rodents Tell Us About Why Humans Love?"
Smithsonian Magazine, February 2014. https://www.smithsonianmag.com
/science-nature/what-can-rodents-tell-us-about-why-humans-love
-180949441/.

Motherly Love

Business Report. "Slimy leeches are devoted parents." July 2, 2004. https://www
.iol.co.za/business-report/technology/slimy-leeches-are-devoted-parents
-216206.

Hamilton, Kristy. "Why You Should Never Squash a Spider." *IFLScience,* April
24, 2015. https://www.iflscience.com/plants-and-animals/mother-wolf
-spider-squashed-hundreds-babies-scatter/.

Hogenboom, Melissa. "Are there any homosexual animals?" *BBC,* February
6, 2015. http://www.bbc.com/earth/story/20150206-are-there-any
-homosexual-animals.

Jenkins, Andrew. "The Protective Mouthbrooding Fish." *PADI,* July 30, 2014.
https://www2.padi.com/blog/2014/07/30/creature-feature-the-protective
-mouth-brooding-fish/.

Yin, Steph. "Nearly a Decade Nursing? Study Pierces Orangutans' Mother–Child Bond." *New York Times,* May 17, 2017. https://www.nytimes.com/2017/05/17/science/orangutans-weaning-nursing.html.

Young, Rosamund. *The Secret Life of Cows.* London: Faber & Faber, 2018.

Grief and Mourning

Bekoff, Marc. "Grief in animals: It's arrogant to think we're the only animals who mourn." *Psychology Today,* October 29, 2009. https://www.psychologytoday.com/us/blog/animal-emotions/200910/grief-in-animals-its-arrogant-think-were-the-only-animals-who-mourn.

Brogaard, Berit. "Can Animals Love?" *Psychology Today,* February 24, 2014. https://www.psychologytoday.com/us/blog/the-mysteries-love/201402/can-animals-love.

Buzhardt, Lynn. "Do Dogs Mourn?" *VCA.* https://vcahospitals.com/know-your-pet/do-dogs-mourn.

Dooren, Thom van. *Flight Ways, Life and Loss at the Edge of Extinction.* New York: Columbia University Press, 2014.

King, Barbara. *How Animals Grieve.* Chicago: University of Chicago Press, 2013.

Krumboltz, Mike. "Just like us? Elephants comfort each other when they're stressed out." *Yahoo News.* February 18, 2014. https://news.yahoo.com/elephants-know-a-thing-or-two-about-empathy-202224477.html.

Langley, Liz. "Do Crows Hold Funerals for Their Dead?" *National Geographic,* October 3, 2015. https://news.nationalgeographic.com/2015/10/151003-animals-science-crows-birds-culture-brains/.

Masson, Jeffrey. *When Elephants Weep.* New York: Dell Publishing, 1995.

Maxwell, Marius. *Stalking Big Game with a Camera in Equatorial Africa.* Literary Licensing, LLC, 2013.

Parker, Laura. "Rare Video Shows Elephants 'Mourning' Matriarch's Death." *National Geographic,* August 31, 2016. https://news.nationalgeographic.com/2016/08/elephants-mourning-video-animal-grief/.

PETA. "The Hidden Lives of Ducks and Geese." https://www.peta.org/issues/animals-used-for-food/factory-farming/ducks-geese/hidden-lives-ducks-geese/.

Sheldrake, Rupert. *Dogs That Know When Their Owners Are Coming Home: Fully Updated and Revised.* New York: Crown/Archetype, 2011.

Animal Empathy

Cheever, Holly. "A Bovine Sophie's Choice." *All-Creatures.org,* Summer 2011. http://www.all-creatures.org/articles/ar-bovine.html.

Holland, Jennifer. "Surprise: Elephants Comfort Upset Friends." *National Geographic,* February 18, 2014. https://news.nationalgeographic.com/news /2014/02/140218-asian-elephants-empathy-animals-science-behavior/.

Resnick, Brian. "Do animals feel empathy? Inside the decades-long quest for an answer." *Vox,* August 5, 2016. https://www.vox.com/science-and -health/2016/2/8/10925098/animals-have-empathy.

Schelling, Ameena. "Mother Cow Hides Newborn Baby To Protect Her From Farmer." *The Dodo,* February 25, 2015. https://www.thedodo.com/dairy-cow -calf-baby-rescue-1010627123.html.

Yong, Ed. "Empathic rats spring each other from jail." *National Geographic,* December 9, 2011. https://www.nationalgeographic.com/science /phenomena/2011/12/09/empathic-rats-spring-each-other-from-jail/.

The Joy of Play

Choi, Charles. "Gorillas Play Tag Like Humans." *Live Science,* July 13, 2010. https://www.livescience.com/10718-gorillas-play-tag-humans.html.

Play to Survive

Blank, David, and Weikang Yang, "Play Behavior in Goitered Gazelle, Gazella Subgutturosa (Artiodactyla: Bovidae) in Kazakhstan." *Folia Zoologica* 61: 2 (2012): 161–71.

Coley, Ben. "Why Do Lions Play?" *Africa Geographic.* January 18, 2016. https:// africageographic.com/blog/why-do-lions-play/.

Fagen, Robert, and Johanna Fagen. "Play Behavior and Multi-Year Juvenile Survival in Free-Ranging Brown Bears, *Ursus arctos." Evolutionary Ecology Research* 11: 7 (2009): 1053–67.

Gray, Peter. "Chasing Games and Sports: Why Do We Like to Be Chased?" *Psychology Today.* https://www.psychologytoday.com/us/blog/freedom -learn/200811/chasing-games-and-spor.

Remy, Melina. "Why Do Squirrels Chase Each Other?" *Live Science,* August 2, 2010. https://www.livescience.com/32740-why-do-squirrels-chase-each-other-.html.

Social Play

Farooqi, Samina, and Nicola Koyam. "The Occurrence of Postconflict Skills in Captive Immature Chimpanzees." *International Journal of Primatology* 37: 2 (2016): 185–99.

Kerney, Max, Jeroen Smaers, P. Thomas Schoenemann, and Jacob Dunn. "The Coevolution of Play and the Cortico-Cerebellar System in Primates." *Primates* 58: 4 (2017): 485–91.

Koyama, Nicola. "How Monkeys Make Friends and Influence Each Other." *The Conversation,* September 17, 2016. https://theconversation.com /how-monkeys-make-friends-and-influence-each-other-65906.

Melnick, Meredith. "Monkeys, Like Humans, Made Bad Choices and Regret Them, Too." *Time,* May 31, 2011. http://healthland.time.com/2011/05/31 monkeys-play-rock-paper-scissors-and-show-regret-over-losing/.

Playing for Kicks

Goldman, Jason. "Why Do Animals Like to Play?" *BBC,* January 9, 2013. http:// www.bbc.com/future/story/20130109-why-do-animals-like-to-play.

Sharpe, Lynda. "So You Think You Know Why Animals Play . . ." *Scientific American,* May 17, 2011. https://blogs.scientificamerican.com/guest-blog /so-you-think-you-know-why-animals-play/.

Sharpe, Lynda, and Michael Cherry. "Social Play Does Not Reduce Aggression in Wild Meerkats." *Animal Behaviour* 66: 5 (2003): 989–97.

Romping Puppies

Bekoff, Marc. "The Power of Play: Dogs Just Want to Have Fun." *Psychology Today,* September 5, 2017. https://www.psychologytoday.com/us/blog /animal-emotions/201709/the-power-play-dogs-just-want-have-fun.

Grimm, David. "In dogs' play, researchers see honesty and deceit, perhaps something like morality," *The Washington Post,* May 19, 2014. https://www.washingtonpost .com/national/health-science/in-dogs-play-researchers-see-honesty-and -deceit-perhaps-something-like-morality/2014/05/19/d8367214-ccb3-11e3 -95f7-7ecdde72d2ea_story.html?noredirect=on&utm_term=.759303f99543.

Sommerville, Rebecca, Emily O'Connor, and Lucy Asher. "Why Do Dogs Play? Function and Welfare Implications of Play in the Domestic Dog." *Applied Animal Behaviour Science* 197 (2017): 1–8.

Todd, Zazie. "Why Do Dogs Play?" *Companion Animal Psychology,* November 8, 2017. https://www.companionanimalpsychology.com/2017/11/why-do -dogs-play.html.

Pouncing Kittens

Caraza, Bianca. "Frisky Felines: Why Cats Play." *Global Animal,* June 11, 2011. https://www.globalanimal.org/2011/06/11/frisky-felines-why-cats-play/.

Johnston, Ian. "How Ancient Egypt's beloved cats helped our feline friends colonise the planet." *Independent,* June 19, 2017. https://www.independent .co.uk/news/science/ancient-egypt-cats-colonise-planet-sacred-animals -a7798021.html.

Fun on the Farm

Associated Press. "Goats escape from Idaho rental service. What happened next will not shock you." *Los Angeles Times,* August 3, 2018. http://www.latimes .com/nation/la-na-boise-goat-escape-20180803-story.html.

PETA. "The Hidden Lives of Pigs." https://www.peta.org/issues/animals-used -for-food/factory-farming/pigs/hidden-lives-pigs/.

Elephant Shenanigans

Kivi, Rose. "How Do Elephants Behave?" *Sciencing,* April 24, 2017. https:// sciencing.com/elephants-behave-4567810.html.

Worrall, Simon. "How Burmese Elephants Helped Defeat the Japanese in World War II." *National Geographic,* September 27, 2014. https://news.nationalgeo graphic.com/news/2014/09/140928-burma-elephant-teak-kipling-japan -world-war-ngbooktalk/.

Avian Amusements

Gamble, Jennifer, and Daniel Cristol. "Drop-catch behaviour is play in herring gulls, *Larus argentatus.*" *Animal Behavior* 63: 2 (2002): 339–45.

Newitz, Annalee. "Scientists investigate why crows are so playful." *Ars Technica,* October 19, 2017. https://arstechnica.com/science/2017/10/scientists-inves tigate-why-crows-are-so-playful/.

Frolicking Mollusks

Borrell, Brendan. "Are octopuses smart?" *Scientific American*, February 27, 2009. https://www.scientificamerican.com/article/are-octopuses-smart/.

Courage, Katherine. "Octopus Play and Squid Eyeballs—And What They Can Teach Us About Brains." *Scientific American*, November 18, 2014. https://blogs.scientificamerican.com/octopus-chronicles/octopus-play-and-squid-eyeballs-mdash-and-what-they-can-teach-us-about-brains/.

Nuwer, Rachel. "Ten Curious Facts About Octopuses." Smithsonian.com, October 31, 2013. https://www.smithsonianmag.com/science-nature/ten-curious-facts-about-octopuses-7625828/.

Crocodile Smiles

Dinets, Vladimir. "Play Behaviour in Crocodilians." *Animal Behaviour and Cognition* 2: 1 (2015): 49–55.

SECTION II

Scientific Research

Animals in Science Policy Institute. "Animals in Testing." https://www.animalsinscience.org/why_we_do_it/animals-in-testing/.

Canadian Council on Animal Care. "Three Rs: Replacement, Reduction and Refinement." https://3rs.ccac.ca/en/about/three-rs.html.

Clifton, Merritt. "Fewer Dogs & Cats Used in U.S. Labs Than Ever Before." *Animals 24-7*, June 24, 2017. https://www.animals24-7.org/2017/06/24/fewer-dogs-cats-used-in-u-s-labs-than-ever-before/.

———. "U.S. Labs Now Using More Animals Than Ever, Data Review Finds." *Animals 24-7*, May 1, 2015. https://www.animals24-7.org/2015/05/01/u-s-labs-now-using-more-animals-than-ever-data-review-finds/.

———. "Why Is Animal Use in Labs Up, Even As Public Moral Approval Is Down?" *Animals 24-7*, May 18, 2017. https://www.animals24-7.org/2017/05/18/why-is-animal-use-in-labs-up-even-as-public-moral-approval-is-down/.

Committee for the Update of the Guide for the Care and Use of Laboratory

Animals. *Guide for the Care and Use of Laboratory Animals*. Washington: The National Academies Press, 2011.

Cruelty Free International. "Alternatives to Animal Testing." https://www.cruel tyfreeinternational.org/why-we-do-it/alternatives-animal-testing.

Foundation for Biomedical Research. "Love Animals? Support Animal Research." https://fbresearch.org/love-animals-support-animal-research/.

Franco, Nuno. "Animal Experiments in Biomedical Research: A Historical Perspective." *Animals* 3: 1 (2013): 238–73.

Gluck, John. "Second Thoughts of an Animal Researcher." *New York Times*, September 2, 2016. https://www.nytimes.com/2016/09/04/opinion/sunday /second-thoughts-of-an-animal-researcher.html.

Hajar, Rachel. "Animal Testing and Medicine." *Heart Views* 12: 1 (2011): 42.

Hastings Center. "Alternatives to Animals Fact Sheet." http://animalresearch .thehastingscenter.org/facts-sheets/alternatives-to-animals/.

———. "Animal Research and Pain." http://animalresearch.thehastingscenter .org/facts-sheets/animal-research-and-pain/.

National Anti-Vivisection Society. "Alternatives to Animal Research." https:// www.navs.org/what-we-do/keep-you-informed/science-corner/alternatives /alternatives-to-animal-research/#.XIfiPy2ZOne.

———. "The Animal Welfare Act." https://www.navs.org/what-we-do/keep -you-informed/legal-arena/research/explanation-of-the-animal-welfare-act -awa/#.XIfg4y2ZOnc.

National Institute of Environmental Health Studies. "Alternatives to Animal Testing." https://www.niehs.nih.gov/health/topics/science/sya-iccvam /index.cfm.

PETA. "Alternatives to Animal Testing." https://www.peta.org/issues/animals -used-for-experimentation/alternatives-animal-testing/.

———. "Trauma Training 101." http://features.peta.org/TraumaTraining/101 .asp.

Smith, Jane. "Ethics in Research with Animals." *Monitor on Psychology* 34: 1 (2003): 57.

Clothing

Alchon, Suzanne. *A Pest in the Land: New World Epidemics in a Global Perspective*. Albuquerque: University of New Mexico Press, 2003.

Backwell, Lucinda, Francesco d'Errico, and Lyn Wadley. "Middle Stone Age bone tools from the Howiesons Poort layers, Sibudu Cave, South Africa." *Journal of Archaeological Science* 35: 6 (2008): 1566–80.

Cartner-Morley, Jess. "Fur flies as Stella McCartney unveils 'skin-free skin' in Paris." *Guardian,* March 6, 2017. https://www.theguardian.com /fashion/2017/mar/06/fur-stella-mccartney-unveils-skin-free-skin-paris -fashion-week.

Conniff, Richard. "Why Fur Is Back in Fashion." *National Geographic,* September 2016. https://www.nationalgeographic.com/magazine/2016/09/skin-trade -fur-fashion/.

Dindar, Shereen. "World's oldest leather shoe found in Armenia." *National Post,* June 9, 2010. http://news.nationalpost.com/2010/06/09/worlds-oldest -leather-shoe-found-in-armenia-2/.

Grinnell, George. *The Indians of Today.* Whitefish: Kessinger Publishing, 2010.

History.com. "Black Death." https://www.history.com/topics/black-death.

Hodge, Gene Meany. *Kachina Tales from the Indian Pueblos.* Santa Fe: Sunstone Press, 1993.

Holloway, April. "First hemp-weaved fabric in the World found wrapped around baby in 9,000-year-old house." *Ancient Origins,* February 6, 2014. http:// www.ancient-origins.net/news-history-archaeology/first-hemp-weaved -fabric-world-found-wrapped-around-baby-9000-year-old.

Kadoph, Sara, and Anna L. Langford. *Textiles.* Upper Saddle River: Prentice Hall, 2006.

Laver, James. *The Concise History of Costume and Fashion.* New York: Abrams, 1979.

Lynch, Alison. "Stella McCartney debuts her 'fur-free fur' at Paris Fashion Week." *Metro,* March 9, 2015. http://metro.co.uk/2015/03/09/stella -mccartney-debuts-her-fur-free-fur-at-paris-fashion-week-5095084 /?ito=cbshare.

Miller, Michael. "Meet Chris, the insanely overgrown sheep that nearly died for the sake of our fashion." *Washington Post,* September 3, 2015. https://www .washingtonpost.com/news/morning-mix/wp/2015/09/03/meet-chris-the -insanely-overgrown-sheep-that-nearly-died-for-the-sake-of-our-fashion/.

Montaigne, Michel de. "Of sumptuary laws." *Quotidiana.* Edited by Patrick Madden. September 23, 2006. http://essays.quotidiana.org/montaigne /sumptuary_laws/.

Mooney, James. *The Ghost Dance Religion and Wounded Knee.* Mineola: Courier Dover Publications, 1973.

Outwater, Alice. *Water, A Natural History.* New York: Basic Books, 2008.

Schweig, Sarah. "Sheep Decides to Keep Wool, Hides Out in Cave for 6
    YEARS." The Dodo, August 27, 2015. https://www.thedodo.com/wooly
    -sheep-hides-in-cave-1315578823.html.

RSPCA. "What Is Mulesing and What Are the Alternatives?" May 12, 2016.
    http://kb.rspca.org.au/what-is-mulesing-and-what-are-the-alternatives
    _113.html.

Whitfield, John. "Lice genes date first human clothes." Nature, August 20, 2003.
    https://www.nature.com/news/2003/030818/full/news030818-7.html.

Entertainment

Abramowitz, Rachel. "'Every Which Way but Abuse' Should Be Motto." Los
    Angeles Times, August 27, 2008. http://articles.latimes.com/2008/aug/27
    /entertainment/et-brief27.

Associated Press. "Gorilla's Escape, Violent Rampage Stun Zoo Officials." NBC
    News, March 19, 2004. http://www.nbcnews.com/id/4558461/ns/us_news/t
    /gorillas-escape-violent-rampage-stun-zoo-officials/#.XFs3DC2ZPfE.

———. "The Hobbit: Handlers Claim Deaths of Animals Could Have Been
    Prevented." The Guardian, November 19, 2012. https://www.theguardian
    .com/world/2012/nov/20/the-hobbit-animal-deaths-farm.

Bogdanich, Walt, Joe Drape, Dara L. Miles, and Griffin Palmer. "Mangled
    Horses, Maimed Jockeys." New York Times, March 24, 2012. https://www
    .nytimes.com/2012/03/25/us/death-and-disarray-at-americas-racetracks.html.

Busch, Anita. "Sidney Yost & Amazing Animals Prods Hit With Fines, License
    Revocation Over Animal Welfare Act Violations; Appealing Government
    Decision." Deadline, January 18, 2018. https://deadline.com/2018/01/sidney
    -jay-yost-amazing-animals-productions-fined-license-revoked-animal
    -welfare-violations-appealing-decision-order-1202246105/.

Calvo, Amanda. "Tensions Are on the Rise in Spain Over its Bloody Tradition
    of Bullfighting." Time, July 19, 2016. http://time.com/4400516/bullfighting
    -calls-for-ban-spain/.

Diaz, George. "Iditarod Dog Deaths Unjustifiable." Orlando Sentinel, March
    5, 2000. https://www.orlandosentinel.com/news/os-xpm-2000-03-05
    -0003050070-story.html.

Donahue, Bill. "Putin's Persian Leopard Project is an Olympic-Size Farce."
    Salon, February 9, 2014. https://www.salon.com/2014/02/08/putins_persian
    _leopard_project_is_an_olympic_sized_farse_partner/.

Ensley, Gerald. "Case of the 3,600 Disappearing Homing Pigeons Has Experts
    Baffled." *Chicago Tribune,* October 18, 1998. https://www.chicagotribune
    .com/news/ct-xpm-1998-10-18-9810180320-story.html.

Flanagin, Jake. "It's 2015—Time to Pack up the Iditarod." *Quartz,* March 11,
    2015. https://qz.com/358639/the-iditarod-is-exploitative-and-inhumane/.

Four Paws US. "Bans on Circuses." https://www.four-paws.us/campaigns-topics
    /topics/wild-animals/worldwide-circus-bans.

Gruttadaro, Andrew. "The Insane Story Behind Disney's 'Snow Buddies,'
    The Movie That Killed 5 Puppies." *Complex,* December 16, 20. https://
    www.complex.com/pop-culture/2016/12/snow-buddies-killed-five-puppies
    ?utm_campaign=popculturetw&utm_source=twitter&utm_medium
    =social.

Hill, Logan. "The Legacy of Flipper." *New York Magazine,* July 13, 2009. http://
    nymag.com/movies/profiles/57863/.

Hughes, Dana. "Mugabe's Ghoulish Gift for North Korea's Kim Jong Il." ABC
    News, May 14, 2010. https://abcnews.go.com/International/mugabe-sends
    -exotic-animals-north-korean-death/story?id=10650497.

Hunt, Julia. "Alan Cumming Seeking Sanctuary for Chimpanzee He Once
    Starred With." *Independent,* June 5, 2017. https://www.independent.ie/style
    /celebrity/celebrity-news/alan-cumming-seeking-sanctuary-for-chimpanzee
    -he-once-starred-with-35792384.html.

Iafolla, Robert. "Ads Pulled After Claims of Chimp Abuse." *Whittier Daily News,*
    July 1, 2005. https://lists.ibiblio.org/pipermail/monkeywire/2005-July.tx.

McHugh, Jess. "Swedish Zoo Admits to Killing 9 Healthy Lion Cubs." *Travel +
    Leisure,* January 12, 2018. https://www.travelandleisure.com/travel-news
    /zoo-dead-lion-cubs.

Messenger, Stephen. "Captivated: A Brief History of Animals Exploited for
    Entertainment." The Dodo, January 18, 2014. https://www.thedodo.com
    /captivated-a-brief-history-of--394381912.html.

Mott, Maryann. "Wild Elephants Live Longer Than Their Zoo Counterparts."
    National Geographic, December 11, 2008. https://news.nationalgeographic
    .com/news/2008/12/wild-elephants-live-longer-than-their-zoo-counter
    parts/.

PETA. "Graveyard Races: Summary." https://www.peta.org/features/graveyard
    -races/summary/.

Solis, Steph. "Ringling Bros. Circus Closing After 146 Years." *USA Today,*
    January 14, 2017. https://www.usatoday.com/story/news/nation/2017/01/14
    /ringling-bros-circus-close-after-146-years/96606820/.

World Animal Foundation. "Don't Support Marine Mammal Parks." https://worldanimal.foundation/advocate/don-t-support-marine-mammal-parks/.

Zoological Society of London. "The History of the Aquarium." https://www.zsl.org/zsl-london-zoo/exhibits/the-history-of-the-aquarium.

Food

Allen, Arthur. "U.S. Touts Fruit and Vegetables While Subsidizing Animals That Become Meat." *Washington Post,* October 3, 2011. https://www.washingtonpost.com/national/health-science/us-touts-fruit-and-vegetables-while-subsidizing-animals-that-become-meat/2011/08/22/gIQATFG5IL_story.html?utm_term=.8f61c5ba80fe.

Animal Welfare Institute. "Inhumane Practices on Factory Farms." https://awionline.org/content/inhumane-practices-factory-farms.

———. "Subtherapeutic Antibiotics in Agriculture." https://awionline.org/sites/default/files/uploads/documents/fa-antibioticsfactsheet-112511.pdf.

Barber, Nigel. "Do Humans Need Meat?" *Psychology Today,* October 12, 2016. https://www.psychologytoday.com/blog/the-human-beast/201610/do-humans-need-meat.

Bittman, Mark. "Rethinking the Meat-Guzzler." *New York Times,* January 27, 2008. http://www.nytimes.com/2008/01/27/weekinreview/27bittman.html.

Boyle, Rebecca. "Eating Cooked Food Made Us Human." *Popular Mechanics,* October 22, 2012.

Business Wire. "Don Lee Farms Introduces First Organic Raw Plant-Based Burger—Made with Plants, Not with Science." February 15, 2018. https://www.businesswire.com/news/home/20180215006465/en/Don-Lee-Farms-Introduces-Organic-Raw-Plant-Based.

Carrera-Bastos, Pedro, Maelan Fontes-Villalba, James O'Keefe, Staffan Lindeberg, and Loren Cordain. "The Western Diet and Lifestyle Diseases of Civilization." *Research Reports in Clinical Cardiology* 2011: 2 (2011): 15–35.

Chiorando, Maria. "European Meat Alternative Market Spikes by 451% in Four Years." *Plant Based News,* February 13, 2018. https://www.plantbasednews.org/post/european-meat-alternative-market-spikes-451-four-years.

Cordain, Loren, Stanley Eaton, Anthony Sebastian, Neil Mann, Staffan Lindeberg, Bruce Watkins, James O'Keefe, and Janette Brand-Miller. "Origins and Evolution of the Western Diet: Health Implications for the 21st Century." *The American Journal of Clinical Nutrition* 81: 2 (2005): 341–54.

Cordain, Loren, Stanley Eaton, Janette Brand-Miller, Neil Mann, and Karen Hill. "The Paradoxical Nature of Hunter-Gatherer Diets: Meat-Based, Yet Non-Atherogenic." *European Journal of Clinical Nutrition* 56 (2002): S42–S52.

Crawford, Elizabeth. "Vegan Is Going Mainstream, Trend Data Suggests." *FoodNavigator-USA,* March 17, 2015. https://www.foodnavigator-usa.com /Article/2015/03/17/Vegan-is-going-mainstream-trend-data-suggests#.

Davis, John. "The Origins of the Vegans: 1944–46." *Veg Source,* September 2016. http://www.vegsource.com/john-davis/origins_of_the_vegans.pdf.

Despain, David. "Why You Can All Stop Saying Meat Eating Fueled Evolution of Larger Brains Right Now." *Evolving Health,* December 2, 2012. http:// evolving.

Dunn, Rob. "Human Ancestors Were Nearly All Vegetarians." *Scientific American,* July 23, 2012. https://blogs.scientificamerican.com/guest-blog /human-ancestors-were-nearly-all-vegetarians/.

Eaton, Stanley, Loren Cordain, and Staffan Lindeberg. "Evolutionary Health Promotion: A Consideration of Common Counterarguments." *Preventative Medicine* 34: 2 (2002): 119–23.

Eden Farmed Animal Sanctuary. "Interview with Jerry Friedman." July 4, 2014. http://edenfarmedanimalsanctuary.com/animal-flesh-human-brain -evolution-dispelling-myths-2/.

Evans, Katy. "World's First Lab-Grown Chicken Has Been Tasted and Apparently it's Delicious." *IFLScience,* March 16, 2017. http://www.iflscience.com /technology/worlds-first-labgrown-chicken-has-been-tasted-and-apparently -its-delicious/.

The Flaming Vegan. "Vegan Mythbusting #2: Eating Meat Gave Our Ancestors Bigger Brains." September 8, 2014. http://www.theflamingvegan.com /view-post/Vegan-Mythbusting-2-Eating-Meat-Gave-Our-Ancestors -Bigger-Brains.

Food & Water Watch. "Factory Farm Nation." November 2010. https://www .factoryfarmmap.org/wp-content/uploads/2010/11/FactoryFarmNation -web.pdf.

Food Empowerment Project. "Exporting Factory Farms." http://www.foodis power.org/exporting-factory-farms/.

Freston, Kathy. "Shattering the Meat Myth: Humans Are Natural Vegetarians." *Huffington Post,* November 17, 2011. https://www.huffingtonpost.com /kathy-freston/shattering-the-meat-myth_b_214390.html.

Garfield, Leanna. "A Former McDonald's CEO Is Teaming Up With the Vegan

Meat Movement." *Business Insider,* November 10, 2015. http://www.busines
sinsider.com/mcdonalds-vet-don-thompson-joins-beyond-meat-2015-11.

———. "Leonardo DiCaprio Just Invested in the Bill Gates–Backed Veggie
Burger That 'Bleeds' Like Beef—Here's How It Tastes." *Business Insider,*
October 17, 2017. http://www.businessinsider.com/review-leonardo
-dicaprio-beyond-meat-veggie-plant-burger-2017-10.

Gibbons, Ann. "The Evolution of Di." *National Geographic,* February 2013.
https://www.nationalgeographic.com/foodfeatures/evolution-of-diet/.

Gowlett, John. "What Actually Was the Stone Age Diet?" *Journal of Nutritional
& Environmental Medicine* 13: 3 (2003): 143–47.

Haki, Danny. "At Hamburger Central, Antibiotics for Cattle That Aren't Sick."
New York Times, March 23, 2018. https://www.nytimes.com/2018/03/23
/business/cattle-antibiotics.html?rref=collection%2Ftimestopic%2FFa
ctory%20Farming&action=click&contentCollection=timestopics&region=s
tream&module=stream_unit&version=latest&contentPlacement=1&pgtype
=collection.

Hardy, Karen, Jennie Brand-Miller, Katherine D. Brown, Mark G. Thomas,
and Les Copeland. "The Importance of Dietary Carbohydrate in Human
Evolution." *Quarterly Review of Biology* 90: 3 (2015): 251–68.

healthscience.blogspot.com/2012/12/why-you-can-all-stop-saying-meat-eating
.html.

Humane Society of the United States. "Factory Farming in America." http://
www.humanesociety.org/assets/pdfs/farm/hsus-factory-farming-in-america
-the-true-cost-of-animal-agribusiness.pdf.

Jha, Alok. "Synthetic Meat: How the World's Costliest Burger Made It On To
the Plate." *Guardian,* August 5, 2013. https://www.theguardian.com/science
/2013/aug/05/synthetic-meat-burger-stem-cells.

Johns Hopkins. "History of Agriculture." http://www.foodsystemprimer.org
/food-production/history-of-agriculture/.

Kaplan, Hillard, Jane Lancaster, and Ana Hurtado. "A Theory of Human Life
History Evolution: Diet, Intelligence, and Longevity." *Evolutionary Anthropology* 9: 4 (2000): 156–85.

King, Barbara. "Humans Are 'Meathooked' But Not Designed for Meat-Eating."
NPR, May 19, 2016. https://www.npr.org/sections/13.7/2016/05/19/47864
5426/humans-are-meathooked-but-not-designed-for-meat-eating.

Kristof, Nicholas. "Our Water-Guzzling Food Factory." *New York Times,* May
30, 2015. https://www.nytimes.com/2015/05/31/opinion/sunday/nicholas

-kristof-our-water-guzzling-food-factory.html?rref=collection%2Ftimestopi
c%2FFactory%20Farming.

Leneman, Leah. "No Animal Food: The Road to Veganism in Britain,
1909–1944." *Society and Animals* 7: 3 (1999): 219–28.

Luca, Francesca, George Perry, and Anna Di Rienzo. "Evolutionary Adaptations
to Dietary Changes." *Annual Review of Nutrition* 30 (2010): 291–314.

MarketsandMarkets. "Dairy Alternatives Market Worth $29.6 Billion by 2023."
January 2019. https://www.marketsandmarkets.com/PressReleases/dairy
-alternative-plant-milk-beverages.asp.

Morris, Craig. "USDA Graded Cage-Free Eggs: All They're Cracked Up to
Be." *US Department of Agriculture,* September 13, 2016. https://www.usda
.gov/media/blog/2016/09/13/usda-graded-cage-free-eggs-all-theyre
-cracked-be.

Muskiet, Frits, and Pedro Carrera-Bastos. "Beyond the Paleolithic Prescription:
Commentary." *Nutrition Reviews* 72: 4 (2014): 285–86.

Newkirk, Ingrid. "Will In Vitro Meat Help Put an End to Animal Suffering?"
Newsweek, September 23, 2017. http://www.newsweek.com/will-vitro-meat
-help-put-end-animal-suffering-669615.

Nicholson, Ward. "Paleolithic Diet vs. Vegetarianism." *Beyond Vegetarianism,*
October 1997. http://www.beyondveg.com/nicholson-w/hb/hb-interview1c
.shtml.

O'Keefe Jr., James, and Loren Cordain. "Cardiovascular Disease Resulting
From a Diet and Lifestyle at Odds With Our Paleolithic Genome: How
to Become a 21st-Century Hunter-Gatherer." *PlumX Metrics* 79: 1 (2004):
101–8.

PETA. "Are Humans Supposed to Eat Meat?" https://www.peta.org/features
/are-humans-supposed-to-eat-meat/.

PETA. "Factory Farming: Misery for Animals." https://www.peta.org/issues
/animals-used-for-food/factory-farming/.

PETA. "10 Things We Wish Everyone Knew About the Meat and Dairy Industries." December 6, 2013. https://www.peta.org/living/food/10-things-wish
-everyone-knew-meat-dairy-industries/.

Phys.org. "Milk Drinking Started Around 7,500 Years Ago in Central Europe."
Phys.org, August 28 Briana. "Meat-Eating Among the Earliest Humans."
American Scientist, March–April 2016. https://www.americanscientist.org
/article/meat-eating-among-the-earliest-humans.

PR Newswire. "Meat Substitutes Market Worth 6.43 Billion USD by 2023."

February 6, 2018. https://www.prnewswire.com/news-releases/meat-substi
tutes-market-worth-643-billion-usd-by-2023-672903423.html.

Richards, Michael. "A Brief Review of the Archaeological Evidence for Palaeo-
lithic and Neolithic Subsistence." *European Journal of Clinical Nutrition* 56:
12 (2002): 1270–78.

Scheltens, Liz, and Gina Barton. "How Big Government Helps Big Dairy
Sell Milk." *Vox,* May 2, 2016. https://www.vox.com/2016/5/2/11565698
/big-government-helps-big-dairy-sell-milk.

Shapiro, Paul. "Lab-Grown Meat Is on the Way." *Scientific American,* December
19, 2017. https://blogs.scientificamerican.com/observations/lab-grown
-meat-is-on-the-way/.

Shivan, Joshi. "Evolved to Eat Meat? Maybe Not." *Huffington Post,* March 5,
2017. https://www.huffingtonpost.com/entry/evolved-to-eat-meat-maybe
-not_us_58bc7e4be4b02eac8876d020.

Simon, David. "Uncle Sam Says: Eat More Meat!" *Meatonomics,* December 9,
2014. https://meatonomics.com/2014/12/09/uncle-sam-says-eat-more-meat/.

Smithsonian National Museum of Natural History. "Homo Erectus." http://
humanorigins.si.edu/evidence/human-fossils/species/homo-erectus.

———. "Homo Habilis." http://humanorigins.si.edu/evidence/human-fossils
/species/homo-habilis.

———. "Homo Neanderthalensis." http://humanorigins.si.edu/evidence/human
-fossils/species/homo-neanderthalensis.

———. "Homo Sapiens." http://humanorigins.si.edu/evidence/human-fossils
/species/homo-sapiens .

Sorvino, Chloe. "Tyson Invests In Lab-Grown Protein Startup Memphis Meats,
Joining Bill Gates And Richard Branson." *Forbes,* January 29, 2018. https://
www.forbes.com/sites/chloesorvino/2018/01/29/exclusive-interview-tyson
-invests-in-lab-grown-protein-startup-memphis-meats-joining-bill-gates
-and-richard-branson/.

Strom, Stephanie. "Tyson to End Use of Human Antibiotics in Its Chickens
by 2017." *New York Times,* April 28, 2015. https://www.nytimes.com
/2015/04/29/business/tyson-to-end-use-of-human-antibiotics-in-its
-chickens-by-2017.html?rref=collection%2Ftimestopic%2FFactory%20
Farming.

———. "What to Make of Those Animal-Welfare Labels on Meat and Eggs."
New York Times, January 31, 2017. https://www.nytimes.com/2017/01/31
7/dining/animal-welfare-labels.html?rref=collection%2Ftimestopic%2FFa
ctory%20Farming.

Timmins, Beth. "Who Were the World's Very Earliest Vegans?" *Independent,* April 6, 2017. http://www.independent.co.uk/life-style/who-were-the -world-s-very-earliest-vegans-a7668831.html.

Ungar, Peter. "The 'True' Human Diet." *Scientific American,* April 17, 2017. https://blogs.scientificamerican.com/guest-blog/the-true-human-diet/.

University of Hohenheim. "Meat Substitutes and Lentil Pasta: Legume Products on the Rise in Europe." December 2, 2018. https://www.uni-hohenheim.de /en/press-release?tx_ttnews%5Btt_news%5D=39041&cHash=7d337967882 8c2cddf90799cde96b63c.

University of Sydney. "Starchy Carbs, Not a Paleo Diet, Advanced the Human Race." August 10, 2015. https://sydney.edu.au/news-opinion /news/2015/08/10/starchy-carbs--not-a-paleo-diet--advanced-the-human -race.html.

Vegan Society. "History." https://www.vegansociety.com/about-us/history.

World Wildlife Fund. "Overview." https://www.worldwildlife.org/threats /overfishing.

Wrangham, Richard. "The Evolution of Human Nutrition." *Current Biology* 23: 9 (2013): PR354–R355.

Zaraska, Marta. "How Humans Became Meat Eaters." *Atlantic,* February 19, 2016. https://www.theatlantic.com/science/archive/2016/02/when-humans -became-meateaters/463305/.

———. "Lab-Grown Beef Taste Test: 'Almost' Like a Burger." *Washington Post,* August 5, 2013. https://www.washingtonpost.com/national/health-science /lab-grown-beef-taste-test-almost-like-a-burger/2013/08/05/921a5996 -fdf4-11e2-96a8-d3b921c0924a_story.html?utm_term=.f18052f20c2c.

———. "Lab-grown Meat Is In Your Future, and It May Be Healthier Than the Real Stuff." *Washington Post,* May 2, 2016. https://www.washingtonpost .com/national/health-science/lab-grown-meat-is-in-your-future-and-it -may-be-healthier-than-the-real-stuff/2016/05/02/aa893f34-e630-11e5 -a6f3-21ccdbc5f74e_story.html?utm_term=.58dd6c22adfc.

Zeng, Spencer. "The Evolution of Diet." *IMMpress Magazine.* April 13, 2017. http://www.immpressmagazine.com/the-evolution-of-diet/.

Zimmer, Carl. "How the First Farmers Changed History." *New York Times,* October 17, 2016. https://www.nytimes.com/2016/10/18/science/ancient -farmers-archaeology-dna.html.

Notes

1   Maggie Koerth-Baker, "Humans Are Dumb at Figuring Out How Smart Animals Are," *FiveThirtyEight,* May 18, 2018, https://fivethirtyeight.com /features/humans-are-dumb-at-figuring-out-how-smart-animals-are/.

2   William Hodos, "Scala Naturae: Why There is no Theory in Comparative Psychology," *Psychological Review* 76: 4 (1969): 337–50.

3   "Slime Molds: No Brains, No Feet, No Problem," *PBS News Hour,* April 5, 2012, https://www.pbs.org/newshour/science/the-sublime-slime-mold.

4   Jane Lee, "New Theory on How Homing Pigeons Find Home," *National Geographic,* January 30, 2013, https://news.nationalgeographic.com/news/2013 /13/130130-homing-pigeon-navigation-animal-behavior-science/.

5   Peter Brannen, "Tracking the Secret Lives of Great White Sharks," *Wired,* December 19, 2013, https://www.wired.com/2013/12/secret-lives-great-white -sharks/.

6   Joseph Castro, "Wow! Dung Beetles Navigate by the Stars," *Live Science,* January 24, 2013, https://www.livescience.com/26557-dung-beetles-navigate -stars.html.

7   Pallab Ghosh, "Snails 'Have a Homing Instinct,'" *BBC,* August 3, 2010, https:// www.bbc.com/news/science-environment-10856523.

8   Sarah Knapton, "Snails Have Homing Instinct and Will Crawl (Slowly) Back to Motherland if Moved, BBC Wildlife Film Proves," *Telegraph,* June 24, 2017, https://www.telegraph.co.uk/science/2017/06/24/snails-have-homing-instinct -will-crawl-slowly-back-motherland/.

9   Laura Helmuth, "Saving Mali's Migratory Elephants," *Smithsonian Magazine,* July 2005, https://www.smithsonianmag.com/science-nature/saving-malis -migratory-elephants-74522858/.

10 Vlastimil Hart, Petra Nováková, Erich Pascal Malkemper, Sabine Begall, Vladimír Hanzal, Miloš Ježek, Tomáš Kušta, Veronika Němcová, Jana Adámková, Kateřina Benediktová, Jaroslav Červený, and Hynek Burda, "Dogs Are Sensitive to Small Variations of the Earth's Magnetic Field," *Frontiers in Zoology* 10: 80 (2013).

11 Karin Brulliard, "Your Dog Really Does Know What You're Saying, and a Brain Scan Shows How," *Washington Post,* August 31, 2016, https://www.washington post.com/news/animalia/wp/2016/08/30/confirmed-your-dog-really-does-get -you/?utm_term=.7f008d837514.

12 Brian Hare and Vanessa Woods, "Opinion: We Didn't Domesticate Dogs. They Domesticated Us," *National Geographic,* March 3, 2013, https://news.national geographic.com/news/2013/03/130302-dog-domestic-evolution-science-wolf -wolves-human/.

13 "Measuring Animal Intelligence," *CBS News,* March 18, 2018, https://www.cbs news.com/news/measuring-animal-intelligence/.

14 Rosamund Young, *The Secret Life of Cows* (London: Faber & Faber, 2018), 78.

15 University of Lincoln, "It's not just a grunt: Pigs really do have something to say," *ScienceDaily,* June 29, 2016, https://www.sciencedaily.com/releases/2016/06 /160629100349.htm.

16 "It's not just a grunt: pigs really do have something to say," *University of Lincoln,* June 29, 2016, http://www.lincoln.ac.uk/news/2016/06/1240.asp.

17 Denise Herzing, "Could We Speak the Language of Dolphins?" *TED,* https:// www.ted.com/talks/denise_herzing_could_we_speak_the_language_of _dolphins/transcript#t-178120.

18 Jeremy Manier, "Dolphin Cognition Fuels Discovery," *University of Chicago,* September 3, 2013, https://www.uchicago.edu/features/dolphin_cognition_fuels _discovery/.

19 Chris Otchy, "The Hypnotic Power of Repetition in Music," *Medium,* May 5, 2017, https://medium.com/@ChrisOtchy/the-hypnotic-power-of-repetition -in-music-8d59ab12b615.

20 Billy McQuay and Christopher Joyce, "It Took a Musician's Ear to Decode the Complex Song in Whale Calls," *NPR,* August 6, 2015, https://www.npr.org /2015/08/06/427851306/it-took-a-musicians-ear-to-decode-the-complex-song -in-whale-calls.

21 Kenneth Oakley, "The Earliest Tool-Makers," *Antiquity* 30: 117 (1956): 4–8.

22 Frans de Waal, *Are We Smart Enough to Know How Smart Animals Are?* (New York: W. W. Norton & Company, 2016), 62.

23 Benedict Carey, "Washoe, a Chimp of Many Words, Dies at 42," *New York Times,* November 1, 2017, https://www.nytimes.com/2007/11/01/science/01 chimp.html.

24 Victoria Gill, "Chimpanzees' 66 Gestures Revealed," *BBC News,* May 5, 2011, http://news.bbc.co.uk/earth/hi/earth_news/newsid_9475000/9475408.stm.

25 Claire Spottiswoode, Keith Begg, and Colleen Begg, "Reciprocal Signaling in Honeyguide–Human Mutualism," *Science* 353: 6297 (2016): 387–89.

26 Zoe Mendelson, "Traffic Is How City Birds Sing," *Next City,* February 19, 2016, https://nextcity.org/daily/entry/noise-pollution-bird-calls-san-francisco.

27 Joe Pinkstone, "Animals Take Turns to 'Speak' and Are Having Two-Way Conversations All Around Us, Claim Scientists," *Daily Mail*, June 5, 2018, https://www.dailymail.co.uk/sciencetech/article-5804697/Animals-turns -communicating-wait-turn-just-like-polite-humans-do.html.

28 Ashley Sullivan, "Wounda: The Amazing Story of the Chimp Behind the Hug with Dr. Jane Goodall," *The Jane Goodall Institute*, November 21, 2017, http:// news.janegoodall.org/2017/11/21/tchimpounga-chimpanzee-of-the-month -wounda/.

29 Phillip Staines, *Linguistics and the Parts of the Mind* (Cambridge: Cambridge Scholars Publishing, 2018), 68.

30 Joseph Castro, "Animal Sex: How Sea Turtles Do It," *Live Science*, May 5, 2014, https://www.livescience.com/45354-animal-sex-sea-turtles.html.

31 Christine Peterson, "Ten Strange, Endearing and Alarming Animal Courtship Rituals," *The Nature Conservancy*, February 9, 2016, https://blog.nature.org /science/2016/02/09/ten-strange-endearing-and-alarming-mating-habits-of -the-animal-world/.

32 Noah Strycker, *The Thing with Feathers* (New York: Riverhead Books, 2014), 248.

33 Ibid.

34 University of Sheffield, "Biased sex ratios predict more promiscuity, polygamy and 'divorce' in birds," *ScienceDaily*, March 24, 2014, https://www.sciencedaily .com/releases/2014/03/140324090324.htm.

35 Sandra Guzman, "Think Pigeons Are a Nuisance? Meet New York City's Pigeon Whisperer," *NBC News*, October 16, 2015, https://www.nbcnews.com /news/latino/pigeons-nuisance-meet-new-york-city-s-pigeon-whisperer-n44 5506.

36 Brandon Keim, "What Pigeons Teach Us About Love," *Nautilus*, February 11, 2016, http://nautil.us/issue/33/attraction/what-pigeons-teach-us-about-love.

37 "Slimy Leeches Are Devoted Parents," *Business Report*, July 2, 2004, https:// www.iol.co.za/business-report/technology/slimy-leeches-are-devoted-parents -216206.

38 Rosamund Young, *The Secret Life of Cows* (London: Faber & Faber, 2018), 30.

39 Simon Worrall, "How the Current Mass Extinction of Animals Threatens Humans," *National Geographic*, August 20, 2014, https://news.nationalgeo graphic.com/news/2014/08/140820-extinction-crows-penguins-dinosaurs -asteroid-sydney-booktalk/?utm_source=Twitter&utm_medium=Social&utm _content=link_tw20140820news-extinct&utm_campaign=Content&sf4259638=1.

40 Kaeli Swift and John Marzluff, "Wild American Crows Gather Around Their Dead to Learn About Danger," *Animal Behaviour* 109 (2015): 187–97.

41 Konrad Lorenz, *The Year of the Greylag Goose* (San Diego: Harcourt Brace Jovanovich, 1979), 39.

42   Francie Diep, "How Do Gorillas Grieve?" *Pacific Standard,* June 9, 2016, https://
     psmag.com/news/how-do-gorillas-grieve.

43   Roger Highfield, "Elephants Show Compassion in Face of Death," *Telegraph,*
     August 14, 2006, https://www.telegraph.co.uk/news/1526287/Elephants-show
     -compassion-in-face-of-death.html.

44   Jennifer Holland, "Surprise: Elephants Comfort Upset Friends," *National
     Geographic,* February 18, 2014, https://news.nationalgeographic.com/news/2014
     /02/140218-asian-elephants-empathy-animals-science-behavior/.

45   Brian Resnick, "Do Animals Feel Empathy? Inside the Decades-Long Quest
     for an Answer," *Vox,* August 5, 2016, https://www.vox.com/science-and-health
     /2016/2/8/10925098/animals-have-empathy.

46   Ibid.

47   Holly Cheever, "A Bovine Sophie's Choice," *All-Creatures.org,* Summer 2011,
     http://www.all-creatures.org/articles/ar-bovine.html.

48   University of Portsmouth, "Great apes 'play' tag to keep competitive advantage,"
     ScienceDaily, July 14, 2010, https://www.sciencedaily.com/releases/2010/07
     /100713191223.htm.

49   Peter Gray, "Chasing Games and Sports: Why Do We Like to Be Chased?"
     Psychology Today, November 5, 2008, https://www.psychologytoday.com/us
     /blog/freedom-learn/200811/chasing-games-and-sports-why-do-we-be-chased.

50   Karl Groos, *The Play of Animals* (New York: D. Appleton and Company,
     1898), 75.

51   Michael Steele, Sylvia Halkin, Peter Smallwood, Thomas McKenna, Katerina
     Mitsopoulos, and Matthew Beam, "Cache Protection Strategies of a Scatter-
     Hoarding Rodent: Do Tree Squirrels Engage in Behavioural Deception?"
     Animal Behaviour 75: 2 (2008): 705–14.

52   Scott Nunes, Eva-Maria Muecke, Lesley Lancaster, Nathan Miller, Marie
     Mueller, Jennifer Muelhaus, and Lina Castro, "Functions and Consequences of
     Play Behaviour in Juvenile Belding's Ground Squirrels," *Animal Behaviour* 68:
     1 (2004): 27–37.

53   Robert Fagen and Johanna Fagen, "Play Behaviour and Multi-Year Juvenile
     Survival in Free-Ranging Brown Bears, *Ursus Arctos,*" *Evolutionary Ecology
     Research* 11 (2009): 1053–67.

54   Frans de Waal and Angeline van Roosmalen, "Reconciliation and Consolation
     Among Chimpanzees," *Behavioral Ecology and Sociobiology* 5: 1 (1979): 55–66.

55   Samina Farooqi and Nicola Koyama, "The Occurrence of Postconflict Skills
     in Captive Immature Chimpanzees," *International Journal of Primatology* 37: 2
     (2016): 185–99.

56   Lynda Sharpe, "So You Think You Know Why Animals Play," *Scientific
     American,* May 17, 2011, https://blogs.scientificamerican.com/guest-blog/so
     -you-think-you-know-why-animals-play/.

57 Zazie Todd, "Why Do Dogs Play?" *Companion Animal Psychology,* November 8, 2017, https://www.companionanimalpsychology.com/2017/11/why-do-dogs-play.html.

58 Victoria Allen, "'Here's Looking at You Kid': Goats Can Recognise Happy Humans and Are More Drawn to Those With Smiling Faces, Study Finds," *Daily Mail,* August 28, 2011, https://www.dailymail.co.uk/news/article-6108275/Goats-recognise-happy-humans-drawn-smiling-faces-study-finds.html.

59 "The Hidden Lives of Pigs," *PETA,* https://www.peta.org/issues/animals-used-for-food/factory-farming/pigs/hidden-lives-pigs/.

60 "New Caledonian Crows Can Create Tools From Multiple Parts," *University of Oxford,* October 24, 2018, http://www.ox.ac.uk/news/2018-10-24-new-caledonian-crows-can-create-tools-multiple-parts.

61 Rachel Nuwer, "Ten Curious Facts About Octopuses," *Smithsonian.com,* October 31, 2013, https://www.smithsonianmag.com/science-nature/ten-curious-facts-about-octopuses-7625828/.

62 Michael Kuba, Ruth Byrne, and Daniela Meisel, "When Do Octopuses Play? Effects of Repeated Testing, Object Type, Age, and Food Deprivation on Object Play in *Octopus vulgaris,*" *Journal of Comparative Psychology* 120: 3 (2006): 184–90.

63 Katherine Courage, "How the Freaky Octopus Can Help Us Understand the Human Brain," *Wired,* October 1, 2013, https://www.wired.com/2013/10/how-the-freaky-octopus-can-help-us-understand-the-human-brain/.

64 Rosemary McTier, *"An Insect View of Its Plain"* (Jefferson: McFarland & Company, 2013), 162.

65 Ingrid Newkirk, *The PETA Practical Guide to Animal Rights* (New York: St. Martin's Press, 2009), 216.

66 Ibid.

67 Bernice Bovenkerk and Jozef Keulartz, ed., *Animal Ethics in the Age of Humans: Blurring Boundaries in Human–Animal Relationships* (New York: Springer Publishing, 2016), 113.

68 Rachel Hajar, "Animal Testing and Medicine," *Heart Views* 12: 1 (2011): 42.

69 Nuno Franco, "Animal Experiments in Biomedical Research: A Historical Perspective," *Animals* 3: 1 (2013): 238–73.

70 "Experiments on Animals: Overview," *PETA,* https://www.peta.org/issues/animals-used-for-experimentation/animals-used-experimentation-factsheets/animal-experiments-overview/.

71 "8 Expert Quotes Admitting That Testing on Animals Is Unreliable," *PETA,* https://www.peta.org/features/expert-quotes-reasons-animal-testing-unreliable/.

72 "PVM Cancer Researcher Collaborates on Creating Device to Identify Risks for Breast Cancer," *Purdue University,* https://vet.purdue.edu/newsroom/2017/pvr-a2017-breast-cancer-research.php.

73 "Trauma Training 101," *PETA*, http://features.peta.org/TraumaTraining /101.asp.

74 Michael Miller, "Meet Chris, the insanely overgrown sheep that nearly died for the sake of our fashion," September 3, 2015, https://www.washingtonpost.com /news/morning-mix/wp/2015/09/03/meet-chris-the-insanely-overgrown -sheep-that-nearly-died-for-the-sake-of-our-fashion/?noredirect=on&utm _term=.8af09ae71717.

75 "Another Patagonia-Approved Wool Producer Exposed—Help Sheep Now," *PETA*, https://investigations.peta.org/another-patagonia-approved-wool -producer-exposed/.

76 "Dispatches from Paris: Stella McCartney," *Elle UK*, September 3, 2015, https://www.elle.com/uk/fashion/news/a25155/stella-mccartney-autumn -winter-2015-catwalk-review-rebecca-lowthorpe/.

77 Brooke Bobb, "Donatella Versace Says Fur Is Over," *Vogue*, March 14, 2018, https://www.vogue.com/article/donatella-versace-fur.

78 Georgina Safe, "Sans Beast: Vegan Accessories Brand Reflects Global Shift to Ethical Fashion," *Australian Financial Review*, February 26, 2018, https://www .afr.com/lifestyle/sans-beast-vegan-accessories-brand-reflects-global-shift-to -ethical-fashion-20180206-h0un3n.

79 Tess Kornfeld, "Eco-Friendly Stella McCartney Reveals 'Skin-Free Skin' Fabric During Fall '17 Show in Paris," *Us Magazine*, March 7, 2017, https://www .usmagazine.com/stylish/news/stella-mccartney-reveals-skin-free-skin-fabric -at-fall-17-show-w470838/.

80 Pete Norman, "Pamela Anderson Gives UGGs the Boot," *People*, February 23, 2007, https://people.com/celebrity/pamela-anderson-gives-uggs-the-boot/.

81 Hannah Parry, "EXCLUSIVE: Actor Alan Cumming is pleading for the release of his former chimpanzee co-star Tonka from 'cockroach-infested' Missouri sanctuary," *Daily Mail*, June 3, 2017, https://www.dailymail.co.uk/news/article -4568922/Alan-Cumming-pleads-release-chimp-costar-Tonka.html.

82 "Zoos: Pitiful Prisons," *PETA*, https://www.peta.org/issues/animals-in -entertainment/animals-used-entertainment-factsheets/zoos-pitiful-prisons/.

83 "Marine Animal Exhibits: Chlorinated Prisons," *PETA*, https://www.peta.org /issues/animals-in-entertainment/animals-used-entertainment-factsheets /marine-animal-exhibits-chlorinated-prisons/.

84 George Diaz, "Iditarod Dog Deaths Unjustifiable," *Orlando Sentinel*, March 5, 2000, https://www.orlandosentinel.com/news/os-xpm-2000-03-05-00030 50070-story.html.

85 "Graveyard Races: Summary," *PETA*, https://www.peta.org/features/graveyard -races/summary/.

86 Petrine Mitchum and Audrey Pavia, *Hollywood Hoofbeats: The Fascinating Story of Horses in Movies and Television* (Los Angeles: i5 Publishing, 2014).

87   "Animal Actors: Command Performances," *PETA*, https://www.peta.org/issues
     /animals-in-entertainment/animals-used-entertainment-factsheets/animal
     -actors-command-performances/.

88   Rachel Abramowitz, "'Every Which Way but Abuse' Should Be Motto," *Los
     Angeles Times*, August 27, 2008, http://articles.latimes.com/2008/aug/27/enter
     tainment/et-brief27.

89   M. Dimesh Varma, "From Tent to the Stage, Transforming Circus," *The Hindu*,
     October 26, 2017, https://www.thehindu.com/news/cities/puducherry/from
     -tent-to-the-stage-transforming-circus/article19920134.ece.

90   Richard Bowie, "*Jungle Book* Film Awarded for Sparing Animal Lives," *Veg
     News*, April 10, 2016, https://vegnews.com/2016/4/jungle-book-film-awarded
     -for-sparing-animal-lives.

91   Beth Timmins, "Who Were the World's Very Earliest Vegans?" *Independent*,
     April 6, 2017, http://www.independent.co.uk/life-style/who-were-the-world
     -s-very-earliest-vegans-a7668831.html.

92   "Are Humans Supposed to Eat Meat?" *PETA*, https://www.peta.org/features
     /are-humans-supposed-to-eat-meat/.

93   Kathy Freston, "Shattering the Meat Myth: Humans Are Natural Vegetarians,"
     Huffington Post, November 17, 2011, https://www.huffingtonpost.com/kathy
     -freston/shattering-the-meat-myth_b_214390.html.

94   Danny Hakim, "At Hamburger Central, Antibiotics for Cattle That Aren't
     Sick," *New York Times*, March 23, 2018, https://www.nytimes.com/2018/03/23
     /business/cattle-antiobiotics.html.

95   Russell Simmons and Chris Morrow, *The Happy Vegan* (New York: Avery, 2015),
     166.

96   Bert Archer, "The Ethics, Emotion & Logic Behind Going Vegan," *Everything-
     Zoomer*, November 1, 2018, http://www.everythingzoomer.com/food/2018/11
     /01/going-vegan/.

97   Caldwell Esselstyn Jr., Gina Gendry, Jonathan Doyle, Mladen Golubic, and
     Michael Roizen, "A Way to Reverse CAD?" *Journal of Family Practice* 63: 7
     (2014): 356–64.

98   Marl Wahlqvist, Tao Huang, Ju-Sheng Zheng, Guipu Li, Duo Li, and Young
     Bin, "Cardiovascular Disease Mortality and Cancer Incidence in Vegetarians:
     A Meta-Analysis and Systemic Review," *Annals of Nutrition and Metabolism* 60:
     4 (2012): 233–40.

99   Timothy Key, Elizabeth Spencer, Paul Appleby, and Ruth Travis, "Cancer
     incidence in vegetarians: results from the European Prospective Investigation
     into Cancer and Nutrition (EPIC-Oxford)," *American Journal of Clinical
     Nutrition* 89: 5 (2009): 1620–26.

100 "Frequently Asked Questions," *Beyond Meat*, https://www.beyondmeat.com
     /faqs/.

101   Kat Eschner, "Winston Churchill Imagined the Lab-Grown Hamburger," *Smithsonian.com,* December 1, 2017, https://www.smithsonianmag.com/smart -news/winston-churchill-imagined-lab-grown-hamburger-180967349/.

102   Zara Stone, "The High Cost of Lab-To-Table Meat," *Wired,* March 8, 2018, https://www.wired.com/story/the-high-cost-of-lab-to-table-meat/.

103   Adele Peters, "Lab-Grown Meat Is Getting Cheap Enough for Anyone to Buy," *Fast Company,* May 2, 2018, https://www.fastcompany.com/40565582 /lab-grown-meat-is-getting-cheap-enough-for-anyone-to-buy.

104   Rip Esselstyn, *Plant Strong: Discover the World's Healthiest Diet* (New York: Grand Central Life & Style, 2015), 95.

Index

activist organizations, 154
 see also specific organizations
Adélie penguins, 14, 67–68
Admiralty Island, 92
Ado (greylag goose), 82
advertising campaigns, by meat industrial
 complex, 212
Africa, 34–35, 93
African cichlids, 75
African elephants, 32–34, 68
African gray parrots, 56–57
Agnes Scott College, 84
Agriculture Department, US (USDA), 128,
 153, 192, 193, 200, 211, 216
ahimsa silk, 175
AIDS, *see* HIV/AIDS
Alaska Fairbanks, University of, 91–92
albatrosses, 17, 70–71, 78
Alex (African gray parrot), 56–57
alligators, 110–11, 162
Amazing Animal Productions, 192
American Anti-Vivisection Society
 (AAVS), 125
American bullfrogs, 50
American Humane (AH), 192–93
American Journal of Cardiology, 210
American Journal of Clinical Nutrition, 223
American Society for the Prevention of
 Cruelty to Animals (ASPCA), 219
American woodcock, 19
Amphicoelias fragillimus, 206

Anderson, Charles, 31
Anderson, Pamela, 179–80
Andics, Attila, 40
anesthesia, animal experiments and, 125
animal agriculture:
 environmental effects of, 117
 see also meat industrial complex
Animal Behavior, 81
animal behavior, anthropomorphizing of, 13
animal cams, 201
Animal Cognition, 54
Animal Legal Defense Fund, 220
Animal Liberation (Singer), 127
Animal Makers Inc., 196
Animal Navigation (Lockley), 15
animal protection movements, 127, 148–54,
 174–80
 Origins of, 9, 217–20
Animal Rights Foundation of Florida, 220
animals:
 domestication of, 208–9
 historical view of, 2–3
 physical differences between humans
  and, 129
animals, exploitation of:
 changing attitudes toward, 115–16
 see also clothing; entertainment; food;
  scientific research
animal sanctuaries, 201, 203–4
Animal Welfare Act of 1966 (AWA),
 127–28, 151, 193, 200

animatronics, 196–97
Anita's Yogurt, 230
Antarctica, Ice Maidens crossing of, 193, 200
antibiotics, 212–13
ants, 10–11
aplastic anemia, 137
Applied Animal Behavior Science, 97
aquafaba, 227
aquafarming, 216–17
aquariums and marine amusement parks,
    186–87
arctic terns, 14, 19, 26
Aristotle, 8–9, 106, 123
Armani, Giorgio, 169
Asia, 93
Asian elephants, 83
Astley, Philip, 184
atherosclerosis, 137
Atlantic salmon, 25
Aubrey Organics, 148
aurochs, 209
Australian Financial Review, 169
Australian leeches, 74
Australopithecus, plant-based diet of, 207
automobiles, alternatives to leather trim in,
    169, 176
autopsies, 136–37

Baba Yaga, 39
baboons, 121
Bacon, Francis, 123
Baeckler, Sarah, 191
Bahamas, 46
bamboo, fabrics from, 171–72
Bandoola (elephant), 102
Barnard, Neal, 119–21
Barnum, P. T., 184
bar-tailed godwit, 19
Basel Declaration (2011), 127
Bath, University of, 71
bats, 22–23
Bat World Sanctuary, 2
Baum's Sporting Goods, 173

Baywatch (TV show), 179
BBC News, 54
BCBG, 168
bearbaiting, 183
Beauty Without Bunnies (PETA website),
    148
beavers, beaver trade, 159
Beck, Benjamin, 13
bees, 28–29
Beesley, Alec Macbeth, 155
behavior, of animals, *see* animal behavior
Behavioral Ecology and Sociobiology, 94
behaviorism, 85
Bekoff, Marc, 62, 80, 98
Ben & Jerry's, 230
Ben-Hur (films), 191
Bentham, Jeremy, 218
Bergh, Henry, 219
Bernard, Claude, 124, 125
Beyond Meat, 224–25
BHT, 140
Big 5 Sporting Goods, 173
binocular vision, 22
bioinformatics, 134
Biology Letters, 78
bioluminescence, 140–41
birds:
    brains of, 22
    caged, 105–6
    cognitive abilities of, 11
    communication among, 54–58; *see also*
        birdsong
    courtship among, 55
    flight and, 17–18
    migration by, 19–22, 26
    monogamy among, 64, 70–73
    play among, 103–6
    tool-making by, 57–58
Birds & Animals Unlimited, 193
birdsong:
    and human-animal communication, 55
    syntax in, 55
    urban adaptations in, 56

bisexuality, 77–78
bison, 206
Black, Jeffrey, 71
black-capped chickadees, 60
Black Death, 158
Blackfish (documentary), 186
Blaser, Martin J., 213
blind mole rats, 14, 35–36
blue whales, 48
Bob's Red Mill Egg Replacer, 227
body language, 38, 41, 53
Body Shop, 148, 151
Bologna declaration (1999), 127
bone char, 232
bonobos, 51, 53, 78, 129
Borneo (orangutan), 75
Born Free (film), 186
Boston University, 136
botanical gardens, 201
Boulden, Jim, 196
box turtles, 65–66
Boyle, Robert, 124–25
brains:
    of birds, 22
    cortico-cerebellar system of, 94
brain size:
    of bees, 28
    intelligence and, 11
Brazil, aquaculture in, 217
Brazilian torrent frog, 50
breast cancer, 144
Breyer's, 230
Brin, Sergey, 226
British Journal of Animal Behaviour, 90
British Medical Journal, 214
Brooks, Ruth, 31–32
brown bears, 91–92
Brown University, 150
Bruck, Jason, 47
Buber, Martin, 38
Buddy (film), 181
Buffy Comforter, 174
bullfighting, 183, 188, 203

Burberry, 169
Burch, Rex, 127
Burma, 102
Bush, George W., 200
butter, nondairy, 229–30
By Chloe, 233

calcium, milk as poor source of, 214
Calvin Klein, 169
Cambridge, University of, 56
Canada Goose, 166, 175
cancer, 221
    plant-based diet and, 223
cancer research:
    animal-free testing in, 143–44
    and failure of animal studies to result in
        treatments, 129–30
    in vitro, 132
carbohydrates, 221
caribou, 34
carnivores, 209–10
Case for Animal Rights, The (Regan), 127
casomorphins, 228
Catching Fire (Wrangham), 208
cats:
    domestication of, 99
    navigation skills of, 16
    play among, 98–100
    as predators, 99–100
cattle:
    communication between humans and,
        43–44
    domestication of, 209
    in meat and dairy industry, 213–14
    mother-child bond in, 76–77, 86–87
CB2, 175
Cedars-Sinai Hospital (Los Angeles), 139
celestial navigation, 16, 20, 29–30
Cellink, 143
cell lines, 132
Chao, 228
charitable donations, animal testing and,
    149–50

Charlemagne, Holy Roman emperor, 183
Charm School, 231
chase, in play, 88–89, 90, 91, 92
Chaser (border collie), 2
cheese, nondairy, 228–29
Cheese Trap, The (Barnard), 119
cheetahs, chirping by, 60
Cheever, Holly, 86–87
Cheezehound, 229
Cher Ami (homing pigeon), 21
Chicago, University of, 42, 47
chickens:
  cognition abilities of, 45
  domestication of, 209
  genetic engineering of, 215
  misleading "free-range", "cage-free", or
    "pasture-raised" terminology for, 215
  as social animals, 45
child rearing:
  by African cichlids, 75
  by Australian leeches, 74
  by orcas, 75
  by pigeons, 73
  by wolf spiders, 74–75
chimpanzees, 129
  in AIDS research, 116
  cognitive skills of, 13, 52
  communication among, 54
  conciliatory behavior in, 94–95
  diet of, 205–6
  in film and television, 181–82, 191
  homosexuality and bisexuality among, 78
  human-like behavior of, 52
  as humans' closest relatives, 51–52,
    205–6
  poor vocalizing ability of, 52
  promiscuity of, 64
  sign language and, 52–54
  tool-use by, 51, 52
China, 183
  animal testing of cosmetics in, 126, 138
  cruel fur farming practices in, 160
  in vitro meat and, 226

  as world's largest exporter of fur and
    leather, 159–61
chocolate, vegan, 230–31
Chris (sheep), 163, 164
Christianity, animals as viewed by, 123
Christmas Bonnet (cow), 44
chronic traumatic encephalopathy (CTE),
  137
chronometer, 24
Church, Russell, 84
Churchill, Winston, 225
circadian rhythms, 20
Circus 1903, 196
circuses, 184–85
  animal-free, 195–96, 201
Circus Roncalli, 195
Circus Vargas, 201
Cirque du Soleil, 195, 201
Cirque Italia, 201
Clapham, Phillip, 49
Clarabelle (cow), 86
cleaner wrasse, 28
"clean meat," 117
Clever Hans (horse), 38, 42, 53
clinical trials, 135
  animal testing and, 126–27, 130
clothing, 155–80
  advances in nonanimal materials in, 116
  animal-free, 168–69
  anti-cruelty slogans for, 176–77
  charitable donations of, 179
  exploitation of animals and, 116, 156,
    160–67
  fashion and, 158
  as necessity, 156–58
  personal action and, 174–80
  plant-based fabrics in, 170–72
  regulation of, 158–59
  synthetic materials in, 172–73
  vegan accessories and, 176–77
Coast Guard, US, 146
Cobbe, Frances Power, 125, 219
cockfighting, 183, 188, 199–200

Coconut Bliss, 230
cognition, play and, 93–94, 98
Cold War, 48
Coleman Company, 173
Collins, Francis S., 121, 152
Columbia University, 150
communication, 14, 38–61
   among ants, 10–11
   among birds, 54–58
   canine, 39–41
   among domesticated animals, 43–45
   language vs., 45
   among primates, 54
   smell and, 41
   symbol reading in, 43
   two-way conversation in, 58–60
communication, human-animal:
   birdsong and, 55–56
   body language and, 38, 53
   Clever Hans Effect in, 38
   cows and, 43–44
   fMRI scans and, 39–40
   in folklore, 39
   primates and, 51–54
compassion, see empathy
Compassion Over Killing, 220
computer-generated imagery (CGI),
      198–99
computer simulations, 134, 143
Confucius, 167
Congo, Democratic Republic of, 51, 52, 62
contagious diseases, deliberate infection of
      animals with, 116, 121–22
Cook, Thomas, 195
cooking, invention of, 207–8
cooperation, play and, 98
Cornell Lab of Ornithology, 49
Cornell University, 150
cortico-cerebellar systems, 94
corvids:
   grief and mourning among, 80–81
   memory in, 81
   play among, 103

snowboarding by, 104
   tool-use by, 103–4
cosmetics:
   animal-derived ingredients in, 116
   animal-free testing of, 137–39
   animal testing of, 115–16, 126, 137–38
   personal action and, 148–49
cotton, 157, 170–71
courtship rituals, 50, 55, 65–66, 68,
      70–71, 72, 87
Cousteau, Jacques, 3, 186
cows, see cattle
Cowspiracy (documentary), 169
Crate and Barrel, 175
Creature Technology Co., 196
crocodiles, crocodilians, 109–11
   cruel farming of, 162
   evolutionary age of, 109
   play among, 110
crows, see corvids
Cruelty Free International, 148
Cruelty-Free Shopping Guide, 180
Cruelty to Animals Act (British), 125, 127,
      151
CTI Biotech, 143
Cumming, Alan, 181–82

Dacke, Marie, 29–30
Dairy Alternatives Market, 228
dairy products, government subsidies for,
      211–12
Daiya, 228
Dalmatians, 155–56
Danzig, Mac, 221
Dartmouth University, 150
Darwin, Charles, 124
   on animal emotions, 63–64
   on animal intelligence, 8, 63
David, Alki, 194
Davila-Ross, Marina, 88
Days of Jesse James (film), 192
Defense Advanced Research Projects
      Agency, 134

Defense Department, US, animals in training programs of, 145–46
dependency needs, 9
Descartes, René, 123, 217
Descent of Man, The (Darwin), 8
dessert, vegan alternatives to, 230–31
de Vil, Cruella (char.), 155–56
de Waal, Frans, 3, 52, 83–84, 94–95
diabetes, 221
Diamond, Jared, 51–52
Diaz, George, 187
Diaz, Nate, 221
Digital Frog, 145
Dinets, Vladimir, 110
dinosaurs, plant-eating, 206
Direct Action Everywhere, 220
Discours de la méthode (Descartes), 217
Disney, 191
Djokovic, Novak, 221
doctors, vegans and, 237
Dodo, The, 192
dogfighting, 182–83, 188, 199
dogs:
    coevolution of humans and, 42
    communication in, 39–41
    empathy among, 80
    grief and mourning in, 78–79
    human diseases shared by, 42
    play among, 97–98
    in scientific research, 122
dogsled racing, 187, 200
Dolly, Dolly II (cows), 76
dolphins, 46–47, 186–87, 202–3
Donna (elephant), 43
Donna, 168
Donner, Richard, 187
dopamine, 73
dorsolateral prefrontal cortex, 94
Douglas-Hamilton, Iain, 33
down, 166–67
    synthetic alternatives to, 173, 175–76
dragonflies, 31
Draize test, 137

Dr. Cow, 229
drug trials, 135, 141–42
    animal-free testing in, 142
    animal testing in, 126–27, 130, 141
dung beetles, 29–30

Earth:
    magnetic field of, 14, 19–20, 24, 25, 35–36
    undiscovered species on, 8
Earth Balance, 229
Easterseals, 149
echolocation, 23
Edgar's Mission, 86
Edison film company, 190
education and training:
    animal-free, 145–48
    animals in, 144, 150
eggs, vegan, 227
Egypt, ancient, 99, 157, 171
Eleanor (elephant), 83
Electrocuting an Elephant (film), 190
elephants, 202
    compassion among, 83–84
    as herbivores, 206
    musth in, 73–74
    play among, 102–3
    see also African elephants; Asian elephants
Elephant Sanctuary (Tennessee), 196
Ellis, Jason, 78
Ellyndale Organics, 229
emotions, of animals:
    Darwin on, 63–64
    of fish, 27–28
    play and, 98
    see also specific emotions
empathy, 84–87
    of dogs, 80
    of elephants, 83–84
    experiments on, 84–85
    of pigs, 101–2
    play and, 98
Emulate, 141

Encounter: Ocean Odyssey, 197

Endangered Species Chocolate Bar, 231

endocrine disruptors, 139–40

Enjoy Life, 231

Enlightenment, 123

entertainment, animal abuse in, 181–93
    animal fighting and, 182–83, 188,
       199–200, 203
    in antiquity, 182, 184
    aquariums and marine amusement parks
      in, 186–87
    bullfighting and, 183, 188, 203
    dogsled racing and, 187, 200
    in films and television, 181–82, 189–93
    horse racing and, 189
    personal action and, 199–204
    pigeon racing and, 188–89
    rodeos and, 187, 200
    tourism and, 202–3
    zoos and menageries and, 183–84,
      185–86

entertainment, animal-free, 116–17, 193–99
    animal cams in, 201
    animatronics in, 196–97
    CGI and, 198–99
    circuses and, 195–96, 201
    holograms in, 194
    replicas and mechanical animals in, 194
    virtual reality and, 193–94, 197

environment, effects of animal agriculture
    on, 117

Environmental Protection Agency, US, 140

Environmental Science and Technology, 140

Eötvös Loránd University, 39

epidemiology, 136

EpiDerm, 138

EpiSkin, 138

Epithelix Sàrl, 133

Ethics (Spinoza), 123–24

European starlings, 20, 60

European Union, 126

Evan Almighty (film), 193

evolution, modern understanding of, 10

*Expression of the Emotions in Man and
    Animals, The* (Darwin), 63

fabrics, plant-based, 156, 170–72

Falco, Edie, 197

farming:
    family-based, 210–11
    industrial, *see* meat industrial complex
    invention of, 208

fashion, *see* clothing

Fashion Institute of Technology (FIT),
    Sustainability Awareness Week of, 178

fat, dietary, 221

Favreau, Jon, 198–99

Federal Food, Drug, and Cosmetic Act
    (1938), 126, 138

Feld Entertainment, 197

Fern Street Circus, 201

fidelity, 41, 64, 69–74

"Fifty Years Hence" (Churchill), 225

Figo (German shepherd), 78

FilmOn, 194

Finless Foods, 226

fish:
    emotions of, 27–28
    factory farming of, 216
    mouthbrooders, 75

flamingos, 72

flax, 157, 171

Flicka (film), 191

*Flight Ways: Life and Loss at the Edge of
    Extinction* (van Dooren), 80

Flipper (TV series), 186

Florida Atlantic University, 24

Flying High Circus, 201

folklore, human-animal communication
    in, 39

Follow Your Heart, 227, 228

food:
    animal-free, *see* vegans, veganism
    animals as, 205–20

Food and Drug Administration (FDA),
    126, 129, 134

Forager, 230
Ford, Tom, 168
Fossey, Dian, 3
Framingham Heart Study, 136
Franco, Nuno Enrique, 127
Free Willy (film), 187
Friends Committee on National
    Legislation, 151
frogs, 50
Froguts Dissection Simulator, 145
Frontiers in Zoology, 36
functional magnetic resonance imaging
    (fMRI), 39–40
fur, 157–58
    China as world's largest exporter of, 159–60
    cruel farming of, 160
    expanding demand for, 158–59
    faux, 116, 168–69, 174
    practical qualities of, 158
Furla, 168
Future Meat Technologies, 226, 227

Gabon, 52
Gaffin's cockatoos, 57–58
Galdikas, Biruté, 3
Galen of Pergamon, 123, 124
Galliano, John, 168
game farms, 185
Game of Thrones (TV series), 197–98
Gana (gorilla), 83
gazelles, 92–93
geese, 81–82
gelatin, 231–32
Genius of Dogs, The (Hare and Woods), 42
Genoskin, 139
George IV, king of England, 218
George Washington University, School of
    Medicine of, 120, 121
Georgia Institute of Technology, 47
gibbons, 13
GigSalad.com, 203
Giorgio Armani, 169
Givenchy, 168

Global Federation of Animal Sanctuaries
    (GFAS), 201, 203–4
Gluck, John P., 119
goats, 100–101
Goodall, Jane, 3, 51, 52, 54, 62, 191
Gore-Tex, 176
gorillas, 82–83, 88, 206
Gosse, Philip Henry, 186
Govedich, Fred, 74
government accountability, animal testing
    and, 151–52
GPS, 15
Grace (elephant), 83
Gray, Peter, 89
gray whales, 26
Great Ape Trust, 53
Great Britain:
    Cruelty to Animals Act of, 125, 127
    royal menagerie in, 183
great chain of being, 9
greater honeyguide, 55
Great Migration, 34–35
great snipe, 19
great white sharks, 26–27
green sea turtles, 23–24
Grey, Clark, Shih and Associates, 212
grief and mourning, 78–84
    in human-animal relationships, 78–79
    ritualistic behavior in, 82–83
Groos, Karl, 89
Grumeti Game Reserve (Tanzania), 35
Gucci, 168
Guinea, 52
Gurnemanz (greylag goose), 82
gut-on-a-chip, 142

Häagen-Dazs, 230
Hachi: A Dog's Tale (film), 79
Hachikō (Akita), 79
Hagstrum, Jon, 21
Hamilton, Lewis, 222
HappyCow (app), 234
Hare, Brian, 42

Harlow, Harry, 9

Harold (pigeon), 72–73

Harvard Brain Tissue Resource Center, 137

Harvard University, 150

Harvey, William, 124

heart disease, 221, 222

heart-in-a-jar, 142

Heaven's Gate (film), 191

Heisenberg, Werner, 13

Hellmann's, 227

hemp, fabrics from, 171–72

Henry I, king of England, 183

Herbivore Clothing Company, 177

herbivores, 206, 209–10

Herbivorous Butcher, The, 225

Herodotus, 169–70, 172

Heron Tree, 194

herring gulls, 0

Herzing, Denise, 45–47

high-throughput screening, 140–41

Hilfiger, Tommy, 169

hippocampus, 11–12

Histories (Herodotus), 169–70

History of Animals (Aristotle), 106

HIV/AIDS, 116

    failure of animal studies to result in
        treatments for, 129–30

Hobaiter, Catherine, 54

Hobbit, The: An Unexpected Journey (film),
    191–92

Hodgson, Dave, 32

Holly (cat), 16

Hollywood Hoofbeats (Mitchum), 190–91

Hollywood Reporter, 191, 192

holograms, 194, 195

Hologram USA, 194

homing pigeons, 21

Hominins, as scavengers of meat, 207–8

homosexuality, 77–78

honey, 232–33

horse racing, 189

horses, symbol reading by, 43

How Animals Grieve (King), 83

"How Cats Took Over the Internet"
    (museum exhibit), 2

Howie (cat), 16

How to Train Your Dragon (arena show),
    196

Huizinga, Johan, 88

Human Corneal Epithelium Eye Irritation
    Test (HCE EIT), 139

human exceptionalism, 80

humans:

    chimpanzees as closest relatives of,
        51–52, 205–6

    coevolution of dogs and, 42

    courtship rituals among, 68

    divorce rates of, 71

    and invention of cooking, 207–8

    as natural herbivores, 209–10

    physical differences between animals
        and, 129

    prehistoric spread of, 157

hummingbirds, 17, 18

humpback whales, 49

Hundred and One Dalmatians, The (Smith),
    155–56

hunter-gatherers, 207

hyoid bones, 60

"I, Calf" (VR program), 197

"I, Orca" (VR program), 197

I Can't Believe It's Not Butter, 229

Ice Maidens, 193, 200

Iditarod dog race, 187, 200

"Ill Treatment of Horses and Cattle Bill"
    (British), 218–19

Imperial Circus, 201

imprinting, 19, 29

India, ancient, 157, 170

induced pluripotent stem cells (iPSCs),
    132

Inky (octopus), 107

insects:

    metamorphosis in, 30

    navigation by, 28–31

intelligence:
    brain size and, 11
    collective, 10–11
    cross-species comparisons of, 7–8, 63,
        107
    human, 8, 10, 98
    mistakenly viewed as continuum, 8–9,
        63, 218
    species-specific criteria for, 10–14
Interagency Coordinating Committee on
        the Validation of Alternative Methods
        (ICCVAM), 130
International Whaling Commission, 26, 48
Introduction to the Principles of Morals and
        Legislation, An (Bentham), 218
in vitro meat, 225–26
in vitro techniques, 132–34, 138–39
IQ tests, interspecies, 9–10
Irving, Kyrie, 222
isinglass, 232

Jane Goodall Institute (JGI), 62
Japanese great tits, 55
Japanese macaques (snow monkeys), 77
Japanese puffer fish, 67
JBS, 161
jellyfish, 12
Jesse James (film), 191
John, king of England, 183
John Galliano, 168
Johns Hopkins University, 68–69
Jorgensen, Sal, 27
Journal of Family Practice, 222
Journal of Medical Ethics, 122
Journal of the American Medical Association,
        129
Journal of Tropical Ecology, 31
Juicy Couture, 180
Jungle Book (film; 2016), 198–99
Jurassic World (live tour), 197
Jurassic World: The Exhibition, 196
Jurek, Scott, 221
Justin's, 231

Kakaley, Elizabeth Medlock, 140–41
Kant, Immanuel, 218
Kanzi (bonobo), 53
Karan, Donna, 168
Keim, Brandon, 72–73
Kenya, 34, 35, 83
Kerr, Christopher, 226
King, Barbara, 83
King Kong (stage show), 196
Kite Hill, 228, 229, 230
Kite's Nest Farm, 43–44
Klausner, Richard, 130
Klein, Calvin, 169
Klepetan (stork), 17
Kobuk (dog), 80
Koko (gorilla), 53
Konno, Masamitsu, 143
Kornegay, Joseph, 122
Kors, Michael, 168
Kouilou River, 62
krill, 48

LaBante, 169
Land of Nod, 175
language, 45
Lassie (collie), 190
Lassie Come Home (film), 190
Lauren, Ralph, 168
Laver, James, 158
Laysan albatrosses, 78
Leading Cloud, Jenny, 4
Leakey, Louis, 51
Leakey, Richard, 207, 210
Leaping Bunny certification, 148
leather:
    animal cruelty in manufacture of, 160–61
    China as world's largest exporter of,
        160–61
    faux, 168–69, 174
leatherback sea turtles, 66
Legionnaires' disease, 137
Leiden University, 142
Lelièvre, Sophie, 144

life expectancy, 222
Life of Pi (film), 191
light, polarization of, 29
LightAnimal, 198
Liker, András, 71–72
Lindbergh, Charles, 15
Lindt Excellence Dark Chocolate, 231
linen, 157, 171
Lion King, The (film), 34–35
lions, 90
Lister, Joseph, 124
liver-on-a-chip, 141
Live Science, 29–30
Locke, John, 218
Lockley, Ronald, 15
Loi Grammont, 219
London, 1854 cholera outbreak in, 136
London *Mirror,* 101–2
London Zoo, 186, 194
loons, 18
L'Oréal, 138–39
Lorenz, Konrad, 3, 81–82
Los Angeles, Calif., sale of fur banned in, 177–78
Los Angeles Times, 192
Louis XIV, king of France, 183
love, 14, 62–87
   Darwin on, 64
   difficulty of defining, 64
   fidelity and, 41, 64, 69–74
   mate choice and, 65–69
   maternal, 74–77, 86–87
   see also emotions, of animals
Luck (TV series), 191
Luther, David, 56
Lyocell, 156, 172, 175

Maasai Mara National Reserve (Kenya), 34, 35
Maastricht University, 226
macaques, 95

McCartney, Linda, 240
McCartney, Paul, 174, 240
McCartney, Stella, 156, 168, 169, 180
Macedonia, ancient, 182
McGill University, 85
McKenna, Virginia, 186
Magendie, François, 125
magnetic field, of Earth, 14, 19–20, 24, 25, 35–36
magnetoreception, 16, 19–20, 24, 25
   in blind mole rats, 35–36
male canaries, 69
Malena (stork), 17
Mali, 33
mallard ducks, 71
manatees, 206
March of Dimes, 149
MarketsandMarkets, 224, 228
Marmot, 173, 176
Martin, Richard, 218–19
masked boobies, 69, 71
mate choice, 65–69
maternal separation, 9
mating, chase and, 91
Matt & Nat, 169
MatTek Corporation, 133, 138
Maude (pigeon), 72–73
Max Planck Institute for Evolutionary Anthropology, 7
Maxwell, Marius, 84
meadow voles, 70
meat:
   US consumption of, 211
   in vitro, 225–26
meat industrial complex, 210–17
   advertising campaigns by, 212
   antibiotic overuse by, 212–13
   government subsidies for, 211–12
meat substitutes, 224
Meat the Future, 226
medical education and training:
   animal-free, 120–21, 146–48
   animals in, 124, 145–46

medical research:
  animal-free testing in, 143–44
  animals in, 142–43
meerkats, 95–97
memory, 33, 47, 81
Memphis Meats, 226
Mesopotamia, 209
mesotocin, 73
Mexico, ancient, 157, 170
mice, 87, 122
Michael Kors, 168
microdosing, 135
migration:
  of African elephants, 32–33
  of birds, 17, 19–22, 26
  of caribou, 34
  of gray whales, 26
  of great white sharks, 26–27
  of green sea turtles, 23–24
  of monarch butterfly, 30–31
  of oceanic life, 23–27
  of Pacific salmon, 24
  of wandering glider (dragonfly), 31
milk:
  nondairy, 228
  as poor source of calcium, 214
Mimco, 169
Mimetas, 142
Minding Animals (Bekoff), 80
minks, 160
Missouri Primate Foundation, 181
Mitchum, Petrine Day, 190–91
Miyoko, 228, 229
mockingbirds, 59
modal, 172, 175, 176
Modular IMmune In vitro Construct
  (MIMIC©), 142
Mogil, Jeffrey, 85
monarch butterflies, 30–31
Monk's Meats, 225
monogamy, 41, 64, 69–74
monsoons, 31
Montaigne, Michel de, 159, 217

MooShoes, 174
Morgan, C. Lloyd, 12–13
Morgan's Canon, 12–13
MosaMeat, 226
motor skills, development of, 97, 99
mouflons (wild sheep), 163, 208
mouthbrooders, 75
Mozambique, 55
Mugabe, Robert, 183
Muir, John, 112
mulesing, 165
Murka (cat), 16
Murphy, Michael P., 146
muscular dystrophy, 122, 129–30
Museum of the Moving Image, 2
musth, 73–74
Muybridge, Eadweard, 189–90
MyHeart Platform, 142

NadaMoo!, 230
Nahmias, Yaakov, 227
Namib Desert, 33
Namibia, 33
National Academies of Sciences, US, 131
National Academy of Medicine, 221
National Anti-Vivisection Society, 219
National Aquarium (New Zealand), 107
National Football League, CTE and, 137
National Geographic, 80, 84, 197, 203
National Heart, Lung and Blood Institute,
  136
National Human Dogsled Championship,
  200
National Institute for Mathematical and
  Biological Synthesis, 58
National Institutes of Health, 121, 128,
  134, 152
Native Americans, 159
Natural Harmony, 175
Natural History (Pliny the Elder), 182
natural history museums, 202
natural selection, 89, 96
Nature Communications, 53, 140

Nature's Gate, 148
navigation, 15–37
    by birds, 17, 19
    by blind mole rats, 14
    by cats, 16
    celestial, 16, 20, 29–30
    Earth's magnetic field and, 19–20, 24,
        25, 35–36
    by humans, 15, 24, 36–37
    imprinting and, 19, 29
    by insects, 28–31
    of mammals, 32–36
    oceanic, 23–27
    smell and, 19–20, 25
    sound and, 21
Navy, US, 48
NBC, 165
Nellie's Free Range Eggs, 216
Net-a-Porter, 169
New Crop Capital, 226
New York Times, 213
Ngorongoro Conservation Area (Tanzania), 34
Niassa National Reserve (Mozambique), 55
Nim Chimpsky (chimpanzee), 53
Ninja (cat), 16
No Animal Food (Wheldon), 219
North America, European voyages to, 157,
    159
North American blue grouse, 19
North Face, 173, 176
North Korea, 183
Northwest Animal Rights Network, 220
Norwegian University of Life Sciences, 43
Novoheart, 142
Nutiva, 229, 231

Oakland Zoo, 43
Oakley, Kenneth, 51
O'Barry, Ric, 186
oceans:
    navigation in, 23–27
    sound waves in, 47–48
    thermocline layer of, 48

O'Connell-Rodwell, Caitlin, 43
octopuses, 106–9
Oculus Rift, 193–94, 198
omega-3, omega-6 acids, 221
Omni-Heat, 176
orangutans, 75–76
orbitofrontal cortex, 94
orcas, 75
Organization for Economic Cooperation
    and Development, 139
organoids (organelles), 132–34
organs-on-a-chip, 133–34
Orlando Sentinel, 187
Ornish, Dean, 223
Osaka City University, 28
Osten, Wilhelm von, 38
osteoporosis, 214
ostriches, 162
Owens, Dave, 66
owls, 21–22
oxytocin, 70, 73

Pacific salmon, 24
Pac-Man (arcade game), 88
pain, animals' ability to feel, 28, 84–86,
    123–24, 164–66, 186, 217–18
    animal experiments and, 119–22, 124,
        128, 141, 143, 154
pain contagion, 85
Paleolithic Age, diet in, 205
Pallas's long-tongued bats, 22–23
Panchatantra, 39
Parliament, British, 158
parrots, 56–58
Partnership in Birds (Black), 71
Pasteur, Louis, 124
Patagonia, 173
Payne, Katy, 49
Payne, Roger, 49
PCRM, see Physicians Committee for
    Responsible Medicine
peacocks, 55, 68
pecking orders, 45

PeerJ, 83
Pennsylvania, University of, 150
Pepperberg, Irene, 56–57
Peregrine falcons, 18
Performing Animals Welfare Society, 220
Pershing, John J., 21
personalized medicine, 133, 143–44
PETA, 152–53, 189, 195, 197, 239
  Animal-Friendly Destination list of, 203
  Beauty Without Bunnies website of, 148
  Cruelty-Free Shopping Guide of, 180
PETA International Science Consortium,
  133, 138, 150
PFOA, 140
*Philosophical Transactions of the Royal Society
  B: Biological Sciences,* 59
Physicians Committee for Responsible
  Medicine (PCRM), 119, 120–21, 150,
  154, 220, 222–23
Physics and Philosophy (Heisenberg), 13
pigeon racing, 188–89
pigeons, 20–21
  child rearing by, 73
  monogamy among, 72–73
pigs:
  communication among, 44
  domestication of, 208–9
  empathy among, 101–2
  intelligence of, 101
  in meat industry, 214
  play among, 101
  testing of burn treatments on, 116
piping plovers, 71
Pittsburgh, Pa., rodeo law in, 200–201
Pittsburgh, University of, 122
Planet of the Apes (film), 51
plant-based diet, 220–23
play, 14, 88–112
  chase in, 88–89, 90, 91, 92
  cognition and, 93–94, 98
  cooperation and, 98
  in motor skill development, 97, 99
  "purposeless," 95–97

socialization and, 93–95, 98–99
survival skills and, 89–93, 98–99
tool-use and, 103–4
ubiquity of, 89
play-fighting, 90, 91–92, 98
Play of Animals, The (Groos), 89
Pliny the Elder, 182
PLOS Genetics, 42
PlumaFill, 173
Plumtech, 176
Pongo (dog), 155
Popular Mechanics, 225
Post, Mark, 226
post-mortem organ studies, 137
Pottery Barn, 175
prairie voles, 69
praying mantisses, 65
Predators in Action, 193
pregnancy tests, 115
prescription drugs, 222
Presidential Advisory Council on
  Combating Antibiotic-Resistant
  Bacteria, 213
Preventive Medicine Research Institute, 223
Prevot, Jean, 229
PrimaLoft, 173, 176
primates, communication among, 51–54
Princeton University, 150
problem solving, 7
Proceedings of the Royal Society B, 26, 47
product safety testing, 126
prostate cancer, 223
protein, 221
Pru (pig), 101
Public Health Service, US, 128
Purdue University, 144
Purgatorius (ancestral primate), 206–7
Putin, Vladimir, 183

Queen Mary University of London, 29

Raaka Chocolate, 231
Rajamani, Uthra, 140

Ralph Lauren, 168
Rao, Sharanya, 195
rats:
    empathy among, 84–85
    in laboratory experiments, 119–20
Ratsky (rat), 119–20
REACH law (European Union), 151
reading comprehension, of animals, 42
reconciliation, play and, 94–95
red foxes, 36
red jungle fowl, 209, 215
Regan, Tom, 127
regret, 94
restaurants, vegan options in, 233–34,
    236–37
Restoration Hardware, 175
Rhesus macaques, 94
rhesus monkeys, 9
Richter, Jacob and Bonnie, 16
Rico (border collie), 7
Ringling Bros. and Barnum & Bailey
    Circus, 184
Rin Tin Tin (German shepherd), 190
risk-on-a-chip device, 144
Riverdel, 229
Roberts, William C., 210
rock hyrax, 59
rodeos, 187, 200–201
Rome, ancient, 182–83
Ronnen, Tal, 229
Rosa, Karen, 192
Royal de Luxe, 194
Royal Society for the Prevention of Cruelty
    to Animals (Australia), 163
Royal Society Open Science, 44
rPET (recycled polyethylene terephthalate),
    156, 173, 176
ruffed grouse, 54–55
Russell, William, 127
Russo, Rene, 181

Sahara Desert, 33
Sahelanthropus, 207

St. Andrews, University of, 54
Samburu National Reserve (Kenya), 83
sandhoppers, 29
San Francisco, Calif.:
    noise level in, 56
    sale of fur banned in, 177–78
Sanofi Pasteur VaxDesign, 142
Sans Beast, 169
Sareen, Dhruv, 140
Save Movement, 220
Save the Duck, 177
Save the Elephants, 33
Scala Naturae, 8, 9
Science, 217
Scientific Reports, 143
scientific research, 119–54
    animal protections in, 125, 127–28
    cruelty to animals in, 115–16, 119–27,
        131
    and differences between animals and
        humans, 129
    and failure of animal studies to result in
        human treatments, 129–30
    personal action and, 148–54
    3Rs and, 127
scientific research, alternative,
    bioinformatics in, 134
scientific research, alternatives to animal
    testing in, 115–16, 130–48
    autopsies and post-mortem organ studies
        in, 136–37
    clinical trials in, 135
    computer simulations in, 134,
        143
    cosmetics and, 137–39
    drug trials and, 141–42
    in education and training, 145–48
    epidemiology and, 136
    human volunteers in, 135
    medical research in, 143–44
    microdosing in, 135
    as more efficient than animal studies, 131
    noninvasive medical imagery in, 135

scientific research, alternatives to animal testing in (*cont.*)
    toxicity testing and, 139–41
    in vitro techniques in, 132–34, 138–39
Screen Actors Guild, 192
scuba diving, 201
SeaCell, 172
Sea Shepherd Conservation Society, 220
sea turtles, 23–24, 65–67
seaweed, fabrics from, 171–72
SeaWorld, 186, 195, 197, 201
Secret Life of Cows, The (Young), 44, 76
self-awareness, of fish, 27–28
Selfridges, 169
Selma (greylag goose), 82
S. E. Massengill Company, 126
Semi-Pro (film), 193
Serengeti, 34, 35
serotonin, 73
sextants, 20
Sharpe, Lynda, 96
sheep, 162–65, 208
Sheffield, University of, 71
shoes, vegan, 174, 180
shopping, for cruelty-free products, 148–49
Shrek (sheep), 164
sign language, chimpanzees and, 52–54
silk, 167
    alternatives to, 175
Silverstone, Alicia, 178, 197
Simulab Corporation, 146
Singer, Peter, 127
SkinEthic, 138
skin-free skin, 156, 168, 169
slime molds, 11–12
smell:
    communication and, 41
    navigation and, 19–20, 25
Smith, Dorothy Gladys "Dodie," 155–56
snails, 31–32
snorkeling, 201
Snow, John, 136
Snow Buddies (film), 191

socialization, play and, 93–94, 98–99
social media, veganism and, 237–38
Society for the Prevention of Cruelty to Animals, 219
So Delicious, 230
sound:
    anthropogenic, 56
    speed of, 47–48
southern right whales, 65
soybeans, fabrics from, 171–72
spatial awareness, spatial memory, 12
Spiegel, Frederick, 11
Spinoza, Baruch, 123–24
squirrels, 90–91
Stagecoach (film), 191
Stalking Big Game with a Camera in Equatorial Africa (Maxwell), 84
Standard American Diet, 222, 224
Stanford, Leland, 189–90
Statute Concerning Diet and Apparel (England; 1363), 158–59
Ste Martaen, 229
stem cells, 132, 139, 143
Stray Dog Capital, 226
Strycker, Noah, 70
suffering, *see* pain
sugar, 232
Sultan (dog), 79
Sumatra (orangutan), 75
sundials, 20
SuperMeat, 226
survival skills, play and, 89–93, 98–99
swans, 71
symbols, animals' reading of, 43
syntax, in birdsong, 55
synthetic materials, 172–73

tamarin monkeys, 13
Tanzania, 34–35, 51
Tarangire Elephant Project, 33
TBT, 140
Tchindzoulou Island (Congo), 62–63
Terrace, Herbert, 52–53

testosterone, 73

Texas A&M University, 122

Texas Biomedical Research Institute, 121

Theo Chocolate, 231

theory of mind, 98

   see also empathy; self-awareness

ThermaCheck, 176

Thermafill, 176

ThermoBall technology, 173, 176

Thermogreen, 176

Thing with Feathers, The (Strycker), 70

Third Chimpanzee, The (Diamond), 51–52

3-D printing, 132, 134, 143

3Rs (animal research principles), 127, 130

365 (Whole Foods), 148

Tika (dog), 80

Times (London), 218

Timmers, Romain, 195

tofu scramble, 227

Tofutti, 230

Tom Ford, 168

Tommy Hilfiger, 169

Tonka (chimpanzee), 181–82

tool-use:

   by birds, 57–58, 103–4

   by chimpanzees, 51, 52

   play and, 103–4

Topsy (elephant), 190

"Top Trends in Prepared Food," 220

tourism, animal-based attractions in, 202–3

Tower of London, 183

ToxCast, 140

toxicity:

   animal-free testing of, 139–41

   animal tests of, 139

Toxicity Testing in the 21st Century (report), 131

Trader Joe's, 227, 230, 231

TraumaMan, 146

tree frogs, 50

Treeline, 229

Trietsch, Sebastiaan J., 142

TripAdvisor, 195

Truman, Harry, 101

Tyson, Neil deGrasse, 2

Tyson Foods, 211, 226

Ueno, Hidesaburō, 79

Uganda, 54

Uggs, 179

United Nations, 151

United States:

   life expectancy in, 222

   meat consumption in, 211

Universities Federation for Animal Welfare, 127

U-SENS, 139

Utah, University of, 150

vaccines, synthetic, 116

Van Amburgh, Isaac, 184

van Dooren, Thom, 80

van Gogh, Vincent, 69

Van Leeuwen, 230

vasopressin, 73

vasotocin, 73

veal, 213–14

vegan design, 178

VeganEgg, 227

vegan leather, 116, 174

Vegan Outreach, 220

vegans, veganism, 117, 170, 219–22, 239–40

   doctors and, 237

   myths about, 235–36

   personal action and, 234–38

   social media and, 237–38

   see also plant-based diet

Vegan Society, 220

Vegans UK, 204

Vegenaise, 227

vegetarians, 219

Vegg, 227

veggie burgers, 224

Veggie Grill, 233

Verdolin, Jennifer, 69–70

Versace, Donatella, 169
Victoria, queen of England, 125
Victoria Street Society for the Protection of
    Animals Liable to Vivisection, 125
Violife, 229
Vioxx, 130
Virgin Holidays, 195
Virry VR, 198
virtual reality, 193–94, 197–98
vivisections, 122–27, 130
    opposition to, 124–25
vocalization:
    in canines, 40, 41
    in whales, 48–49
Vogue, 169
von Bayern, Auguste, 104
von Furstenberg, Diane, 156
Vtopia, 229

Wake Forest Institute for Regenerative
    Medicine, 132
Walking Dead, The (TV show), 199
Walking with Dinosaurs (arena show), 196
wandering glider (dragonfly), migration
    of, 31
Washington Post, 162, 212
Washoe (chimpanzee), 53
Watson, Donald, 219–20
Watson, Dorothy, 220
Wayne State University, 150
West Elm, 175
whales:
    vocalizations by, 48–49
    see also specific species
whale-watching tours, 202
Wheldon, Rupert, 219
whistle-blowers, 153
White Shark Café, 27
white-tailed deer, 92
Whittlesey, Charles, 21
Wild Connection (Verdolin), 69–70

wildebeasts, 34–35
Willett, Walter, 222
Williams, James Howard, 102–3
Williams, Venus and Serena, 221
Williams Sonoma, 175
William the Conqueror, king of England,
    183
Wills, Cathryn, 169
Wilson's Snipe, 55
wolf spiders, 74–75
wolves, 40, 41
wood, fabrics from, 171–72
Woods, Vanessa, 42
wool, 162–65
    alternatives to, 171–72, 175, 176
    cruelty to sheep in production of,
        164–66
World Animal Protection, 195–96
World Congress on Alternatives and
    Animal Use in the Life Sciences,
    130–31
World's Richest Cat, The (film), 196–97
Wounda (chimpanzee), 62
Wrangham, Richard, 208
Wyss Institute for Biologically Inspired
    Engineering, 150

yaks, 206
Yale School of Medicine, 94
Yale University, 150
Year of the Greylag Goose, The (Lorenz),
    81–82
yellow-naped Amazons (parrots), 58
yogurt, nondairy, 230
Yost, Sidney, 192
Young, Rosamund, 44, 76
Your Body in Balance (Barnard), 119

Zoocheck, 220
zoos and menageries, 183–84, 185–86
    roadside, 185, 200

About the Authors

Ingrid E. Newkirk is the president and founder of People for the Ethical Treatment of Animals (PETA)—the largest animal rights organization in the world, with more than 6.5 million members and supporters. Among her many victories: she coordinated the first arrest and conviction in US history of a scientist on cruelty-to-animals charges, helped pass the first anti-cruelty law in Taiwan, and obtained the first felony charges of cruelty to animals involving a factory farm and the first felony charges of cruelty to factory-farmed birds. She also spearheaded the closure of the Department of Defense's underground "wound laboratory," the closure of the largest horse slaughterhouse in North America on grounds of cruelty, and all car-crash tests on animals internationally. Ingrid's campaigns to promote cruelty-free living have made the front pages of virtually every newspaper in the US, the UK, and India. She was named a top businessperson of the year by *Fortune* magazine and Washingtonian of the Year by the *Washingtonian*. She has been profiled in the *New Yorker*, the *New York Times Magazine*, the *London Times*, *Forbes*, and *People*, appeared on numerous TV shows including the *Colbert Report*, *Today*, the *Oprah Winfrey Show*, *Nightline*, and *60 Minutes*, and has been the subject of two documentaries: the BBC's *Ingrid Newkirk: The Naked Revolutionary* and HBO's award-winning *I Am an Animal*.

A graduate of Stanford and Harvard, **Gene Stone** (www.genestone .com) is a former Peace Corps volunteer, journalist, and book, magazine, and newspaper editor for such companies as Simon & Schuster,

Bantam Books, the *Los Angeles Times*, and *Esquire*. He has also written, cowritten, or ghostwritten forty-five books (fifteen of which were national bestsellers) on a wide range of subjects, but for the last dozen years he has concentrated on plant-based diets and their relationship to animal protection, health, and the environment. These books include, among others, *The Engine 2 Diet*, *How Not to Die*, *Forks Over Knives*, *The Awareness*, *Eat for the Planet*, *Living the Farm Sanctuary Life*, *Mercy for Animals*, and *Rescue Dogs*.